D0114561

ORGANIZ'D INNOCENCE

BLAKE'S *Milton*
(BRITISH MUSEUM COPY)

ORGANIZ'D INNOCENCE

The Story of Blake's Prophetic Books

by

MARGARET RUDD

GREENWOOD PRESS, PUBLISHERS
WESTPORT, CONNECTICUT

The Library of Congress has catalogued this publication as follows:

Library of Congress Cataloging in Publication Data

Rudd, Margaret, 1925–
   Organiz'd innocence.

   Reprint of the 1956 ed.
   Bibliography: p.
   1. Blake, William 1757–1827. I. Title.
[PR4147.R83 1973]   821'.7   72–6209
ISBN 0-8371-6458-3

First published in 1956
by Routledge & Kegan Paul, London

Reprinted with the permission
of Routledge & Kegan Paul Ltd.

First Greenwood Reprinting 1973

Library of Congress Catalogue Card Number 72-6209

ISBN 0-8371-6458-3

Printed in the United States of America

For

M.M.R.

J.H.R.

Unorganiz'd Innocence: An Impossibility.
Innocence dwells with Wisdom, but never with Ignorance.
BLAKE: note written on a page of *The Four Zoas*.

CONTENTS

PREFACE

I WOULD like to take this opportunity to say something about how this book came to be written. Its nature is in many ways unorthodox, and it may seem to lie rather confusingly in the area between formal scholarly criticism and a more creative form of writing, something like a biographical novel about how the troubles of Blake's life affected his strange poems known as the prophetic books.

Although entirely sympathetic to what they praise as exciting and original insight into the meaning of Blake's prophecies, my publishers are a little worried because I have refused to back up my interpretation with the usual heavy machinery of scholarship —the extensive references to other critics, the digressions on possible esoteric sources and parallels, the lengthy footnotes on changes in the values of Blake's never static symbols—all, in fact, that I have deliberately left out or pruned away in order to reveal something that I hope is far more simple and human than any such display of erudition would convey.

The long poems known as the prophetic books tell, like all epics and myths, a very wonderful story about universal human events of the spirit. I believe that the primary value of the poems lies in this story, and that I would be foolish to let even 'scholarship' in any way obscure the fine thread of Blake's tale as I attempt to unwind it. It is a thread that has many twists and knots of its own to untangle without adding further pedantic snarls.

I feel very strongly that such an explication as I am attempting should be kept as simple as possible and as free from all that is extraneous as can be managed. To my way of thinking, rather than erring on the side of too little formality and scholarly pretentiousness, my study is not nearly simple or colloquial enough.

ix

There is no doubt at all in my mind that Blake meant *The Four Zoas, Milton,* and *Jerusalem* to form one long narrative, coherent only as a dynamic whole, and not simply, as Robert Hillyer put it, 'as a trove for lyric selection'. It is the story of these three poems taken together that Blake must be talking about in the following much quoted passage from a letter to his friend, Butts, written in April of 1803. The story of *Milton* alone is much too short and slight to be compared to Homer's epics or *Paradise Lost.*

'None can know the Spiritual Acts of my three years' Slumber on the banks of the Ocean, unless he has seen them in the Spirit, or unless he should read My long Poem descriptive of these Acts; for I have in these three years composed an immense number of verses on One Grand Theme, Similar to Homer's Iliad or Milton's Paradise Lost.'

Blake's earlier shorter prophecies, although often of great loveliness and significance, are only hints and forerunners of the last three poems, the prophetic books proper, with their One Grand Theme. It is this single Grand Theme and narrative that I am trying to follow through in this study.

The impetus for my interpretation of these poems came from an altogether different direction than the reading of Blake criticism, with the single exception of Middleton Murry's book on Blake. This is why I thought it unnecessary and even misleading to add a formal bibliography or list of books about Blake that I have learned from in the past, but did not once consult during the writing of my own book.

Blake's narrative or story, although rarely in itself lucid or simple, is a tale much more readily understandable to our psyche-conscious age than it would have been to Blake's own contemporaries. That this story of the prophetic books is Blake's own psychological drama I firmly believe, and have tried to point out the evidence for believing. However, I do not wish to labour overmuch this secondary point in my book, namely, the identification of Albion and Jerusalem with William and Catherine Blake, but rather simply to tell the story as it unfolds in the prophetic books, after briefly indicating in the first chapter why I believe the experience to be Blake's own. It would be a mistake to try to press an identification too hard, for

always Blake widens out what is personal to universal significance if he succeeds, and simply to cosmic proportions when he
fails, as in the equation of Hayley with Satan, and the soldier,
Scofield, with a devil. Even Blake's removal from London to
Felpham suffered a sea-change towards the eternal, although in
this instance with great lyric charm. It may be a self-evident
comment on the artistic process in general to underscore the
idea that the experiences of Albion and Jerusalem may well be
based on the experience of their creator, and it is not my primary
point.

My awareness that a moving story of turbulent and disturbed
emotion was the mainspring of the prophetic books, came long
after I had first 'read' them and set them aside with a rather
smug sigh of relief that I had 'got through' them at all. At that
time their significance had not dawned upon me, and I agreed
with most critics that one could have only the dimmest notion of
what was going on in their turgid pages, and that the few
passages of fine poetry should by all means be lifted out of their
context in order to be understood.

It was some years after I had put the prophetic books back
on the shelf that my efforts to understand a troubled human
situation in real life threw a white blaze on to the pages of my
neglected Blake, illuminating something of such significance
that I could not look away. 'So *that* is what Blake is talking
about,' became my daily conversation with myself, and it
became more and more imperative to write this book. After
the initial decision it was comparatively easy. Everything fell
into place. Everything confirmed my hunch and I had only to
follow it through the pages of the text, pointing out what now
seemed so obvious, although far from simple in its nature.

To bring into focus the story of the prophetic books is all that
I have tried to do or wanted to do in this study. It is something
that has not been done before and it seemed worth doing. Many
aspects of Blake's work I am content to leave to other critics,
and a large part of this preface consists in listing the things that
I have not done and my reasons for not doing them.

I am very much aware that there are biblical and platonic
overtones in Blake's poems that I have not discussed at all.
That Blake read widely in cabbalistic writings is established,

and it seems likely that he knew the work of the antiquarians Stukeley and Davies, as well as of Bryant. It seems fairly safe to deduce that there are gnostic and occult parallels if not sources for Blake's more esoteric ideas, and others are working on this aspect of his work, while much has already been said on the startling similarity of many of his ideas not only to Freudian and Jungian psychology, but also to some of Marx's beliefs. An impressive study like Northrop Frye's *Fearful Symmetry* is almost frightening when we see the hypnotic way in which any given symbol of Blake's, dropped into the pool of the critic's mind like a stone, stirs up ever-widening circles of learned association. All such fascinating and valid minor aspects of Blake's work I have left regretfully to one side, but not too regretfully, for Blake's main trouble is that he did not know when to stop piling diverse meanings on to his basic structure, which, of course, soon became lost to sight. It is this almost hidden skeleton of plot and meaning that I have set out to reveal in the prophetic books, and to achieve this I must eschew in them much that is rich and interesting.

I have not even allowed myself to make use of any of the illustrations to the prophetic books that have not a significant bearing on the text of the poems, for often Blake tells two quite different stories in his illustrations, and although those that go with the text are very important, those that do not are merely confusing. Some of the most interesting of the latter group, however, I have described without comment in footnotes, especially in the case of the drawings that accompany *Vala, or The Four Zoas*, a poem that exists only in the form of a single manuscript which is in the British Museum and whose illustrations are rarely reproduced. The text of the poem has, of course, been reproduced many times, but in varying versions, for it is almost impossible to place passages and even to read them, since every available corner of the MS. is filled up with scribbled afterthoughts. I might add what most Blake scholars know, that there is no generally agreed upon system for numbering the lines of Blake's long poems, since not only lines but whole plates were switched around, omitted, or inserted. This makes it very difficult for the reader to check my quotations, but I am afraid that there is nothing I could do but to use a readily available

and inexpensive edition (the Modern Library, since the Nonesuch text had not appeared when I started work on this book)
and to follow the poems straight through in order, scrupulously
noting the divisions into chapters, books, and 'Nights'. I hope
that this will make it fairly easy for the reader to turn the pages
with me if he cares to do so. The only alternative would have
been to use the page numbers of such a grand edition as that of
Geoffrey Keynes, published in 1925, but since this is now fast
becoming a rare book, it did not seem a practicable solution. For
Jerusalem I used the fine new facsimile in black and white issued
recently by the Trianon Press.

I believe that my most original contribution to Blake interpretation is in the chapter on *Vala, or, the Four Zoas*. As late as
December 26, 1889, Yeats could write to Katherine Tynan that
he and Edwin Ellis were the first ever to have read the poem.
And even today critics sedulously avoid this poem, which is
considered Blake's most difficult, but is to me the most interesting, being as it is the closest to the cause of Blake's spiritual
upheaval. What the youthful Yeats wrote is interesting and
worth quoting here:

'. . . Did I tell you that we have found a new long poem of Blake's?
Rossetti mentioned its name, no more. We are the only people who
ever read it. It is two thousand lines long or so and belongs to three
old men and their sisters who live away at Red Hill in Surrey. Ellis
and myself go from time to time and do a day's copying at it. The old
men are very hospitable and bring out thirty-year-old port-wine for us,
and, when I am copying, the oldest of the old men sits beside me with a
pen-knife in his hand to point my pencil when it blunts. Their house is
a great typical bare country house. It is full of Blake matters. The old
men and their sisters are like "a family of pew-openers", Ellis says.
Blake is their Church; at the same time they are no little troubled at
the thought that maybe he was heretical . . . (September 7, 1890) . . .
"Vala", a poem of great length and beauty, never having been printed
or even read before.'[1]

I mentioned that my one debt of gratitude to a critic is to
J. Middleton Murry for suggesting that Albion and Jerusalem
are probably William and Catherine Blake. My gratitude, how-

[1] W. B. Yeats, *Letters to Katherine Tynan*, ed. Roger McHugh, New
York, 1953.

ever, seems to have expressed itself in the rather odd way of roundly scolding Mr. Murry in the first chapter because he could so well have written this book in 1933 had he cared to follow through on his excellent suspicion with a careful investigation of the facts and the text rather than with a few careless and unfounded conjectures. I am, all the same, rather glad that Mr. Murry did not write this book, for I have had fun doing it, and have felt it worth while, for, as someone said of Ibsen, 'it takes two people to tell the truth, one to speak it and one to understand what is spoken, the last lesson to be learned by all prophets.'

ACKNOWLEDGEMENT

I would like to thank the American Philosophical Society of Philadelphia for the grant that helped me to complete this book.

M.E.R.

Part One

MR. AND MRS. BLAKE

CATHERINE BLAKE AND THE SPECTRE

'And my sweet Shadow of Delight stood trembling by my side.'

MIDDLETON MURRY was the first critic to point out that the troubled relationship of Albion and his bride, Jerusalem, in Blake's prophetic books, may well have been based on the marital difficulties of William and Catherine Blake. This is a brilliant intuition, and, one would feel, a right one thus far. But Mr. Murry, instead of attempting to establish the point with sufficient evidence, rushes off into what seems to me unfounded conjecture about the exact nature of Blake's conjugal troubles.

Murry's position is this. Basing his interpretation on two poems from *Songs of Experience* and a poem from Blake's notebook—and poems are always a shaky foundation on which to build theories about a poet's life if not supplemented with more concrete data—Murry writes as follows: 'There cannot be much doubt about the story these three poems tell, or conceal. Blake had loved someone not his wife, and had straightway told his wife of his love, and the result had been disaster.'[1] This is, of course, pure guesswork on Mr. Murry's part.

There is no evidence at all that Blake after his marriage fell in love with someone other than his wife, giving Catherine cause for jealousy, and Catherine knew all about his unfortunate experience with 'Polly' before he met his wife. Indeed, if we can

[1] *William Blake*, Middleton Murry, London, 1933, pp. 45–6.

3

credit the legend about the Blakes' courtship, it was the telling of this unhappy experience which led directly to their marriage. And in spite of Blake's theories about free love, or rather, his theories about loving in freedom, and despite the threatened, and altogether theoretical, concubine, to outside eyes Blake and his wife were an ideal couple. The existence of another woman and her identity would not easily have gone unobserved, especially with Blake's own outspokenness. Had he believed in taking such a step, he would have been the first to tell us of its accomplishment, in the same spirit in which he walked the streets of London flaunting the red cap of freedom, although he was the only person with sense enough to see that Tom Paine left the country.

Secondly, assuming at the outset that the three poems Murry cites are dealing with Blake's relation to his wife and not with an imaginary situation, it is still obvious from the wording of the key poem that there is something wrong with Murry's guess:

> Never seek to tell thy love
> Love that never told can be;
> For the gentle wind does move
> Silently, invisibly.
>
> I told my love, I told my love,
> I told her all my heart,
> Trembling, cold, in ghastly fears—
> Ah, she doth depart.
>
> As soon as she was gone from me
> A traveller came by
> Silently, invisibly—
> O was no deny.[1]

Murry assumes that this is Blake speaking to his wife about his love for another woman, and that her withdrawal is out of jealousy. There is nothing at all in the poem to indicate this. In fact such an assumption makes the poem much more complicated than it really is, and much less coherent, assuming three or even four people and two 'loves' which Blake does not differentiate

---

[1] Bronowski brackets together these poems, but in a different context.

at all! The only possible paraphrase of this poem is to repeat what is quite clear: the poet is saying simply that it is a mistake for a lover to try to tell his beloved of the extent of his love for her, that he had done so, and his beloved had retreated in fear of his declared passion. If this is about Catherine, the most we can assume is that at some point Blake frightened his wife pretty thoroughly by focussing on her some of the almost diabolically impersonal energy we feel, for example, in *The Marriage of Heaven and Hell*, and that he called this 'love'. The poem says nothing at all about *her* jealousy, or about any woman except the beloved herself, although it does seem to indicate that *she* turned to the 'traveller'.

This severs immediately the arbitrary connection that Murry makes, based on this faulty interpretation, between the poem above and the one called 'My Pretty Rose-Tree', a poem that *is* about feminine jealousy, but not at all in the same context. This poem tells of another situation, one that might well have arisen after Catherine's (or the abstract beloved's) initial withdrawal from the poet, because she was then afraid that he might turn to someone more responsive. But it does not at all suggest that he did, as Mr. Murry contends, at any point turn to another woman. Quite the contrary—he *could* have turned to an exotic creature, someone who was in love with him and offered herself to him, but instead he turns *away* from her in loyalty to his true love, the pretty rose-tree, even though she is now jealous and puts out her thorns to hurt him.

> A flower was offered to me,
> Such a flower as May never bore;
> But I said 'I've a Pretty Rose-tree'
> And I passed the sweet flower o'er.
>
> Then I went to my Pretty Rose-tree,
> To tend her by day and by night;
> But my Rose turned away with jealousy,
> And her thorns were my only delight.

The third poem on which Mr. Murry bases his erroneous hypothesis is 'The Clod and the Pebble', too universal a statement of love become its opposite to bear such a particular interpretation without further evidence.

It is interesting to note in passing that, from the wording of 'Never seek to tell thy love', it would appear that it was the *woman* and not the poet who actually turned towards someone else in her distress, thereby giving her lover cause for complaint. The figure of the 'traveller' in this poem, which Mr. Murry disregards entirely, is probably the same as that of the 'angel' in the ironic little poem written about the same time. The poet speaks of his love, but the 'angel' and 'traveller' simply take what they want, silently:

> I asked a thief to steal me a peach:
> He turned up his eyes.
> I asked a lithe lady to lie her down:
> Holy and meek she cries.
>
> As soon as I went an angel came:
> He winked at the thief
> And smiled at the dame,
> And without one word said (spoke)
> Had a peach from the tree,
> And still as a maid (And twixt earnest and joke)
> Enjoy'd the lady.

The facts may be nothing more than that Catherine took refuge in the idea of a husband who loved with less articulate energy and violence, and that this ideal husband in her imagination seemed to Blake like a treacherous angel who enjoyed her without physical passion. Or, it could be that she, a simple woman of a naïvely religious and puritan cast, took her trouble to some sympathetic cleric who sided with her attitude that her lover's excessive demands spelled lust rather than love. This would have seemed to Blake a betrayal, the basest treachery, spiritual fornication in fact.

It still remains for us to determine, if we can, the validity of Murry's initial assumption that there were some difficulties that William and Catherine Blake had to overcome in their marriage and that the story of Jerusalem and Albion is, by and large, the story of how this was accomplished. Is there any evidence outside of the prophetic books themselves to suggest this, for Middleton Murry never bothers to give us any?

I think there is, although from the outset I would like to

suggest that the trouble was of a psychological nature and took place only on the stage of Blake's imagination rather than, as Middleton Murry would have us believe, in actual fact and with the protagonists of Blake, Catherine, and a concrete 'other woman'. 'I have indeed fought thro' a Hell of terrors and horrors (*which none could know but myself*) in a divided existence,' writes Blake on December 4, 1804; 'now no longer divided nor at war with myself, I shall travel on in the strength of the Lord God, as Poor Pilgrim says.'

On October 23 of the same year Blake wrote a letter to Hayley. It is remarkable not only for its content which does indicate the reality of a long-endured domestic crisis (since, in fact, immediately after their marriage), but also for its language which is that of the prophetic books, making this letter almost the single exception in Blake's correspondence which otherwise deals almost wholly with ordinary practical matters of the artistic life in a style that is always clear, spare, and objective even when he speaks of depression and of his visions. But this letter tells of an experience, actual and personal, which, by the time Blake wrote to Hayley, was already clothed in the language and symbolism of mythology. This is, of course, not the only experience of Blake's which passed into the prophetic writings. Events such as his encounter with the abusive soldier, Scofield, and his stay in the cottage at Felpham, were woven into the tapestry of the prophetic books. Yet none of these comparatively minor happenings as they are related in Blake's letters are so clearly in the process of being translated into myth as is the following major experience. The letter opens with the practical matters more usual to Blake's correspondence—the receipt of cash, the progress of engravings, his wife's rheumatism, the health of friends—but suddenly breaks into something quite different:

'O Glory! and O Delight! I have entirely reduced that spectrous fiend to his station, whose annoyance has been the ruin of my labours for the last passed twenty years of my life. He is the enemy of conjugal love, and is the Jupiter of the Greeks, an iron-hearted tyrant,[1] the ruiner of ancient Greece. I speak with perfect confidence and certainty of the fact which has passed upon me. Nebuchadnezzar had

[1] Reason was the tyrant of the Greeks too.

7

seven times passed over him; I have had twenty. Thank God I was not altogether a beast as he was; but I was a slave bound in a mill among beasts and devils. These beasts and these devils are now, together with myself, become children of light and liberty, and my feet and my wife's feet are free from fetters.'

It is abundantly clear from this that there were difficulties that William and Catherine had to overcome in their marriage, and that these difficulties were precisely the same as those of Albion and Jerusalem whose whole struggle was to rid themselves of the fetters of the rational Spectre in order to overcome their 'divided existence' and achieve togetherness and wholeness in Christ.

However, to outside eyes these fetters were not visible. I quote from a letter of Hayley's which I will discuss at greater length shortly, which tells of Blake's great happiness in his 'Wife, for Heaven has bestowed on this extraordinary mortal perhaps the only female on Earth who could have suited Him *exactly*—[She] . . . is so truly the Half of her good man that they seem animated by one soul, and that a soul of indefatigable Industry and Benevolence.' The 'divided existence' was indeed far from visible.

Thus far my evidence for the theory that Albion and Jerusalem grew out of the experiences of William and Catherine Blake is contained in the letters quoted above. Half-way between these letters and the prophetic books lies an obscure and apparently personal poem from Blake's private notebook that seems to me to constitute further evidence. It was written some time between 1800 and 1803, the same time that Hayley was writing of the Blakes' ideal marriage, and at least a year before, according to Blake himself, he had freed his marriage from fetters! Blake *ought* to be the one who knew best, but it seems to me at least conceivable that they were both right—that to all practical purposes it was an extremely good partnership, even though in Blake's analytical soul a dire battle was going on to make perfect what was yet imperfect and appeared to him to threaten the whole structure. In the poem that I speak of, it is clear that Blake has not yet 'reduced that spectrous fiend to his station', and that his and his wife's feet are still in 'fetters'. On the one hand, this poem bears out the description of the letter—notice

8

particularly Blake's emphasis on the bestial nature of the Spectre
—and on the other hand, it points to the situation in Blake's
first prophetic book, *Vala, or, The Four Zoas*, and is similar even
down to the wording of one or two lines. This poem, linking
the wholly personal letters to the situation of the prophetic
books, seems to me to establish without a doubt the close connection between Mr. and Mrs. Blake and Albion and Jerusalem, but not at all in the way Middleton Murry suspects

> My Spectre around me night & day
> Like a Wild beast guards my way.
> My Emanation, far within,
> Weeps incessantly for my Sin.
>
> A Fathomless & boundless deep,
> There we wander, there we weep;
> On the hungry craving wind
> My Spectre follows thee behind.
>
> He scents thy footsteps in the snow,
> Wheresoever thou dost go
> Thro' the wintry hail & rain.
> When wilt thou return again?
>
> Dost thou not in Pride & scorn
> Fill with tempests all my morn,
> And with jealousies & fears
> Fill my pleasant nights with tears?
>
> Seven of my sweet loves thy knife
> Has bereaved of their life.
> Their marble tombs I built with tears
> And with cold & shuddering fears.
>
> Seven more loves weep night & day
> Round the tombs where my loves lay,
> And seven more loves attend each night
> Around my couch with torches bright.
>
> And seven more Loves in my bed
> Crown with wine my mournful head,
> Pitying & forgiving all
> Thy transgressions, great & small.
>
> When wilt thou return & view
> My loves, & them to life renew?
> When wilt thou return & live?
> When wilt thou pity as I forgive?

'Never, Never, I return:
Still for Victory I burn.
Living, thee alone I'll have
And when dead I'll be thy Grave.

'Thro' the Heaven & Earth & Hell
Thou shalt never never quell:
I will fly & thou pursue,
Night & Morn the flight renew.'

Till I turn from Female Love,
And root up the Infernal Grove,
I shall never worthy be
To Step into Eternity.

And, to end thy cruel mocks,
Annihilate thee on the rocks,
And another form create
To be subservient to my Fate.

Let us agree to give up Love,
And root up the infernal grove;
Then shall we return & see
The worlds of happy Eternity.

& Throughout all Eternity
I forgive you, you forgive me.
As our dear Redeemer said:
'This the Wine & this the Bread.'

And the additional stanzas:

O'er my Sins thou sit & moan:
Hast thou no sins of thy own?
O'er my Sins thou sit & weep,
And lull thy own Sins fast asleep.

What Transgressions I commit
Are for thy Transgressions fit.
They thy Harlots, thou their slave,
And my Bed becomes their Grave.

Poor pale pitiable form
That I follow in a Storm,
Iron tears & groans of lead
Bind around my aking head.

This is a long poem and an incoherent one, and yet we cannot
say it is really a bad poem, although Blake was right not to

publish it. It is intermediate between a private document and a public poem; and it is moving because of this. It has passages that affect us in precisely the way great poetry affects us. It is as irrational in its mixture of the sublime and petty, the disappointing and the transcendent, as are the moods of ordinary life.

It points, as can readily be seen, not only to the letters I have quoted about the bestial Spectre who ruins love and about the 'divided existence', but also to *The Four Zoas*. Not only is the situation similar, but lines as 'When wilt thou return' and 'There we wander' are caught up into the prophetic books as 'O when will you return, Vala the wanderer?'

The poem tells the story which I have tried to indicate is the story of the three lyrics Murry cites. That is, the poet is being accused by his beloved of the sin of loving too passionately. The Spectre of puritan guilt keeps them apart like a wild beast, yet pathetically dogs her footsteps in the snow as she wanders through the wintry night of love. The beloved is full of conflicting pride, scorn, tears, and unreasonable jealousy, and she murders his loves with these moods. For surely Blake uses 'seven loves', in opposition to Magdalene's seven devils, to indicate his moments of love for her which she rejects each time they arise. They are not, as Mr. Murry might guess, a harem of other women!

The poet asks her to return and live again, pitying him as he forgives her. But still she flees crying that she will never return, still burning for the victory of making him give up his lustful way of loving. And he, suddenly, childishly almost, gives in, saying wearily and patiently—yes, let us then give up this difficult thing called human love and try to return to the mood of happy innocence which was our first glimpse of paradise before passion made its ugly presence felt. And without irony we reach the climax:

> And Throughout all Eternity
> I forgive you, you forgive me . . .

It is a healthy anger we glimpse when the poet suddenly leaves this exalted mood, and, turning to her, asks her if she has no sins of her own that she must always be bewailing his, and adds, quite reasonably, that his own merely complement hers. It is all the more wonderful to find as if inevitable, the cosmic pity and love returning in the last stanza in which the poet sees and forgives and loves, albeit wearily.

It is interesting to see that here, as so often in Blake, the mood of love is suggested by the weather. Just as in 'Never seek to tell thy love' the passage of love was indicated by the shift from a 'gentle wind' that moved 'silently, invisibly' to a cold wind that made the beloved tremble, so in this poem the 'hungry craving wind' sets the note of love's despair. In the previous poems the beloved turned away from the poet towards the 'traveller' or the 'angel'. In this poem she turns simply towards an ideal of love that is sinless and pure. There is an irony as well as submission in the poet's agreement 'to root up the infernal grove' of love, for it postulates an asceticism that is anathema to Blake.

This points to what is the most significant paradox of Blake's work, and there are many. Blake's highest vision of human life cries out against the cruel and false chastity that is based on guilt and jealousy and fear, and sings praises to its opposite, incarnate love. But none the less it is apparent that when Blake slips from this height of vision, he himself is hopelessly caught in Urizen's web of guilt. The more so because he has rebelled. What if Urizen is right after all? What if he *is* God? With the doubt and loss of faith in his own vision comes this suffocating web of rational guilt feelings, and the consequent paradox in his work. This is the work of the Spectre who is the puritan conscience born of the 'Holy Reasoning Power'. It ruins, as he said in his letter, both his poetry and his marriage relationship. It accounts, too, for the feeling of ambiguity, almost dualism, we so often feel in Blake's work, often when he is saying most loudly that there is no dualism. This feeling that his message was somehow guilty may have been one reason why Blake neglected his audience and wrote for himself alone in the prophetic books. But it arose partly, too, just because he had no audience and this bred doubts. Whichever way round it was, and it was probably both, a vicious circle, this feeling of doubt, ambivalence, whatever you wish to call it, towards his work and his marriage, is certainly what the prophetic books are *about*, and they were written in a titanic struggle to overcome it and return to love and faith and imaginative certainty.

The only possible way out of this dilemma is found in this poem, too, at least in terms of marriage. The only way to live at the point of highest vision and to achieve incarnate love without guilt or doubt or ambiguity, is freely to admit one's guilt and forgive it over and over in oneself as well as in the marriage partner. Perfectionism, guilt, and self-righteousness are distortions of the rational spectre and only forgiveness can overcome their disastrous effects in a relationship. In all of life, but especially in the relationship of love, one must tide over the negative and flat moments which cannot help but come, by faith in the blazing meaningful moments which have been and will return in other forms.

> And throughout all Eternity
> I forgive you, you forgive me.
> As our dear Redeemer said:
> This the Wine and this the Bread.

The very probable connection between the experiences of William and Catherine Blake that are revealed in the letters I have quoted and are echoed in this poem, and the myth of Albion and Jerusalem in the prophetic books, will perhaps emerge more clearly if I end this section with a schematic summary of what happens to Albion and his bride in *The Four Zoas*, *Milton*, and *Jerusalem*.

The drama of the prophetic books takes place within Albion who is universal man. To a lesser extent it takes place within Jerusalem, his bride, and until the end, only inasmuch as she represents the feminine half of himself. In a sense there is only one character. The myth tells the story of Albion's 'Fall into Division and his Resurrection to Unity', that is, of his struggle to be reunited with his true bride, Jerusalem, as with the feminine half of himself. Blake implicitly assumes that every man has to go through a microcosmic version of the Fall—a breaking up and a remaking—in order to achieve spiritual wholeness and the consequent acceptance of life and foursquare entry and participation in it. The relationship of Albion and Jerusalem—like that in *The Song of Solomon*—is a series of conversions and lapses and reconversions to incarnate love. When at last such love grips the whole man, then male and female incompleteness is overcome in a union that is not only the marriage of a man and a woman, but an inner marriage of the two halves of the soul in a mystical union with Christ.

Albion is separated from his bride when the four faculties within him are jarred out of harmony. This happens because Albion allows Christ to be replaced in the centre of his soul by one of his own faculties, his intellect or Urizen (Your Reason). In pride Urizen sets himself up as superior to the other faculties which are: the passions or Luvah (lover); imagination or Los (loss); and Tharmas, or sensation.

Thus Albion is no longer guided from the centre of a four-fold being by Christ, but is being dominated by a part of his own Selfhood, his overly analytical reason, which treats him like a tyrannical father-god, Nobadaddy. The Spectre is the puritan sense of guilt which rises up to attend this false god, and the Spectre is continually reminding Albion that his non-rational activities are sinful. Christ is no longer being reborn continually within Albion. Instead, on the level of the imagination, of archetypal parents, there is born the bound *enfant terrible* named Orc. Orc appears to be the ascetic, and is even mistaken for Christ, but he is really the serpent, Satan, anti-Christ. Thus, because Albion is out of harmony within himself and is separated from his emanation, we get not only a false moral law, but a false Father, Son, and Holy Ghost in the persons of Urizen, Orc, and the Spectre. The tragedy is that they are so very often mistaken for true Christian values.

This inner confusion of course keeps Albion from loving spontaneously. In fact he must go so far as to deny his love for his wife because sexual love is forbidden by the rational god, and so seems all the more alarming and guilty when it breaks out from time to time with all the force of repression.

Jerusalem withdraws, sensing the fact that their love now is become lust. But she has no way of knowing exactly what has happened to Albion, and so she reacts in the worst possible way. She feels guilty too, and hurt, and so she flees from him, and at the same time tries to draw from him the kind of love that seems lost. To counterbalance Albion's rational bias she becomes

14

exaggeratedly insistent on the validity of the passions which come to dominate her as Reason dominates Albion. The two sides of human nature which are vital and healthful when operating together, now become destructive when each is trying to be the whole truth. On the one hand we find Albion bowing down to his god, Urizen, while on the other hand Jerusalem sets up Vala, her own passions, as goddess. She becomes the priestess of a kind of nature religion, or so she seems to Albion, fascinated by her possessive and elusive mystery, and he goes to her as he would to Lilith. In her effort to counterbalance Albion's subjugation to reason, she has fallen into the equally disastrous over-emphasis on the earth-passions, and to Albion she seems full of 'beautiful Witchcrafts' of which he is deathly afraid yet which draw him irresistibly. For he is now the high priest of reason and must feel that his non-rational desires are sinful. And yet he has such desires and he feels more and more guilty as she goes all out to provoke them and then flees from the intensity of what she has provoked, verifying his guilty suspicion that love is lust. And yet she beckons him and flees and he follows, feeling unutterable guilt, and as if he were being lured to destruction by the angry father-god he is betraying, his own Reason, which now seems external and vengeful.

Within Jerusalem, who is now dominated by her own passions, the emanations, or female counterparts of the four faculties within Albion, are also out of harmony. None of the faculties within Albion can find its rightful mate within Jerusalem. This accounts for the confusing parade of lamenting figures that part and come together and redivide endlessly throughout the prophetic books. For just as Albion and Jerusalem fight and come together again in brief moments of understanding, so within them their faculties struggle to find one another.

Such moments of peace and resolution are 'windows into eternity', and, Blake insists pathetically, 'there is a moment in every day that Satan cannot find.' But for the most part, despite such rare moments, within Jerusalem Ahania flees from Urizen within Albion and there is no understanding between them on the intellectual level. On the level of imagination Los and Enitharmon are highly discontented. Luvah and Vala stir up the passions, but with torments of jealousy. And on the basic

15

level of instinct or touch, Tharmas and his emanation, Enion, keep losing each other.

And thus, because Albion has forsaken Christ in the pride of his own intellect, he loses touch with Jerusalem at every level. In neither Albion nor his bride is there left anything resembling fourfold Christ-centred love, but instead only passions that are determined to assert the claims of self.

And it is basically the man's fault, Blake comes to see in the prophetic books, although he blames Jerusalem for her 'shadowy female' tactics. 'Let the men do their duty', Blake writes in a marginal comment on Lavater, 'and the women will be such wonders.' And every man's duty is precisely to become a man with all of his faculties functioning in harmony because Christ is at their centre. Although this is very difficult, anything less is impotence. Albion has become less than a man by being persuaded that his own reason is omnipotent and the passions sinful. In trying to become more than man—or, at least, some-thing other than human—he has become less. And it is the refusal of the human reason to be limited, and the allowing of it to impose god-like laws of 'perfection' that cause the false body-soul dualism which, in turn, causes discord, impotence, and destructive action or inaction.

Jerusalem, too, is not herself. More correctly, she is beside herself. Albion is only dominated by the Reason within him. Jerusalem becomes her own passions. She *becomes* Vala, another woman, the 'other woman', all that she has feared. From now on we glimpse Jerusalem herself at very brief intervals only. We are dealing instead with Vala, her Shadow, just as what we now see of Albion is his Spectre. Jerusalem's centre has moved outside herself into Vala who is Luvah's rightful mate.

From here on in the prophetic books, Albion, dominated by his Reason, remains in a state of death-like trance and night-mare impotence, bound, like Hamlet, to ceaselessly questioning inaction. Jerusalem, on the other hand, ruled by passion, becomes over-intense, larger than life and more ceaselessly active. She keeps changing back and forth from herself into Vala, thus bearing a close resemblance to the witchlike 'belle dame sans merci', the glimmering *femme fatale* who lures the spell-bound romantic lover towards his death.

Both Albion and Jerusalem are now in the position of all 'romantic' lovers who flee towards some impossible image but do not in fact want to embrace it for all their agony of desire. And this false image of the beloved, by remaining unattainable, destroys as surely as it would heal were it stripped of illusion and embraced in its more limited and miraculous actuality.

It is death-in-life that Albion pursues in pursuing Vala rather than loving his wife, Jerusalem. And he has by this time almost resigned himself to death as a punishment for desiring when his god Urizen has prohibited desire. Because he has allowed his reason to pronounce sexual love guilty, it looms large all out of proportion, and he can think of his wife only in terms of passion, of Vala. No wonder that she is no longer a human being to him, but Vala, Woman, the primitive female writ large. He has forced her into this position, but all of her hurt reactions only make it worse.

She, seeing his death-like trance, tries to snatch a kind of life-from-death, striving for total possession of the impotent Albion. But Albion treats her as a harlot. He both hates and desires her provocation. Partly to regain the manhood he suspects he has lost and partly to minimize the appearance of his commitment to the passions, he must pretend to himself that she is not his wife, not the sensitive living creature and gentle wise companion he has loved, but a looming impersonal Temptress. And, treated as one, in spirit she becomes undifferentiated Woman with all her wiles who might as well be anyone (Enion) or Ahania or Enitharmon for all Albion apparently cares.

This is why she is jealous even as she flees from him, beckoning, and why the impossible image each flees towards is that of the unattainable, the possession of which must spell death. Everyone is exceedingly unhappy to say the least, and Albion mourns:

> When I first Married you, I gave you all my whole Soul.
> I thought that you would love my loves & joy in my delights,
> Seeking for pleasure in my pleasures, O Daughter of Babylon.
> Then thou wast lovely, mild & gentle; now thou art terrible
> In jealousy, and unlovely in my sight . . .
> Therefore I shew my Jealousy & set before you Death.

I have tried to indicate something of the difficulties that beset Albion and Jerusalem in the prophetic books, and it seems obvious that the fetters that bound them bear more than a passing resemblance to the spectral fetters Blake describes as the ruination of his work and marriage.

The only possible way out of such a predicament is, as Blake says, to 'reduce that Spectrous fiend to his station', that is, put in right perspective the perfectionist rules that the human reason proclaims, and so be willing to forgive imperfection in oneself and in the beloved. This is the only climate in which love can exist and break the bond of Selfhood. Then and only then, when patience and forgiveness have placed Christ again in the centre of the soul, and Urizen is no longer a tyrant but mild Rintrah, an important conscience and guide, can Albion and his bride come together in an affirmation of human love that is also mystical union in Christ, because they now see what the Spectre has long denied, that the senses are the gateway to eternity. It is important to remember that Blake *never* advocates doing away with reason altogether, as many critics think. Rather, Reason must be put in its right place where it becomes commonsense and intelligence applied to particular situations rather than cruel and impossible general laws.

Such an attempt to summarize briefly the main events of Blake's prophetic book, may well read like a case history or a gnostic nightmare. I have purposely left out any indications of the similarity of Blake's myth to the myths that the psychologists explore. The material speaks loudly enough for itself. Again, I have avoided drawing any parallels between Blake's work and the symbols and beliefs of those gnostic sects to which there is often such startling resemblance, from the early gnostics themselves down to Swedenborg whose writings Blake knew intimately and owed much to. Many studies of Blake's sources have been made and continue to appear, and I leave to their authors the tracking down of influences and similarities. I am more fascinated with the new things Blake is trying to say, using whatever of the past that seemed useful to him, but always in his own unique context.

What seems to me the exciting and unparalleled achievement of the prophetic books is their moving and human portrayal, long before the days of depth psychology, of what goes on in the fluid dream-like world of breakdown, breakdown above all of the vision that had held life together. Not only this, but instead of getting entirely lost in the inner guilts and despairs of Albion alone, we are given a clear picture of the frightening effects of his illness on the person closest to him, her resulting insecurity and the consequent breakdown of their relationship.

And still more important, we are shown the way out of this nightmare world, not through being told to let go completely on the analyst's couch, but in an example of human courage and valiantly maintained love that seems to triumph like the dawn after seemingly endless night. It is a way out that worked in Blake's own experience and one, he claims, that is a universal remedy for a necessary and universal illness. For Blake dared to see such breakdown as an almost inevitable consequence of original sin which is intellectual curiosity and pride. Breakdown is simply a stage in every man's journey from innocence through the necessary anguish caused by experience, to that 're-organized innocence' which is liberty and freedom.

WILLIAM'S SHADOW

HAVING tried to give some answer to the frequent wail—
'but I can't make out what the prophetic books are about!'
—I must now tackle the more serious complaint that they are not
poetry. If they are not poetry, what are they? And what of the
undoubted poetry that they contain? How do they stand in
relation to Blake's early lyrics? And what do they mean in terms
of his personal life and development?

Rex Warner in his review of a recent edition of Blake's
Jerusalem gives voice almost apologetically to the conventional
fair-minded and intelligent but baffled point of view. This view-
point could be said to constitute almost a school of thought as
regards Blake, and is, unfortunately, much to be preferred to
the many cranks who have defended Blake, or more often something they read into Blake, with wild and embarrassing
enthusiasm. The attitude taken by such critics as Mr. Warner
most ably represents is, on the whole, mistrustful of Blake,
head-shaking and impatient, and yet more than half open to the
'vision' Blake talks about *if* it were not so buried in what they
respectfully and too loosely call 'mysticism'. Mr. Warner
writes:

'It must be admitted, however, that no beauties of typography or of
presentation can make the poem anything but exceedingly difficult.
There are, of course, many passages where the verse must sweep
the reader along in its own fine frenzy and lead him to behold with
delight and admiration something of the terrific vision of the mystic
poet. But there are other passages which are most bleak and for-
bidding. Not only do "Four Universes round the Mundane Egg remain
Chaotic", but much else besides. And I imagine that there are many

people who, when reading the Prophetic Books and after sticking on such a line as "The Hermaphroditic Condensations are Divided by the Knife", will turn back to the earlier poems and will wonder whether all these visionary pages are worth a single one of the Songs of Innocense or of Experience.

'Such an impatient attitude, though natural, is not to be commended. The author of "Jerusalem" and "Milton" is the same man as the author of "Tyger, Tyger" and "O Rose, thou art sick!" Everything we have from his pen must be respected, and almost everything can be admired. And if, in his later works, he becomes difficult to follow because of the peculiarity of his own system of mythology, we are not entitled to dismiss this mythology as a fraud or to deplore it as an unfortunate accident. This is what Mr. T. S. Eliot seems to do when he writes of Blake: "What his genius required, and what it sadly lacked, was a framework of accepted and traditional ideas which would have prevented him from indulging in a philosophy of his own, and concentrated his attention upon the problems of the poet." To me it seems that, while nearly everybody does "need" this "framework of accepted and traditional ideas", Blake is one of the great exceptions to the rule. He was a self-educated mystic, and had this not been so, his peculiar and powerful vision would certainly have been different. One must be bold indeed to suggest that it would have been in any way "better".'

Remembering that it was Eliot who, in the same essay from which Mr. Warner quotes, put his finger on the phrase 'a peculiar honesty' to describe Blake, and who also commented that Blake 'was naked, and saw men naked' and that his 'poetry has the unpleasantness of great poetry'[1] we cannot altogether discard Eliot's judgement on the prophetic books, for it is sure to be a considered and a sensitive one. But I join Mr. Warner in decrying Eliot's too facile dismissal of Blake's 'ideas', and his insistence that Blake would have been better off writing from within a tradition. Mr. Eliot of all people with his critical acumen should have taken into consideration that more than anything else Blake's vision is a severe criticism of most frameworks 'of accepted and traditional ideas'. Such traditions, to Blake's mind, were simply veils that must be torn away to reveal true art and true Christianity. We can hardly blame him, then, for not using one of these traditions for a vehicle as Mr. Eliot finds himself able to do. And, going a little deeper, we

[1] T. S. Eliot, *Selected Essays 1917–1932*, New York, 1932: 'William Blake', pp. 275–280.

find that after all Blake did belong to a tradition, albeit an untidy one, and this is the tradition of the prophets.

One does often wish, with Eliot, that Blake had concentrated more on the problems of the poet, or alternatively, that he had not tried to put his prophecies into verse. The latter would almost seem preferable, since Blake states firmly that the poetry is second to the vision, and he seemed to know that he would never have the patience to polish the vast *farouche* bulk of the prophetic books into poetry.

His setting down of his prophecies into what is for the most part uneven and often blatantly careless verse has caused endless confusion, and the general tendency is to dismiss most of what Blake is saying simply because it is such a colossal failure as poetry, and especially since we know from his early lyrics what Blake is capable of achieving *qua* poet. Nevertheless, the prophetic books contain rare but lovely passages of poetry, and it is significant that these passages coincide with the most clearly articulated and deeply felt 'vision'. But more of this later.

It seems to me only fair to give what Blake is *saying* a hearing even if we consider that it fails as poetry. This is especially true since Blake told us at the outset that the poetry was secondary, almost incidental. The prophetic books have not yet been given this thorough and impartial hearing. At best critics have generalized or abstracted passages from their context and used them to illustrate Blake's views on some particular point, despairing of the whole as indecipherable nonsense.

It is such a sympathetic hearing that I am trying to give Blake in this study of the prophetic writings. As it becomes more and more clear to me what Blake is saying, I become more and more convinced that he has made in these poems a truly remarkable exploration of the human psyche. The probing of juxtaposed areas which we now, rightly or wrongly, separate into the business of psychology, theology, aesthetics, and so on, goes far beyond anything that has been written before or since, Freud not excepted, with a profundity that frightens those who do not want to see beyond the familiar and manageable. It is easy to dismiss, as many have done, such strangeness as nonsense, particularly since Blake had none of the language signs that we have today in the jargon of psychology, and he had to invent signs as he went along.

Blake's vision is a modern one, and we may be only now catching up with it. What I mean by modern is that it represents a view of life, internal and external, that man today can recognize as a valid articulation and ordering of his particular form of chaos and *angst*. Such a view of life was almost wholly out of context amidst the rational and sentimental literature of Blake's own day, and only now seems to be reaching a period that is ready for it. The prophetic books should, of course, have been written in the form of a psychological novel or fable, but psychology as such had yet to be invented, and the novel was still formal and externalized.

I think from his repeated prose remarks about the verse form of the prophetic books that Blake himself was very uneasy about it and dissatisfied. He himself confessed that he had used 'inferior' verse for the 'inferior' parts. He who was capable of writing 'The Sick Rose' must have realized that the poetry in the prophetic books was sparse. But although uneasy, he was not able to care enough to do much about it, so great was the pressure of the visions 'dictated' to him by the 'supernaturals'.

Jack Lindsay, in a little known book on Blake, accuses him of a kind of 'regional laziness', and I think he is right. He phrases well, too, without making a study of the prophetic books at any length, one aspect of their value:

'We have been permitted, in the spectacle of Blake's mind, by some freak of the gods, to see something not ordinarily permitted. We have a number of examples of the finished image; but here we have been admitted into the subterranean or is it sublunary factories of the soul. As if a sudden side-section had been made of the various layers of the creative energies, like a landslide that exposes the stratification of a hill, we behold the whole plain of cosmos laid open before our eyes. A brief vision of fumes of light, and we fall through congealing plains of anguish; then we see a vast hand descend and grab the twisting little images worming about in the split darkness. We see the conflict, the long process of tempering, of amalgamation, of revolt, of subjection and of slow digestion. After all this universe of furious preparation we expect to find at least a Shakespearean world of imagery appearing. But instead we discover at the top scarcely more that a bubbling up of flowers and a handful of birdsongs. Still, they are

23

very beautiful, and we have been shown all the vaults and corridors and sunken spaces of the spirit. It would be ungrateful to cavil.'[1]

Mr. Lindsay in his little book which is full of purple patches, but also full of insight, gives what seems to me the best description that I have seen of what Blake means by contrasting the masculine Spectre and the feminine Emanation, those predominantly male or female aspects of the soul which go bad if either tries to separate itself off from the whole human being and become its sole truth:

> 'Blake uses two contrasted symbols to express those two conditions which beset the soul (dividing it). He calls them Spectre and Emanation. The first is all that tends to harden, to parch, to lose vital contact with life and set up an intellectual or moral abstraction in place of the living image. The other is all that tends to loosen, to weaken the bonds of individuality, to dissolve it in the common and glucose mass of life.'[2]

Blake, in the prophetic books, not only describes these two states of the divided soul, but often gives every evidence of being in both himself, which ruins his poetry. He is, at these times, at the mercy of both Urizen and Vala. On the one hand, his writing is over-analytical and abstract and out of contact with any living image, individual to the point of eccentricity. On the other hand, it is full of undifferentiated characters who dissolve boringly into the glucose mass of life with their identical orgies of groaning, wailing, and jealousy.

I believe, too, that in the slipshod craftsmanship of the prophetic books there is more than a hint of defiance towards an audience too stupid to recognize the perfect lyricism of the *Songs*. Certainly it is there in Blake's deliberate obscurity. There is in the prophetic books, besides this carelessness and defiance, a kind of lonely talking to himself, a grave buffoonery undertaken in order to keep up his own flagging spirits. It would seem, at first glance, akin to the solemn game that Jonathan Swift is playing in *Gulliver* and in *A Modest Proposal*. But whereas in Blake the game is a naïve even though esoteric one that he uses in his hurt to disguise his deep love of

---

[1] Jack Lindsay, *William Blake*, London, 1927, p. 37.
[2] *Ibid.*, p. 31.

humanity, in Swift, we cannot help feeling that the delightful fantasy is a sophisticated device employed to keep at bay an almost pathological horror of human nature. Blake has much of the 'unpleasantness' Eliot speaks of, but it is more often like that of a wilful child determined to mystify and repel rather than Swift's delicate disguise of his repugnance. Like Swift, Blake invents strange nonsense words and names, and like Swift too, takes infinite pains to measure out the topography and proportions of his strange landscape and relate them to each other and to actual life with absorbed precision.

A digression in order to discuss Blake's invention of names is perhaps relevant, since so much nonsense has been written on the possible derivations of such names. Granted that Blake may well have read much occult and oriental lore, still the main motivation behind his invention of names is a kind of playfulness, an almost naïve whimsy.[1] Thus while Orc probably does go back to the early English word meaning 'demon' Urizen means simply 'Your Reason', and the following type of solemn pedantry on the subject, which is fairly common unfortunately, becomes merely ludicrous, even when it contains some truth:

'Perhaps some of Blake's extraordinary names have been partly inspired by some of Bryant's disquisitions—we shall see later that India may also have had a part to play in the matter.

'Ur (Aur, Our) is given as a root for light and fire, and Blake's *Ur*izen is the Prince of Light.

'On, eon, refer to the Sun.

'Is, az, ees, also refer to light, fire and the Sun.

'Zan refers to the Sun.

'Is it too much to imagine Blake mixing up all these sounds, Ur, is (ees), Zan (eon) and coming to Urizen?

'Bryant also tells us of an Urchon, God of fire, or Orchan, Orchanes, who might have produced Blake's Orc.'

(DENIS SAURAT, *Blake and Modern Thought*, p. 61.)

Saurat goes on with this kind of conjecture:

'The names even in Sonnerat are suggestive of Blake's names. We come across Chittere-Parouvan (p. 123), the giant Erenien, Addi

[1] Foster Damon writes (p. 69): 'Their names were created at random. Some were anagrams; some were found in strange books such as Agrippa's Occult Philosophy; some came from Ossian; one from the Bhagvad-Geeta; but the majority were invented for the sake of the sound alone.'

pouran (124), Aotan (130), Ouricati-Tirounal, Ananda-Perpena-desouomi (132), Paor Nomi (138), Tirounomaley, Paeni-Caori (144), Ani (154), Narissen (208), Allemaron (226), Amnemanta (39), Rudden Ruddiren. In the *Bagavadan*, Emadarmen (100), Outama-baden Pravetiden, Rouguen (73), Ouroucenem (334).

'These can surely compare with Blake's best such as Urizen, Enitharmon, Allamanda, Entuthon-Benython, Tiriel, Oothoon, Rin-trah, Palamabron, etc. There is to the ear a similarity in the use of vowels and consonants in entirely un-English fashion, and Blake's verbal imagination seems to me to produce births more comparable to these versions of Hindoo names than to anything else' (p. 113).

Mr. Saurat goes on to deal with symbolism equally thoroughly, shedding more darkness than light on Blake's poems:

'Thus in the *Zohar*, Man's brain is surrounded by shells (vol. I, pp. 119, 130, 137, de Pauly) but the shells have cracks which let the divine light come in and on men's senses.

'We shall here therefore merely tabulate some of the expressions of that order used by Blake:

Shells: 303, 312, 492, 532, 535, 539, 600–1, 660.
Egg: 513, 532–3, 572, 696, 702, 720, 740.
Windows: 232, 290, 291 (cf. also *Zohar*, vol. III, p. 433: where immortality dirties the windows).
Tent that cuts Man off from Heaven: 252, 59 (*Zohar*, vol. IV, p. 317).
Light: 350, 354, 428, 447–8, 523, 616, 698, 941.
Cold: (cf. Fludd—quoted in Saurat: *Milton et le matérialisme chrétien*, p. 26), 601, 620.
The two Suns, one dead and one living (Swedenborg and Cabala): 937.
The two forces: centrifugal and centripetal: the Prolific and the Devourer: 191–198.
Limits (gnostic: Oros): 340, 381, 398, 401.
Vortexes: 359, 360, 490, 641: Wheels: 427, 634–5 (*Zohar*, vol. IV, pp. 261–77, and vols. V, VI, notes p. 182).
Polypus: 534, 536, 574, 583, 643, 680, 683.   (p. 157).

Having duly admired the research, one might, after reading this and other efforts like it, comment feebly that one would have thought there would be more references to Egg! The most natural reaction is, like Blake's characters, to go off in howls and shrieks and groans.

The intricacy and crudeness of the prophetic books in the bulk, which many of Blake's critics like Saurat vie to outdo, bring us back forcibly time and again to the delicate passionate lucidity of Blake's early lyrics. And we are left with an enormous question mark. How? When? Why? And above all—What happened to Blake that he should turn from writing what may well be the most simply expressed profundity in English poetry to writing the most bafflingly incoherent poems in our literature?

Is there not, we ask, more vision, and of a kind that embraces the heights and depths of the human situation, in one such lyric as 'The Sick Rose', than in all the vast and complex panorama of the prophetic books? They tell the same story. The prophetic books are simply the many levels of the mysterious rose torn off petal by petal and laid out in a row to dry. The prophetic books could be described as a long and vague and cerebral explanation of the precisely felt and thought-out and incredibly alive image of the Sick Rose, which, in fact, needs no analysis to add to its bounded richness.

Is not the single phrase, 'the invisible worm that flies in the night', more graphic to describe the dark guilt within the very nature of love that destroys its living beauty and innocence, than the generation and history of Orc who is the 'invisible worm' explained? Is not this phrase more expressive of love's terror at the self-destruction it helplessly carries within it than all the shrieks and howls and groans of the prophetic books?

The answer is and must be an unqualified yes. No defence of the prophetic books can alter this fact. Such ability to express in one sure stroke the whole beauty and sickness of human life, and also the hope for recovery, is the work of genius, and remains the high point of Blake's career as poet. I am not setting out in this study to deny this in any way. What I hope to do is simply to give a fair hearing to the less poetically successful work of the same genius, which he none the less felt was his finest production because of the message it contained. I hope, too, in some way to evaluate it in terms other than those of poetry alone and yet not simply push it off into a pigeon-hole labelled 'mysticism' and of interest only to initiates. We do not need to plead for such a hearing for 'The Sick Rose'. It speaks for itself and by its mysterious clarity draws fascinated listeners.

The Book of Thel and *The Marriage of Heaven and Hell* are the last of Blake's poems which have this quality to any degree. After these books we begin to need 'keys' and the poems are a chore to read unless regarded as a kind of riddle. The subject matter of these two poems set side by side explains a good deal of the conflict which exploded into the prophetic books, no longer able to focus itself in one image. On the one hand, in *The Marriage of Heaven and Hell,* although the duality is present, we get a predominant impression of tremendous delight in naked beauty and energy of the intellect and senses combined. But in *Thel* we are given a moving picture of the virginal soul fleeing in horror away from the unbearable energy and fleshly beauty of sexual passion back to the father in the quiet garden, and the direct question—'Why a little curtain of flesh on the bed of our desire?' The difficulties of Blake's marriage, plus this ever-present antithesis, plus his lack of success which made him doubt his own message of the beauty of passionate life, seems to me to suggest what made Blake attempt the analysis of the prophetic books. These unhappy poems were born of doubt.

And it is clear that doubt as well as 'pity divides the soul'. In passing I would like to voice a long-standing curiosity as to whether Blake was thinking of his wife when he wrote that 'pity divides the soul'. Pity is the clearest picture we have of Catherine because of the famous story of their courtship. 'I pity you,' she said, and Blake is supposed to have replied, 'Then I love you.' But we do not hear that Catherine answered, 'I love you, too.' Los' downfall—and Los is imagination—is due to Enitharmon's pity. That Blake mistrusts pity emerges clearly.

Did Blake doubt that his wife loved him when she fled from his passion? And that she fled is clear. Was her pity and flight, instead of the love that should have proved his vision of the goodness and innocence of passion, what made him doubt it? And when he was not a success and she pitied rather than blamed him for that, did he doubt even more that she really could love him? Did he then have to prove his vision to her and to his audience and most of all to himself through the analysis of the prophetic books? Such interesting questions are unanswerable.

Thel is not only Catherine fleeing from passion, but one side of Blake. And it is this woman who is both Catherine and Blake's anima or emanation that we are watching in his poems from now on. She is the Sick Rose. Blake is preoccupied with her, one would almost say obsessed, and he is trying to understand and explain her behaviour, for she is out of his control whether she is Vala or Thel or Oothoon. She veers too far in one direction and then in another. By different names and in different moods we follow her through the prophetic books, and we get the impression of one person, the Blakean woman. She emerges much more clearly as a person than Albion even although at times she is only a part of him. I think this was because Blake was watching her closely as he could not watch Albion who was himself. It is in the Blakean woman, drawn or written about, that we get the flavour of a real person and she is much beloved though it is hard to tell how much she loves, for she is at the mercy of her own moods and fears. Only when she is Jerusalem can Blake see the possibility of her maturity and liberation, and Jerusalem's first name was America, her last, Liberty.

And so we get the prophetic books which are a kind of prose-in-the-form-of-poetry working out and analysis of why vision fails—in love, in art, and in religion—and road directions as to how it should be found again, rather than vision itself in the sense Blake meant it and had had it. We find precepts for life and poetry rather than these things themselves, the actual living belief that leaps joyously out from the incomparable early lyrics. The prophetic books, a record of the breakdown of vision and gropings back towards it, are highly interesting and necessary documents. There are indications that, had Blake lived long enough, he would have emerged from the prophetic books capable of writing 'Songs of Reorganiz'd Innocence' as lovely and profound as his early lyrics. 'To see the world in a grain of sand' and the lyric known as 'Jerusalem' are very late poems and prove that Blake could still write with gnomic lucidity. They hint at the lyrics he might have written had not the battle with the prophecies taken so long and consumed all his poetic energies. For we must remember that as an artist Blake's career is directly the reverse of his career as a poet. He did his finest designs at the end of his life, and some of the Job engravings and Dante drawings are the artistic equivalent of the Songs.

Blake in the prophetic books is protesting too much that he has vision. There is something too insistent in his loud cries that he is the prophet and knows he has truth. The louder he cries the more we suspect that he is doubting his vision. And this is precisely what it was that plunged him into the heart of the sick rose and lost him his god's-eye-view. 'If the Sun and Moon should Doubt, They'd immediately go out.' Blake's poetic genius went out because he doubted what was essential to his vision, the fundamental goodness of life, and of the passions.

What made Blake doubt? It is obvious that he himself is not clear what it was—he casts around blaming it first on Urizen, then on Vala, and concocted the whole maze of the prophetic books to explain his doubt and overcome it. He still is not clear.

But his poetry knows what it was. We are told with startling clarity what the answer is, and it is a much simpler, more human and pathetic one than Blake's cosmic explanations. In *The Four Zoas*, which is the first and therefore the closest-to-the-cause statement of Blake's troubled state of mind, there is only one passage of beauty and pathetic inevitability that strikes the reader as heartfelt poetry. It is the finest passage in the prophetic books, and it is not about Albion's subjection to Urizen, his loss of Christ, or his troubled relation with his wife.

Rather, it is about the desolate market where none come to buy wisdom. The lament is sung by Enion who has been driven out into 'the deathful infinite':

> What is the price of Experience? do men buy it for a song?
> Or Wisdom for a dance in the street? No, it is bought with the price
> Of all that a man hath, his house, his wife, his children.
> Wisdom is sold in the desolate market where none come to buy.

The wording of the first line, 'What is the price of *Experience?* do men buy it for a *song?*' takes on more particular meaning when we think of Blake's *Songs of Experience* that were not bought. And the last line, 'Wisdom is sold in the desolate market where none come to buy', is a cry from the heart and out of Blake's own experience.

Can anything be plainer? The experience that lies behind these lines is the main experience that lies behind the prophetic books. The primary cause of Blake's doubt and confusion was his complete neglect by what should have been his audience.

This initial doubt of the value of his vision set into motion all of the other ways in which a man can doubt himself, especially in relation to his wife and to his God. These latent doubts are the underlying causes of the prophetic books, and they tell an interesting psychological story.

By the time Blake came to write the prophetic books, he had virtually no audience. The purest work of his genius, the *Songs*, were totally disregarded. The difficult time at Felpham was preceded by an even more difficult time in London. Blake had no commissions and little money. No one seemed to care about what he was trying to say, and Blake began to doubt the vision of life that had once so confidently pervaded his whole being. It was a time of desperate neglect. Art was judged solely by the standards that made Hayley the popular poet of the day. It is no exaggeration to say that there was not a soul to comfort Blake about his work except Catherine, his wife. And this may have seemed too like pity.

It was probably she who told him not to mind, that neglect was the price he had to pay for wisdom. If she did say something of the sort in an effort to comfort him, he might easily in his hurt have banished her to 'the deathful infinite' where false rational standards hold sway. Seeing 'rational' men like Hayley praised and successful while his own far greater talent went ignored, he could have replied to her comfort he *must* doubt his own vision which had gotten him nowhere *until* he could prove it, or else disprove the standards of reason, but in the terms of reason itself. For that Blake had a residue of guilt about not 'getting anywhere' is apparent in a letter to Cumberland: 'I thought my pursuits of Art a kind of criminal dissipation and neglect of the main chance.' And even if his wife had continued to beg him not to be so foolish as to doubt his own vision, that of imagination, he might, like Urizen casting Ahania away for such advice, tell her that vision itself must be subjected to reason and 'proved' once intellectual doubts have set in and faith departed.

This surprising theme of the wife holding out for true vision, begging her deluded husband not to neglect imagination for what he suspects may be a higher intellectual vision, occurs again and again in the prophetic books. And again and again the wife is cast off, derided as weak and feminine for this advice. And thus begins marital strife in the prophetic books. Ahania is banished by her husband, Urizen, for the feminine wisdom of pleading with him not to become a tyrant over the other faculties; Enitharmon in the guise of Enion is banished by Los; and Jerusalem herself is deserted by Albion, although regretfully, as he leaves her and goes off into the dazzling abstract world of pure intelligence that she is afraid of, to 'converse with fathers and brothers', and 'talk man to man'.

Blake, being no fool, himself suspected that the manly fourfold vision he was always harping on—that clear intellectual gnosis which even Urizen must bow to and which Blake calls 'Eternity'—was not really so much to be preferred to 'three fold' vision—which is the artistic vision of Beulah—as he would like to persuade us, and possibly himself. Again, it is his poetry that knows more clearly than Blake does. The suspicion of the reader, that Blake is for the most part simply talking through his hat about the superiority of fourfold vision, is verified by the greatly contrasting quality of the poetry about Beulah and about Eternity. Contrast, in the following passage, the differences in quality and interest. The poetry about Beulah, the realm of artistic vision and marital harmony, is warm and tender and many-levelled, and most certainly contains thought. The lines about Eternity which I have underscored, are thin, pompous and didactic, and often shrilly insistent on the poet's ability to reach his abstract pinnacle. So great is the difference not only in quality but in quantity, that it is as if Blake could hardly bear to fill out a minimum number of lines concerning Eternity, and he fills them out carelessly with a number of stock generalities and abstract tags, and turns with relief to telling us about Beulah where his real interest lies. But to admit outright that he preferred Beulah, would be to admit that the weak feminine advice had been right! None the less, Blake comes pretty close to admitting this.

There is a place where Contrarieties are equally True:
This place is called Beulah. It is a pleasant lovely Shadow
Where no dispute can come, Because of those who Sleep . . .
. . . Beulah's moony shades & hills . . .
Beulah is evermore Created around Eternity, appearing

To the Inhabitants of Eden around them on all sides.
But Beulah to its Inhabitants appears within each district
As the beloved infant in his mother's bosom round incircled
With arms of love & pity & sweet compassion. But to
The Sons of Eden the moony habitations of Beulah
Are from Great Eternity a mild & pleasant Rest.

And it is thus Created. *Lo, the Eternal Great Humanity,*
To whom be Glory & Dominion Evermore, Amen,
Walks among all his awful Family seen in every face:
As the breath of the Almighty such are the words of man to man
In the great Wars of Eternity, in fury of Poetic Inspiration,
To build the Universe stupendous, Mental forms Creating.

But the Emanations trembled exceedingly, nor could they
Live, because the life of Man was too exceeding unbounded.
His joy became terrible to them; they trembled & wept,
Crying with one voice: 'Give us a habitation & a place
In which we may be hidden under the shadow of wings:
For if we, who are but for a time & who pass away in winter,
Behold these wonders of Eternity we shall consume;
But you, O our Fathers & Brothers, remain in Eternity.
But grant us a Temporal Habitation, do you speak
To us; we will obey your words as you obey Jesus
The Eternal who is blessed for ever & ever. Amen.'

So spake the lovely Emanation, & there appear'd a pleasant
Mild Shadow above, beneath, & on all sides round.

Into this pleasant Shadow all the weak & weary
Like Women & Children were taken away as on wings
Of dovelike softness, & shadowy habitations prepared for them.
But every Man return'd & went still going forward thro'
The Bosom of the Father in Eternity on Eternity,
Neither did any lack or fall into Error without
A Shadow to repose in all the Days of happy Eternity.

The lines about Beulah speak for themselves. But does not
Blake succumb to just that Miltonic error he is trying to correct?
He is not here speaking through Milton to show us Milton's
error, but is, for the moment, in dead earnest when he relegates
woman to a lower order than her husband. In fact, he implies
that she is of baser material altogether, as lovely as a flower, but
also as transient. since she is unable to bear those pure visions

of the intellect which are alone eternal. It is not until the end of *Jerusalem* that Blake corrects himself and Albion on this score, and, incidentally, Milton.

What do they mean, we may well ask, those capitalized abstractions and ludicrous generalities in the lines about Eternity? They convey no image. And have they anything at all of the Minute Particularity that Blake insists must be in all fine art? We get no sense of dazzling vision, but simply of vague and empty ideas, as unsatisfying as Milton's Heaven.

Blake's complete giveaway is in the single word 'unbounded'. It is the measure of his unconscious insincerity here, that in every other instance in his writing it is a term of severe disapproval. He condemns other artists for not possessing the 'wirey bounding line' in thought and execution. There can be no true vision, he insists, without the bounding line. This he says over and over again. Yet in the passage above he would have us believe that only the 'unbounded' fourfold vision is manly and can be considered the highest.

This is one aspect of the ambiguity in Blake's thinking, and it always appears when he is trying to convince us of the supreme desirability of fourfold vision. That he himself is not altogether convinced of its superiority to threefold poetic vision is apparent, although he uses all the terms of conviction. Another indication of his uncertainty is that on the one hand he states that Christ is the only true God, and he equates art with Christianity. Since Beulah is the realm of love and art, one would think that it would also be the realm of Christ and the highest vision. But we find, on the other hand, Blake is persuading us that there is yet a higher realm in fourfold vision, and here we hear nothing of Christ, but only of union with God the Father. Is this Urizen? we wonder in astonishment, for we are faced with one of many contradictions.

All of Blake's longing that Albion might be allowed to stay in the peaceful moony realms of poetic insight and marital harmony emerges in the poetry about Beulah. But Albion, like Blake, must believe that it is too easy, too feminine a solution to remain where he is happy, while intellect is doubting the very existence of such happiness. And so, instead of expressing his truest vision of what Foster Damon describes as ordinary human life *intensified*, Blake sets out instead to 'prove' it. It is as if he feels that such felicity must first be contained and examined by the intellect before it can be enjoyed. Such a lack of spontaneity is often the price paid when the analysing intellect is regarded as more authoritative than the more earthy faculties. This is certainly one of Urizen's most elementary illusions.

Because the emanation trembles to see him go off into the realm of abstract certainties, Albion accuses her of not being interested in the things he is interested in, of not 'loving his joys'. Yet the predominant tone of this passage is that of his great tenderness because she remains in the realm he must regretfully leave, and because she insists on its validity despite his doubts and scorn.

I believe that Blake's search for fourfold vision was the downfall of his poetry. It was tempting to him not only because such an inquiry seemed to be *proving* poetic vision in terms of the rational analysis admired by his contemporaries, but because this theory rounds off his fourfold pattern very neatly. Indeed, to talk about fourfold vision makes it seem as if some sort of beatific vision has been achieved, unless we look closely at the sterility of the actual vision on the page in front of us, and notice its contradiction of Blake's much more glowing earlier statements about Christ and art and love being one. The Eden or Eternity of fourfold vision is a place without Christ or imagination or love. It has only the thin and terrible whiteness of the Father in whose light the songs of innocence would surely wither away, just as they must thrive in the sunny warmth and moony radiance of Beulah, the poet's state of mind, or rather, state of being. Beulah was the place or state that Blake loved, there is no doubt about that, and it is where his Songs were written, even though he now relegates Beulah to a lowly position, describing it as simply a place of rest from the more arduous labours of eternity.

The idea of postulating a higher realm than Beulah came with the need to prove his vision intellectually to those who by their neglect made him doubt its validity. 'If the Sun & Moon should Doubt, They'd immediately go out.' And for Blake they did go out when he came to doubt his vision of gold-green days and children playing, the white starry night and amber mornings when lost children were found again. Such heightened and clear reality can be perceived only in the soft sunlight and moonglow of Beulah which is a land of maternal love and compassion, and not a realm of purgation where the only reality is to talk 'man to man' about the 'Universe stupendous' and the 'fury of Poetic Inspiration' under the terrible eye of the Father.

If to the amateur psychologist this would seem to open up significant vistas back to Blake's childhood, let it do so without undue pressure, for there are many such glimpses if we look for them, and they all help to round out the portrait of an extraordinary and sensitive being, rather than a neurotic. We are told by Gilchrist of the small boy crying ecstatically that he had seen angels singing in a perfectly ordinary tree, 'and only through his mother's intercession escaped a thrashing from his honest father, for telling a lie' (p. 6). We know that this same father was sympathetic enough to finance Blake's training as an engraver and to give him enough money to buy prints to copy, but none the less like many practical fathers he continually wanted reassurance that he was not wasting his money, and we can see the adolescent talking big and abstract 'man to man' about the fury of poetic inspiration. And yet, from Blake's letter to Cumberland we know that he was somehow made to feel that Art was 'a criminal neglect of the main chance' and as guilty as an illicit love. But more of this when we come to Blake's strange relation with his patron, Hayley. It is enough to suggest that such a rich passage as the one we have been discussing reveals not only that it was Blake's neglect by his contemporaries that made him doubt his vision and write the prophetic books to prove it, but that this doubt opened up a long corridor of doubts going back to his childhood.

If Blake is a mystic, his true mystic vision like his best poetry is shaped in Beulah's realm, not in the negation of fourfold Eternity. For the burden of his religious vision, like that of his best poetry, is 'Thy own Humanity learn to adore.' But this is not what we are told in the so-called higher vision of Eternity. Here we find something more like gnosticism in its desire for a destructive union with the Father in order to contain in the human mind things that only the Creator can know.

All this is, of course, supposed to be Albion's story, not Blake's. Yet, even if we did not have the evidence of letters to connect Blake's situation to Albion's, it is easy to see that while Blake was writing the prophetic books, he himself was half caught in Albion's state of confusion and subjection to Urizen. He refutes Urizen, or says he does, but remains confused on the question of whether Beulah's vision or that of Eternity is more to be desired, although his poetry tells us where his real interest lies. There is a faint possibility that Blake deliberately wrote thinly about Eternity and richly and movingly about Beulah in order to imitate Milton. But this would defeat his own fourfold scheme, and I do not think that his writing in the prophetic books is nearly controlled enough to support this possibility, especially since in every other instance where he gives an ironic parody of Milton or Swedenborg in order to point out their errors, he gives us plenty of warning that he is doing this. Finally, in *Milton* such a parody would be a confusion rather than a subtlety, for he points out quite didactically the errors that Milton made which he, Blake, is going to correct.

The painful contradictions in the prophetic books stem largely from the fact that although Blake tells us he is overcoming the tyrant, Urizen, he tries to do it with Urizen's weapons rather than those of poetry and Christ. And just when we are told that Urizen is routed, we are apt to find that once more he is tyrannizing over Blake's poetry. In *Jerusalem* Blake is back on the right track, and it is Los or imagination who begins to win out. Los is once more Blake's friend and brings back Jerusalem to Albion and sometimes wears the guise of Christ.

The question of Blake's lack of an audience and popular success brings us to the problem of his relationship with his patron, William Hayley. It is a relationship which puzzles critics, and in which, one cannot help feeling, there is more than meets the bewildered eye that scans Blake's rude epigrams on the subject. I think that it is a puzzle which can be more or less cleared up if it is examined in the light of those inner difficulties of Blake's that I have been trying to piece together. And I feel it is a situation that can and ought to be clarified in such a way that Hayley regains a little of the dignity that he has lost through Blake's epigrams and through Blake's champions among the critics. Poor Hayley is usually dismissed by the irate Blakeans as, at best, a well-meaning but painfully obtuse buffoon whose only assets were a kind heart and considerable wealth. At the worst, he is made out to be the ruination of Blake's genius, the Satan of *Milton*, as Blake would like to have us believe for want of a better scapegoat. Neither of these comfortable assumptions fits the facts closely enough.

At the time that Hayley suggested that Blake and his wife move from London to a cottage at Felpham, near his own mansion, Hayley was all that Blake was not. He was, in fact, *the* successful eighteenth-century man of letters, by far the most popular poet of his day, and a landed gentleman of culture and charm to boot. Hayley was fifty-five to Blake's forty-three.

Blake, on the other hand, had been going through a period of total neglect. His vision and his expression of it seemed wholly unwanted. In London he and his wife had been near starvation with little work on hand and no commissions forthcoming. The invitation to Felpham seemed to come as a godsend. And there is no evidence that in suggesting this removal Hayley was motivated by anything but concern for Blake, whose genius he recognized, and by the kindness that seems to have characterized him in all of his dealings with the less fortunate artists he befriended. Hayley really cared for the cause of the arts, and, not content with personal success, set out to help other artists. It is almost harder to strike the right note of tact in being a benefactor than it is to be the grateful recipient of *largesse*. And Hayley was no fool. He knew an artist when he met one, and Cowper and Romney were among his debtors as well as Blake, so he could not have been so obtuse or as much the enemy of true art as he has been made out to be.

And it is clear that at first Blake accepted Hayley's kindness in the same spirit in which it was offered. If anything, his first hopes and his initial ecstasy upon finding himself installed at Felpham were too blown up to last. It is significant that Blake hoped for a great revival of inspiration at Felpham.

What happened then was unforeseen, but wholly natural. In close proximity to the successful and charming man of letters who presided over the town from his walled estate, The Turret,

Blake felt more than ever inferior. What was more, astute Hayley could see no hope of success for the first of the prophetic books, *Vala, or, the Four Zoas*. Quite reasonably, since Blake had no money and could not always live off his bounty, Hayley tried to turn Blake's interest towards commissions that would be profitable, but which soon seemed to Blake mere hackwork designed to keep him from his own work. Blake had that stubborn kind of artistic pride that would rather starve than prostitute his art, even though his art sometimes seemed to him like a forbidden passion.

How like the repetition of an old parental pattern Hayley's advice must have seemed to Blake. For although Blake's father helped him to study art, he *had* wanted to whip him for saying he had seen a vision, and he did make Blake feel that his art was a guilty because unrewarding occupation: 'I myself remember', Blake writes to Cumberland, 'when I thought my pursuits of Art a kind of criminal dissipation and neglect of the main chance, which I hid my face for not being able to abandon as a Passion which is forbidden by Law and Religion.' It was Blake's mother with her 'arms of love and pity and sweet compassion' who protected Blake from his father, and she probably became equated with his art. Is there any wonder that Hayley with his concern that Blake leave his unmarketable visions and take advantage of opportunity, began to be confused with archetypal images in Blake's mind and in his myth? It was only a short step to further confusions. Note particularly the metaphor of illicit passion that Blake uses to describe his art. There is no doubt at all that the two images were inextricably connected in Blake's mind. I do not want to labour the fact that Catherine was playing the role begun by Blake's mother while Hayley was in the position of the condemning father. A number of images could have merged to account for Blake's subsequent attitude.

It looks as if Blake, secure with a roof overhead, forgot, as it is easy to do, the near starvation of London from which Hayley had rescued him, and took it into his head to be touchy about the work Hayley had found for him to do. Hayley had taken considerable pains to persuade wealthy friends and neighbours to give Blake commissions, and, quite naturally, these commissions were for painted miniatures, not prophecies. To Blake it seemed a plot to keep him from doing his own work.

It is always galling to see genius expending itself in making fashionable gew-gaws for a livelihood, and Blake had genius. But what must have rankled most of all was that a man of third-rate talent was in a position to advise and dictate as if he were top authority, and at the same time was himself raking in all the sweets of success. But this was not Hayley's fault, and, recognizing Blake's genius, he did his charming best to compensate for the unequal distribution of material goods without hurting Blake's touchy pride in another way, that of making him an out and out charity case. And so we find Hayley popping over to the thatched cottage from his walled estate, commissions in hand, and Blake growing more and more annoyed and having to suppress it.

Hayley not only subscribed to all the eighteenth-century canons of sensibility and sweet reasonableness, but typified them. Moreover, he was always preaching them to Blake, urging above all a more prudent way of life than that of a visionary. And he had a large audience who agreed without reservation with his way of thinking.

We can see how Blake, already full of doubts about his own vision of life, began to have even worse doubts, and how Hayley seemed to be the cause of them. Blake must at this time have felt he was failing his wife, too, for he was forty-three and had had no success at all, and he had subjected her to all the deprivations of the artistic life without justifying it. He may have felt that no matter how she stuck by him, in her heart of hearts she was comparing him unfavourably with the successful and suave Hayley. Catherine Blake was pretty and vivacious, and it is clear that she charmed Hayley who had an eye for pretty women. He had much affectionate regard for her which doubtless pleased her, particularly as she was completely unsophisticated and Hayley was a man of the world as well as a poet, and possessed charm and breeding.

It would seem that, starting from his own feeling of inferiority and a doubting of all that he stood for as an artist, Blake began to feel vaguely jealous of Hayley in relation to Catherine. If he thought at all he would have had to base such jealousy on the very shaky ground of Hayley's open regard for Catherine and his reputation as a ladies' man. Yet there remains Blake's curious verse:

> When H(ayley) find out what you cannot do,
> That is the very thing he'll set you to.
> If you break not your Neck, 'tis not his fault,
> But pecks of poison are not pecks of salt.
> And when he could not act upon my wife
> Hired a Villain to bereave my Life.

There is no existing evidence outside this verse that Blake actually had grounds for jealousy, and after the Blakes returned to London we find them friends once again with Hayley which is not likely were these accusations true. But who knows how much of a benevolent and romantic 'father figure' Hayley may have become to Catherine during the stay at Felpham, and, dazzled, she may have sung his praises until Blake was sick of the very name of their generous patron. And the more Blake seemed ungrateful, the more would she have done so, until Blake dashed off this doggerel in pure spite. However it happened, it remains true that, starting with good will on both sides, Hayley gradually became to Blake the Satan of his poem, *Milton*, which was written at Felpham. Hayley may even be the 'traveller' and the 'angel' of the lyrics. It is apparent that at close quarters the comparison of himself with Hayley became too painful to Blake.

And all this misunderstanding and shunting off of good will is a great pity. For there is in existence a letter written by Hayley, which Blake never saw, written in Blake's defence to one of Hayley's unperceptive and critical friends, a letter which seems to me to reveal a sensitive, albeit over-simplified, understanding of the nature of Blake's genius and its basic disturbance that no one else even glimpsed. Far from being the obtuse patron who exploited Blake's genius more than helping it, Hayley is here revealed as a most perceptive and willing friend to a man who needed a friend more than most and who quarrelled with all the people who tried to be his friends. Hayley understood Blake's self-doubts and his self-torture, and, what's more, recognized that Blake's talent was genius and far beyond his own.

41

The letters which passed between Hayley and Lady Hesketh are as follows: Lady Hesketh wrote at the instigation of a disgruntled octogenarian who fancied himself a critic, to the effect that Blake lacked or 'wanted perfection'. She writes:

'May I be *forgiven* if I say to *you*, that some, among the *very* few now here, who have any pretensions to Taste, find many defects in your friend's engravings. . . . *Yet*, if Mr. Blake is but new in the world, may it not be *in reality kinder*, to point out his failing than to suffer him to think his performance faultless—surely it may stimulate his endeavours after Perfection!'

Obviously, Hayley had already cautioned his friends not to criticize Blake's work. Lady Hesketh complains that Blake pays little attention to the 'Human Face Divine', and, sin of sins, 'the faces of his *babies are not young*'. This is, perhaps, a deeper insight into what Blake meant than Lady Hesketh ever knew:

> My mother groan'd! my father wept.
> Into the dangerous world I leapt:
> Helpless, naked, piping loud:
> Like a fiend hid in a cloud.
>
> Struggling in my father's hands,
> Striving against my swaddling bands,
> Bound and weary I thought best
> To sulk upon my mother's breast.

Hayley replies to Lady Hesketh at length, taking pains to mollify the good lady in an effort to win her support of Blake by drawing parallels between his case and that of her beloved relative, Cowper. He flatters her capacity for sensitive perception, and finally, by painting a pathetic picture of William and Catherine ill in bed, he makes a pointed appeal to her maternal and charitable instincts. The tone of Hayley's letter is awkward and even clumsy, but it is a warming plea for kindness towards an artist whom Hayley realizes needs moral support and encouragement even more than bread. That is, of course, precisely what Blake did need. Whether Hayley himself was ever articulate enough to praise Blake to his face is doubtful from the turn of events and from Blake's lines:

> My title as a Genius thus is prov'd:
> Not Prais'd by Hayley nor by Flaxman lov'd.

Hayley's admiration may well have been expressed only in the form of material aid that was supposed to speak for itself, and in his activities among his friends on Blake's behalf, and, of course, in companionable literary talk, man to man, chiefly about his own projects!

He writes to Lady Hesketh on July 15, 1802:

'Pray suffer no mortal, my dear Lady, however you may give them *credit for refined taste in Art,* to *prejudice* you against the works of that too feeling artist, whose designs met with so *little mercy* from your Octogenaire admirable! . . . (there is) great spirit and sentiment in the engravings of my friend. . . . Whatever the Merits, or the Failings of my diligent and grateful artist may be, I know I shall interest your Heart and Soul *in his Favour,* when I tell you, that he resembles our Beloved Bard in the Tenderness of his Heart, and in the perilous powers of an imagination utterly unfit to take due care of Himself. With admirable Faculties, his sensibility is *so dangerously acute,* that the common rough treatment which true genius often receives from *ordinary minds* in the commerce of the world, might not only wound Him *more than it should do,* but really reduce Him to the Incapacity of an Ideot, without *the consolatory support of a considerable Friend.* From these excesses of Feeling, and of irregular Health (forever connected with such excesses) His productions must ever perhaps be *unequal,* but in all He does, however wild or hasty, a penetrating eye will discover true Genius, and if it were possible to keep his too apprehensive spirit for a Length of Time *unruffled* He would produce works of the pencil, almost as excellent and original, as those works of the pen, which flow'd from the dear poet, of whom He often reminds me— when his mind is darkened with any unpleasant *apprehension*—He reminds me of him also by being a most fervent Admirer of the Bible, and intimately acquainted with all its Beauties—I wish our beloved Bard had been as happy in a *Wife* for Heaven has bestow'd on this extraordinary mortal perhaps the only female on Earth who could have suited Him *exactly*—They have now been married more than seventeen years and are as fond of each other, as if their Honey Moon were still shining—They live in a neat little cottage, which they both regard as the most delightful residence ever inhabited by a mortal; they have no servant:—the good woman not only does all the work of the House, but she even makes the greater part of her Husband's dress, and assists him in *his* Art—she draws, she engraves, and sings delightfully, and is so truly the Half of her good man that they seem animated by one soul and that a soul of indefatigable Industry and Benevolence—it sometimes harries them to labour *rather too much,* and I had some time ago the pain of seeing both confin'd to their Bed —I endeavour to be as kind as I can to two creatures so very interesting and meritorious.'

43

This seems to me to be a very fine and unsparing effort on Hayley's part to win over an influential friend for Blake despite the obstacle of her mistrust. He flatters Lady Hesketh's intelligence, not too subtly, but subtly enough, and he blatantly observes the note of elegiac reverence and precedence due to her dead relative, the poet Cowper. There is full recognition of Blake's genius, but also of his tendency to be wild and hasty, and, best of all, of the psychological causes behind the uneven quality of his work. That adverse criticism might reduce Blake 'to the incapacity of an Ideot' is a very strong statement to make, but it shows that Hayley knew exactly where Blake was most vulnerable, and did not hesitate or mince words in an effort to save him from such a breakdown. Last but not least in this letter, there is to Hayley's credit much pure and simple loving-kindness towards the Blakes as people, and an appreciation of Mrs. Blake's good qualities as well as those of her husband. His description of her is not, incidentally, the description that would be written by a man who was amorously interested in his friend's wife. It speaks well for Hayley's delicacy that he refrained from mentioning that the delightful cottage that the Blakes were living in was his idea.

Hayley's whole intention, it would seem, was to protect and help this vulnerable genius and the wife who was so suited to him. It is significant that Hayley clearly had no inkling of either the jealousy concerning Catherine or the irritation about work that he was provoking in Blake. Not the least interesting information that we get from his letter is that to eyes that had more opportunity to observe the Blake household than anyone else ever had, it seemed that this couple had indeed achieved the marriage ideal of male and female completeness that Albion and Jerusalem are always struggling towards in anguish. Whatever the difficulties of the marriage—and we have Blake's word for it that there were 'fetters'—they did not appear on the surface. It is tempting to conclude that Blake's misgivings about his marriage like his hostility towards Hayley were dissatisfactions born of his self-doubt concerning his work, and had actuality only in the realm of imagination. What seemed to Hayley an ideal harmony in the little cottage, was probably torturing Blake because it just fell short of some impossible ideal, and as such the fetters could have seemed very real. But any theory like Murry's that Blake 'fell out' with his wife or that he fell in love with another woman is surely off the track.

And Blake's accusation of Hayley as 'the other man' or, potentially so, surely stems also from what Blake himself terms his 'abstract folly'. Poor Hayley was the only person close enough to the Blakes to get personally involved in the myth, and his involvement may even be taken as a back-handed compliment from Blake, a kind of love! For it is assuredly true that although for mankind in general Blake had the greatest tolerance, at least theoretically, for those near and dear to him he held up superhuman standards, assuming them like himself capable of perfection, and any small lapse assumed monstrous proportions, and his suspicions became almost paranoid. We can hardly blame Hayley that in seeing and setting out to protect Blake from his own self-doubts, he did not also see the vast mythological ramifications of such doubt and the part he himself would play in them.

There is something pathetic and ridiculous about the whole misunderstanding. Hayley, whatever his limitations, could have become the sympathetic audience Blake so badly needed, instead of the focus for Blake's projected doubts. Prepared to be the fatherly benefactor, Hayley was turned by the fertile imagination of his protégé genius into Satan, the arch-enemy of artistic vision, and would-be seducer of his wife.

It is apparent that at first Blake was wholly in agreement with the general opinion about Hayley's charm and kindness. He was altogether delighted with his good fortune in finding such a patron. Since illustrating Young's *Night Thoughts* in 1797 he had had no commissions, and his patron, Butts, was desperately overstocked with Blake's work and could do no more for him. Therefore, Blake's tone upon discovering such a willing patron as Hayley was one of joy and wonder only—'And now Flaxman has given me Hayley, his friend, to be mine . . . Mr. H. acts like a Prince, I am at complete Ease . . . my several engagements are in Miniature Paintings. Miniature has become a Goddess in my Eyes, and my Friends in Sussex say that I Excel in the pursuit.' And this is about the same work he later chafed at as mere hackwork unworthy of his genius. At this time

Hayley was writing to Lady Hesketh about Blake: 'As he has *infinite genius*, and a most engaging simplicity of character, I hope He will execute many admirable things in this sequestered scene, with the aid of an excellent wife, to whom he has been married seventeen years, and who shares his Labour and his Talents.' Once again, Hayley emerges as perceptive rather than obtuse in seeing that Blake's character was essentially joyous and simple, and that it was only through self-doubt that it turned into complexity and gloom. And Hayley set about quietly, wanting no thanks and not even letting Blake know, to ward off occasions for doubt. It is significant that it was Hayley to whom Blake wrote after the break had been made and the Blakes had returned to London, about the fetters that had bound his work and his marriage. Hayley needed no further explanation—he knew exactly the nature of these fetters that had made themselves felt at Felpham despite his vigilance.

For Blake soon became restive at Felpham executing his trivial commissions and with his inability to get on with his own work, and with, perhaps, being a kind of secretary to Hayley while Hayley himself was achieving tremendous success with his *Cowper*.

Blake writes ominously on September 11, 1801, his dissatisfaction with himself tremendously apparent, and his subjugation to abstraction instead of imagination become worse rather than better in the Hayley *milieu*. But nevertheless, he is still blaming *himself* for his own 'abstract folly' rather than casting around for a scapegoat: 'I labour incessantly, and accomplish not one half of what I intend, because my Abstract Folly hurries me often away while I am at work, carrying me over Mountains and Valleys which are not Real, in a Land of Abstraction where Spectres of the Dead wander.' Few more moving passages have been written to describe the bleak inner landscape of an artist who is in the bondage of his own fine intellect, which abstracts and analyses and dries up the spontaneous flow of images rather than channelling and shaping them.

Blake's sense of unreality, of self-doubt and self-hatred emerges in another letter. Here again he is still aware that he can blame no one but himself, and if the visions have departed, it is because he is not worthy: 'If it was fit for me, I doubt not

46

that I should be Employ'd in Greater Things.' But the letter
ends with an accusation of Hayley.

After reading Hayley's letters to Lady Hesketh, it is sad to
find that Blake was writing unhappily to his brother that he
must leave Felpham because of what he imagines is Hayley's
antagonism:

'I did not mention our Sickness to you and should not to Mr. Butts
but for a determination which we have lately made, namely to leave
This Place, because I am now certain of what I have long doubted,
Viz that H. is jealous as Stothard was and will be no further my friend
than he is compelled by circumstances. The truth is, As a Poet he is
frightened at me and as a Painter his views and mine are opposite; he
thinks to turn me into a Portrait Painter as he did poor Romney, but
this he nor all the devils in hell will never do. I must own that seeing
H. like S., envious (and that he is I am now certain) made me very
uneasy, but it is over and I now defy the worst and fear not while I
am true to myself which I will be. This is the uneasiness I spoke of to
Mr. Butts, but I did not tell him so plain and wish you to keep it a
secret and to burn this letter because it speaks so plain. . . . But again
as I said before, we are very Happy sitting at tea by a wood fire in our
Cottage, the wind singing about our roof and the Sea roaring at a
distance, but if *sickness* comes all is unpleasant.'

It is plain to see that at least a part of the sickness that
destroys the pleasant atmosphere in the cottage is not physical
but is the mental unease of jealousy and self-doubt. And this is
Blake's illness, not Hayley's. The accusation that Hayley is
jealous of *him* is pure projection. Hayley had no reason at all to
be jealous of Blake. But Blake had plenty of reasons to be jealous
of Hayley, some actual, some imaginary. If we turn each
mention of Hayley's name in this letter into the first person
singular, we get something much nearer the truth. For Blake
was uneasy at his own envy of Hayley's success. He speaks of
Hayley's jealousy of him, but ends the sentence most ambi-
guously with what can be a reference only to his own mood of
depression and envy: 'but it is now over and I now defy the
worst and fear not while I am true to myself which I *will* be.'
How could he know that Hayley's jealousy was over? But he
could know about his own mood. The shift to the future tense
here reveals his shame at his present petty jealousy, a state of
soul that keeps him from being true to himself.

47

Hayley, a literary lion of the first order, had no reason whatsoever to be envious of his obscure protégé who was to all eyes a failure. The only possible cause for jealousy would have been if he had suddenly realized that Blake had genius beyond his own. But this he recognized from the outset and had set out to protect and aid it. Nor had he any cause to be 'frightened at' Blake as a poet. What very likely rankled in Blake's mind was that Hayley probably did not think of him as a poet, but rather as a painter and engraver. He, Hayley, was the poet, acclaimed so by all.

Nor was there anything in 'circumstances' to 'compel' Hayley to be friendly to Blake, as Blake implies. It was quite the other way round with the Blakes living so close to Hayley and having to keep up a pretence of gratitude they no longer felt. It is perhaps fair to note in passing that 'poor Romney' did not lose but gained by turning to portraiture at Hayley's instigation.[1]

So much for the effort to see Hayley more clearly from behind the smoke screen of Blake's epigrams and the anger of Blake's defenders. It is important to clarify Blake's relation with his patron not only to vindicate Hayley, but in order to understand Blake.

And though Blake was grossly unfair to Hayley and misunderstood his motivation, we cannot say that Blake was entirely without a point. He had long ago made the choice to put art first and foremost even if it meant becoming a burden to his friends when the visions failed him, and even if it meant being ungrateful to these same friends if they seemed to be trying to turn him away from his own work. He puts the dilemma clearly:

'I find on all hands great objections to my doing anything but the mere drudgery of business, and intimations that if I do not confine myself to this, I shall not live . . . for that I cannot live without doing my duty to lay up treasures in heaven is Certain and Determined, and to this I have long made up my mind, and why this should be made an objection to Me, while Drunkeness, lewdness, Gluttony and even Idleness itself, does not hurt other men, let Satan himself explain.'

Whether Hayley had already become Satan we will never know!

[1] Although later Hayley tried to make Romney give up portraiture, for which Romney's son blames him.

Part Two

VALA, OR, THE FOUR ZOAS

'Can it be that the harmony further from the surface, the
harmony that hides from all but loving eyes, is, once recognized, proportionally dearer?'

OSBERT BURDETT: *The Two Carlyles*, p. 158.

VALA, OR, THE FOUR ZOAS

Most critics have been offended by the enormous welter of detail that obscures, almost defiantly, the meaning of the prophetic books. Taking into account that Blake did not want to be easy,[1] in the following chapters I hope to cut through some of the non-essential padding to lay bare the underlying structure of what appears to me, naïvely perhaps, as primarily a story. It is an enthralling and coherent story when it is seen, as all narrative must be seen, as a dynamically unfolding whole. Oddly enough, or perhaps not so oddly, since the temptation to regard them as an esoteric puzzle is so obvious, the prophetic books have never before been examined as pure and simple narrative.

Often those critics who dismiss the prophetic books as poetry, admit that they would like to possess the key to Blake's mythological labyrinth, for it seems to contain something of extraordinary power and significance. But to find the key seems too great an effort. Other critics, intent on unravelling the puzzle, feel that in tracking down the myriad esoteric sources for Blake's symbols and names, they have the key to what he is saying. Into this category come Denis Saurat and now Miss Kathleen Raine who goes so far as to say that we can explain Blake wholly by his sources, that he was not inspired by the supernaturals as he said he was, but got all of his ideas and images from traditional lore. This seems to me to carry too far what is admittedly an important aspect of Blake criticism, and I would

[1] 'That which can be made explicit to the Idiot is not worth my care,' he wrote. 'The wisest of the Ancients considered what is not too explicit as the fittest for Instruction.'

like to suggest that Blake had in common with many of the esoteric cults his work so resembles, a tapping of that realm we now call archetypal, and that contact with this realm always appears to be a kind of revelation. I would like to maintain that there is a still more important way in which we can understand Blake, and this is to try to understand the *new* tale that Blake is fashioning out of all the bits of ancient lore and out of what he claims is inspiration.

Although Blake's impatience with his form is often felt by the reader, one never feels that he is tired of his material which breathtakingly foreshadows so much of what depth psychology has made us aware of, and more, since Blake does not hesitate to ground the mysterious human soul he is holding under merciless examination in the greater Humanity of Christ.

In the following pages my comments are meant solely for clarification of the story Blake is telling in the prophetic books, and I will not follow up any of the tempting opportunities for relating Blake's ideas to possible outside influences. I would like to make a special plea that the quoted passages be given careful attention, since I wish as far as possible to let Blake tell his own story.

Without further ado, I will start with the first of the prophetic books proper, *Vala, or, The Four Zoas*,[1] which is considered by many to be Blake's most obscure poem. To me it is the most interesting of the prophetic books because it is the first and most spontaneous statement of Blake's troubled state of mind. It exists only in manuscript form. Max Plowman believes that this poem is the missing 'Bible of Hell' which Blake promised his readers at the end of *The Marriage of Heaven and Hell*, and this may well be so. For the breaking apart of the marriage of Albion and Jerusalem is close enough to Blake's definition of Hell in 'The Clod and the Pebble':

> Love seeketh only Self to please,
> To bind another to Its delight,
> Joys in another's loss of ease,
> And builds a Hell in Heaven's despite.

[1] The first page of the manuscript is illustrated by a drawing of Vala, naked and reclining, right arm behind her head, and an intense far-off staring expression.

We rarely see the main characters of this first prophetic book from the outside. Rather we see as if from within Albion the battle of his warring faculties, with an occasional over-all glimpse of a man who seems to be in a death-like trance. Jerusalem, too, is rarely seen from the outside in her status of Albion's wife or emanation, but only as she appears to Albion, which, in his confused state of mind, is usually as the glimmering witch-like Vala. The breaking apart of the marriage relationship, too, is seen almost wholly from Albion's point of view. It is only in *Jerusalem* that Albion's emanation is presented fairly consistently as a whole person even when she lapses from her fullest being.

Until then it is as if Blake forces us to look out from inside Albion at his marriage, and it is an uncomfortable ringside seat that we have purchased. First we find ourselves on one level of consciousness within Albion and then on another, and on each level the process of separation is going on. Each level of consciousness is represented by a male figure within Albion, and the female emanation which is its counterpart within Jerusalem. And this is the history not only of how Albion lost touch with his wife, but of his losing touch with the female principle within himself. This loss does not make him more of a man, but less. In slightly different terms Blake describes this dividing process in *A Descriptive Catalogue*:

'The Strong Man represents the human sublime. The Beautiful Man represents the human pathetic, which was in the wars of Eden divided into male and female. The Ugly Man represents the human reason. They were originally one man, who was fourfold. He was self-divided, and his real humanity slain on the stems of generation, and the form of the fourth was like the Son of God. How he became divided is a subject of great sublimity and pathos. The Artist has written it under inspiration, and will, if God pleases, publish it; it is voluminous, and contains the ancient history of Britain, and the World of Satan and of Adam.'

(KEYNES, p. 110.)

Vala, or, The Four Zoas presents the story of this division in schematic terms rather than in the round as in *Jerusalem*. *Milton*, the middle prophetic book, advances the story slightly, but is more an interlude during which Blake takes time out to rail against Hayley-Satan and all the forces which work against true art.

It is significant that the process of breakdown begins when Albion cannot reach Jerusalem on the level of actual sensory contact. Tharmas, who is instinct or sensation in Albion, cannot reach Enion, his mate within Jerusalem. Blake tells us why this is so. Enion has fled from Tharmas in fear and disillusionment because:

> I have look'd into the secret soul of him I lov'd,
> And in the Dark recesses found Sin and cannot return.

It is thought which has separated instinct from its true goal and has made physical love seem sinful not because of its animality which is good and innocent but because of what is in the beloved's soul. 'And yet I love thee in my terror,' she cries piteously, although insisting that 'All love is lost.'

Blake is not altogether clear about telling us who first saw love as sinful, but the name of Tharmas (Doubting Thomas) may give us a clue as to where the doubts about the goodness of passion originated. If Tharmas is ashamed of his own passion even in his innermost soul, the beloved can sense this and flees from what must now seem lust. This repeats the story of the lyrics I have quoted.

The net result is that, although Blake assures us that Tharmas is 'holy' and 'innocent', as soon as he begins to wonder about the innocence of sexual love, he appears sinful to Enion and she is afraid of his love. She, in turn, appears to him to be like a harlot. And her reaction really does set in motion the train of events which brings to the scene the father-god, Urizen, who pronounces love truly sinful. But this is to anticipate.

Meanwhile, Tharmas pleads with great dignity, begging Enion not to probe too deeply into this feeling of sin:

> Why wilt thou Examine every little fibre of my soul,
> Spreading them out before the sun like stalks of flax to dry?
> The infant joy is beautiful, but its anatomy
> Horrible, Ghast & Deadly; nought shalt thou find in it
> But Death, Despair & Everlasting brooding Melancholy.
> Thou wilt go mad with horror if thou dost Examine thus
> Every moment of my secret hours. Yea, I know

> That I have sinn'd, & that my Emanations are become harlots.
> I am already distracted at their deeds, & if I look
> Upon them more, Despair will bring self-murder on my soul.
> O Enion, thou art thyself a root growing in hell,
> Tho' thus heavenly beautiful to draw me to destruction.
> Sometimes I think thou art a flower expanding,
> Sometimes I think thou art fruit, breaking from its bud
> In dreadful dolor & pain; & I am like an atom,
> A Nothing, left in darkness; yet I am an identity:
> I wish & feel & weep & groan. Ah, terrible! terrible!

This is a most remarkable passage, and one that is fully realized poetry, as well as an extraordinary understanding of the destructiveness of too much self-analysis, which was Blake's own temptation. Tharmas laments further that because Enion is lost to him, the possibility of Jerusalem is lost to Albion:

> Lost! Lost! Lost! are my Emanations! Enion, O Enion,
> We are become a Victim to the Living. We hide in secret.
> I have hidden Jerusalem in silent Contrition. O Pity Me.
> I will build thee a Labyrinth also: O pity me. O Enion,
> Why hast thou taken sweet Jerusalem from my inmost Soul?

But Enion, as in the shorter lyrics, will not pity him, and flees from passion that seems to demand her love as a duty of marriage, rather than as love given in freedom. From now on the quest of the sick Albion is to find again Jerusalem whose name is Liberty, while Jerusalem in the guise of Vala, like the goddesses of mythology, seeks for her lost lover. Enion cries:

> All love is lost: Terror succeeds, & Hatred instead of Love,
> And stern demands of Right & Duty instead of Liberty.
> Once thou wast to Me the loveliest son of heaven—But now
> Why art thou Terrible?

When Albion and Jerusalem have lost contact on the basic level of touch or sensation, represented by Tharmas and Enion, there is no longer much hope that they can communicate on any level. Their whole relationship is thrown out of harmony.

There are three other couples within Albion and Jerusalem, besides Tharmas and Enion, representing three levels of consciousness. Luvah and his wife, Vala, stand for the passionate emotions. Urizen's emanation, Ahania, is feminine wisdom, equivalent to the gnostic Sophia. The faculty of imagination is represented by Los and Enitharmon, significantly the only couple that are generated after the Fall, the children of Tharmas and Enion. Their generation seems to be a kind of compensation to make up for the loss of Eternity, but they immediately prove to be irresponsible creatures who defy the parental realm of sensory fact, and poison Albion with fantasies.

Probably the losing touch between Jerusalem and Albion happened on all levels more or less simultaneously. But we must remember that Urizen did not spontaneously move to the place of tyrant over Albion. It was Enion who set in motion the train of events that called him to the scene by her probing of what seemed to be Tharmas' sin, and their mutual feeling of shame. And shame, Blake tells us elsewhere, is 'Pride's cloak'. Enion's feeling of shame for which she welcomes authority, is verified, not by fact, but by the self-elected authority of 'reason'. And of course Urizen cannot resist decreeing categorically that yes, passion is *ipso facto* sinful. Almost with relief the faculties allow Urizen to set up his laws prohibiting love as sinful because the vague feeling of shame has spread through all of them and has become almost intolerable in its undefined oppressiveness. And there is no valid basis at all for the feeling of shame or for Urizen's tyranny, for Blake tells us clearly that Tharmas is not sinful as he and Enion fear, but 'holy' and 'innocent'.

> Tharmas groan'd among his Clouds
> Weeping: then bending from his Clouds, he stoop'd his innocent head,
> And stretching out his holy hand . . .
> Said: 'Return, O Wanderer, when the day of Clouds is o'er.'

This shame which is pride's cloak persuades each of the couples in turn that it is somehow guilty to be human, and to have human needs and loves. They should try to be gods and since reason is the faculty that is farthest away from the level of animal sensation, reason should be given sole authority. This in itself is the most fallacious type of reasoning. In *Neurosis and Human Growth* (pp. 91–2) Karen Horney writes that 'the pride in intellect, or rather in the supremacy of mind, is not restricted to those engaged in intellectual pursuits but is a regular occurrence in all neurosis.'

Each pair, discontented and ashamed of the human need for a mate which Reason scorns as weak, lose all closeness, and soon all is bitterness and sexual strife. Blake tells the history of each couple's coming to grief. The whole drama of the prophetic books is Albion's 'fall into Division & his Resurrection to Unity'. His fall represents not only his separation from Jerusalem, his wife, but also his separation from the feminine principle in himself. Until he can unite the masculine and feminine sides of his soul—the mother and father within him—and himself be born as a mature person from this union, he is continually trying to unite with his wife, not as a beloved person, but as the other half of himself.[1] We remember the lines from *The Book of Urizen*:

> Eternity shudder'd when they saw
> Man begetting his likeness
> On his own divided image.

This is not to say that love should not have in it at all times something of this element. Human love, as A. P. Rossiter so aptly put it, is partly the marriage of true minds, partly the betrayal of Troilus and Cressida, and partly 'Mummy possest'. But these must be conscious accepted and controlled desires rather than undirected and unconscious moods or drives that cause inner riots. In Albion they are the latter. Although he does wish for the marriage of minds and is unhappy because his wife cannot follow him into the dazzling realm of eternal truths, he does not know that in conflict with this is his need to unite with the mother in himself at the same time that he wants to reject her as a faithless harlot.

Although Blake sees sensory factual knowledge alone as 'single vision and Newton's sleep', it is significant that the losing touch on the level of physical contact is by far the most calamitous thing that could have happened to the marriage of

---

[1] Until then, the sick child Orc is born of such a union on the level of imagination to the archetypal parents of fantasy, Los and Enitharmon, who are also brother and sister.

Albion and Jerusalem. It begins the series of events that leads to total breakdown in the relationship.

For to doubt, as Tharmas does, the value of the sensual side of love, and for Enion to flee like Thel from the experience of the senses, is the betrayal of what can and must be the gateway to eternity in a marriage. To doubt this is to doubt the possibility of Albion's union with Jerusalem.

Perhaps because Tharmas and Enion themselves doubt the goodness of the realm they represent, that of empirical sensation, their children, Los and Enitharmon, immediately reject the parent level. They, brother and sister who are also husband and wife, represent the faculty of imagination in Albion and Jerusalem, but they become imagination that is irresponsible fantasy when they reject the bed-rock of actual fact. They refuse to be grounded in the doubtful evidence of the senses, and consequently begin to create havoc as soon as they are born. It almost seems as if they were born mature in body and turbulent in spirit. Blake with almost frightening psychological insight gives the smallest of hints in passing that Enion is jealous of her husband's relationship to their own daughter, so that Tharmas has to protest:

> It is not love I bear to Enitharmon. It is Pity.
> She hath taken refuge in my bosom & I cannot cast her out.

Enion's suspicions are those of a mother out of touch with her daughter because out of touch with her husband, and she sits in judgement on both until they are almost forced to take refuge together. Blake gives no indication that Enion's suspicions have any foundation in fact, even if Enitharmon is irresponsible and mischievous, and Tharmas, Blake tells us, is holy and innocent although he is made to feel guilty.

Thus it is Enion who first creates the Spectre of guilt in Tharmas:

> he sunk down into the sea, a pale white corse.
> In torment he sunk down & flow'd among her filmy Woof,
> His spectre issuing from his feet in flames of fire.
> In gnawing pain drawn out by her lov'd fingers. . . .
> Wond'ring she saw her woof begin to animate, & not

As Garments woven subservient to her hands, but having a will
Of its own, perverse & wayward. Enion lov'd & wept . . .
'What have I done,' said Enion, 'accursed wretch! What deed?
Is this a deed of Love? I know what I have done. I know
Too late now to repent. Love is chang'd to deadly Hate . . .'

It is interesting to realize that Blake takes this image from his
domestic life, possibly at Felpham by the sea, for Hayley tells
us that Catherine made almost all of her husband's clothes.

For the first time we encounter the realm of Beulah, and the
mild Daughters of Beulah who are that part of Jerusalem which,
even during marital disagreements, watches over the trance-
bound Albion with pity and concern, like a Greek chorus of
lamenting women, or like guardian angels.

There is from Great Eternity a mild & pleasant rest
Nam'd Beulah, a soft Moony Universe, feminine, lovely,
Pure, mild & Gentle, given in mercy to those who sleep,
Eternally Created by the Lamb of God around,
On all sides, within & without the Universal Man.
The daughters of Beulah follow sleepers in all their dreams,
Creating spaces, lest they fall into Eternal Death . . .
They said: 'The Spectre is in every man insane & most
Deform'd. Thro' the three heavens descending in fury & fire
We meet it with our songs & loving blandishments, & give
To it a form of vegetation. But this Spectre of Tharmas
Is Eternal Death. What shall we do? O God, pity & help!'

Next comes a passage reminiscent of 'The Mental Traveller'
in its violent changes in mood and in the swiftly changing roles of
dominance and subjection in a love relationship gone wrong.
There is rapid alternation of power, as each partner plays in
turn the sulky bound child to the other's tyrannical parent.
Never do we find either or both on a mature footing. One is
always the perverse and wayward child, the other the condemning parent.

Tharmas' Spectre starts life as a sullen babe, wholly in
Enion's power because she is for the moment in the false
position of judging and condemning her husband as a parent
judges a child. But suddenly the Spectre gets out of control,
and the babe she has nursed so scornfully swells itself in terrific

adult pride and forces her to worship it, at the same time
despising her as an unworthy audience:

> But standing on the Rocks, her woven shadow glowing bright,
> She drew the Spectre forth from Tharmas in her shining loom
> Of Vegetation, weeping in wayward infancy & sullen youth.

> List'ning to her soft lamentations, soon his tongue began
> To lisp out words, & soon, in masculine strength augmenting, he
> Rear'd up a form of gold & stood upon the glittering rock
> A shadowy human form wing'd, & in his depths
> The dazzlings as of gems shone clear; rapturous in fury,
> Glorying in his own eyes, Exalted in terrific Pride . . .
>   repining in the midst of all his glory
> That nought but Enion could be found to praise, adore, & love.

The tables are now completely turned, and Enion is dominated
by the very Spectre she has created in Tharmas.

And, as the Daughters of Beulah said, the 'Spectre is in every
man insane and most deform'd', because it is trying its best to
make the man it hovers over scorn and reject his own humanity
in an effort to be something other than human. Such a man, if he
submits to his Spectre, punishes human nature, not only in
himself, but all around him in the world that might betray him,
and especially in those nearest to him. This is what Albion does
to his emanation, his own *anima* as well as his wife, in treating
her as a harlot. And when he stops actively flagellating himself
and his wife, then he despairs and longs for death because he
cannot fulfil Urizen's laws of puritan perfection: the seductive
beauty and innocence of human nature enthrals him just when
he is crying out that it is ugly and corrupt. And thus we find
Albion stretched out on the sea-coast in a death-like trance, the
Spectre over him like a great hovering sea-bird.

We remember the fragmentary poem in Blake's notebook
about the Spectre:

> Each Man is in his Spectre's power
> Until the arrival of that hour,
> When his Humanity awake
> And cast his own Spectre into the Lake.

> And there to Eternity aspire
> The Selfhood in a flame of fire
> Till then the Lamb of God . . .

Man casts his own Spectre into the Lake when his humanity reasserts itself. The Selfhood is another name for the Spectre, and there is ambiguity in the lines:

> And there to Eternity aspire
> The Selfhood in a flame of fire

We see the Spectre, as if eternally damned, eternally bewailing the loss of Eternity from the fiery lake. But it is also Blake's conscious or half-conscious condemnation of his own ever-recurring aspiration for the fourfold vision he calls 'Eternity'. It is the Spectre, in its fiery pride, that dares to desire the gnosis of Eternity, rather than be content with the Humanity of Christ.

The Spectre that Enion has drawn from Tharmas and which has swelled itself in terrific pride until it dominates Enion completely, speaks to her with comical and pompous righteousness:

> Who art thou, Diminutive husk & shell? . . .
> If thou hast sinn'd & art polluted, know that I am pure
> And unpolluted, & will bring to rigid strict account
> All thy past deeds; hear what I tell thee! mark it well!

She has not even a name as far as he is concerned. She is beneath contempt and hardly worth noticing except to condemn for sins that the Spectre righteously unearths at every possible point. As far as he is concerned sex is synonymous with Sin and with Woman. Enion is completely cowed by the bombast of the Spectre. She apologizes for being born woman and therefore sinful. She recognizes that this state of affairs is a far cry from her initial idea that Tharmas' love was sinful, and sees that her feeling of guilt has set into motion much more than she had bargained for:

> She trembling answer'd: 'Wherefore was I born, & what am I?
> A sorrow & a fear, a living torment, & naked Victim.
> I thought to weave a Covering for my Sins from wrath of Tharmas.
>
> Examining the Sins of Tharmas I soon found my own.
> O slay me not! thou art his wrath embodied in Deceit.
> I thought Tharmas a sinner & I murder'd his Emanations
> His secret loves & Graces. Ah me wretched! What have I done?

For now I find that all these Emanations were my Children's souls,
And I have murder'd these with Cruelty above atonement . . .
And thou, the delusive tempter to these deeds, sitt'st before me.
And art thou Tharmas? all thy soft delusive beauty cannot
Tempt me to murder my own soul & wipe my tears & smile
In this thy world, not mine: tho' dark I feel my world within.

And the Spectre answers petulantly accusation for accusation—
'Tis *thou* who has darken'd all My World, O Woman, lovely
bane.' Enion is coming to seem more and more like a nature
goddess to Tharmas, just as Jerusalem is to Albion. Notice the
remarkable touches, like records out of Frazer's *Golden Bough*,
with which Blake achieves this effect: the image of the woman as
a naked victim for sacrifice; the idea that the man at conception
provides the soul of the child, the woman the body; and, more
directly, the strange monster, Nature, of the following passage,
which is, however, half the creation of the Spectre:

> Thus they contended all the day among the Caves of Tharmas,
> Twisting in fearful forms & howling, howling, harsh shrieking,
> Howling, harsh shrieking; mingling, their bodies join in
>   burning anguish.
> Mingling his brightness with her tender limbs, then high she
>   soar'd
> Above the ocean; a bright wonder, Nature,
> Half Woman & half Spectre; all his lovely changing colours mix
> With her crystal fairness; in her lips & cheeks his poisons rose
> In blushes like the morning, & his scaly armour softening,
> A monster lovely in the heavens or wandering on the earth,
> With spectre voice incessant wailing, in incessant thirst,
> Beauty all blushing with desire, mocking her fell despair.
> Wandering desolate, a wonder abhorr'd by Gods & Men.

Again we seem to glimpse Albion stretched out along the sea
with the strange bird hovering over him, half Spectre and half
the idea of Nature created by the Spectre. The passage quoted
is curiously ambiguous. It is obviously meant to convey the
picture of a monstrous consummation, a union accomplished in
fascinated revulsion and guilty despair. But the way in which
Blake tries to suggest this, simply by the weak repetition of
shrieking and howling, is offensive in its thin imprecision, not
by what it is trying to convey. And the passage fails completely

in its purpose. The union does not strike the reader as at all monstrous. In fact, what is conveyed is the intense delight in physical union which seems somehow to be a mingling of all the rainbow colours in the painter's box as well as a mingling of bodies. Blake tries to counter this joyous impression with the wailing spectrous voice, and again fails, and is himself forced to apply to this supposed monster the unlikely adjective of 'lovely'. An agonized female figure with hair streaming like flames, and snaky forms twisting around her, is Blake's illustration to this plate.

Out of this union Los and Enitharmon are born, to become the brother and sister who, mated, represent the level of imagination in Albion and Jerusalem. Enion turns away from her husband, Tharmas, who is dominated by his Spectre, and gives all of her love to these children, 'Rehumanizing from the Spectre in pangs of maternal love'. Here Blake sketches a graceful feminine form, seated against a rock, the children at her breast.

But soon the children wander away from her too possessive love,[1] and they become irresponsible and mischievous imagination that causes even more trouble than already exists between the unhappy Albion and Jerusalem. They have tremendous power over time and space and the appearance of the seasons, and can make all appear unreal despite the watchful vigilance of the Daughters of Beulah who know them for 'the Youthful terrors' that they are, and are busy making 'windows into Eden' in the moments that Los wilfully destroys, and opening the centre of 'an atom of space' 'into Infinitude' so that Enitharmon cannot wholly confuse appearance. But still Los and Enitharmon pursue their destructive course:

Alternate Love & Hate his breast: hers Scorn & Jealousy
In embryon passions; they kiss'd not nor embrac'd for shame &
    fear.
His head beam'd light & in his vigorous voice was prophecy.
He could control the times & seasons & the days & years:
She could control the spaces, regions, desart, flood & forest,
But had no power to weave the Veil of covering for her sins.
She drave the Females all away from Los,
And Los drave the Males from her away.

[1] A sketch shows the terrible children rejecting Enion who bows much too humbly before them.

Enitharmon really is a terror. She halts in her plans for mistreating their parents—'for if we grateful prove, they will withhold sweet love, whose food is thorns and bitter roots'— to say to Los: 'Hear! I will sing a Song of Death! It is a Song of Vala.'

She then sings her song about a dream in which she sees Vala, whose rightful mate is Luvah, fly up to sleep on the pillow of Albion, usurping Jerusalem's place. This mischievous make-believe on the part of Enitharmon angers Los, and he replies that her song is not true and so cannot kill, and that Albion would not forsake Jerusalem for Vala, but is simply trying to comfort Vala who has lost her lover:

> I die not, Enitharmon, tho' thou singest thy song of Death,
> Nor shalt thou me torment; for I behold the Fallen Man
> Seeking to comfort Vala: she will not be comforted.
> She rises from his throne and seeks the shadows of her garden
> Weeping for Luvah lost in bloody beams of your false morning;
> Sick'ning lies the Fallen Man, his head sick, his heart faint:
> Mighty achievement of your power; Beware the punishment!

Enitharmon's irresponsible fantasy is, in fact, becoming true although Los tries to believe otherwise. Enitharmon with her misuse of her power has completed the havoc begun by her mother, Enion, when she and Tharmas lost touch. For although Vala is indeed mourning her lost husband, Luvah, the passions within Albion, it is also true that it is Vala rather than all of Jerusalem that Albion is dreaming about. She looms large all out of proportion to him because the Spectre has forbidden the passions which she represents. It seems as if she has indeed taken Jerusalem's place beside Albion's pillow. And Vala, thinking to force her lover to return, welcomes Albion's attentions.

Albion is very sick. We begin to see what this warfare on the different levels of his being has done to him. First, he lost direct contact with his wife because the good of physical love was doubted. Next, Jerusalem's mischievous imagination, repudiating completely the parent level of sense data, makes up a story that Vala has taken her rightful place in Albion's affections. Albion's head is sick and his heart is faint, and 'Urizen sleeps on the porch' not functioning in a helpful way at all, but simply dozing there, ready to stake his claim when the time comes. Albion is no longer a man who can function, but the victim of his disorganized faculties which pull him in several directions. He plays dead rather than act, and so fulfils Enitharmon's prophecy of death.

And 'scorn & indignation rose upon Enitharmon' at the sight of this less-than-man who had been so taken in by her fantasy, which might, had Albion and Jerusalem been in sensitive accord, have afforded instead high imaginative play between husband and wife. In scorn and anger and a wanton wish to prove to the full her own fantastical power, Enitharmon then deliberately calls down Urizen to begin his long tyranny over Albion. Until now it has only been the Spectre of guilt that has held Albion prisoner. Now the father-god himself appears on the scene to back up the false dictates of the Spectre with a false authority.

Then Enitharmon, reddn'ing fierce, stretch'd her immortal hands:
'Descend, O Urizen, descend with horse & chariot . . .'
Eternity groan'd & was troubled at the Image of Eternal Death.
The Wandering Man bow'd his faint head & Urizen descended,—
And *the one must have murder'd the Man if he had not descended*—
Indignant, muttering low thunders, Urizen descended,
Gloomy, sounding: 'Now I am God from Eternity to Eternity.'

Here there is a faint ludicrously crude sketch of Los angry at Enitharmon who seems to ward off a blow. Although 'Enitharmon brighten'd more & more' at what she had done, and looked to Urizen for praise, he pays no attention to her, but smiles upon Los and gives Luvah into his keeping, saying 'Pity not Vala, for she pitied not the Eternal Man.' This he does, promising Los the passions as servants if he will obey his laws. But Los, imagination, is furious at this and cries to Urizen: 'One must be master. Try thy Arts. I also will try mine.'

Urizen is startled, but collects himself and thunders for Los to obey him, mocking Christianity as a soft delusion, and proclaiming the Spectre as the only real part of the man. The imagery of the host proclaims him the Miltonic Satan:

'Obey my voice, young Demon; I am God from Eternity to
    Eternity.
Art thou a visionary of Jesus, the soft delusion of Eternity?

Lo, I am God, the terrible destroyer, & not the Saviour.
Why should the Divine Vision compell the sons of Eden
To forgo each his own delight, to war against his spectre?
The Spectre is the Man. The rest is only delusion & fancy.'
Thus Urizen spoke, collected in himself in awful pride.
Ten thousand thousand were his hosts of spirits on the wind,
Ten thousand thousand glittering Chariots shining in the sky.

Los had smitten Enitharmon in rage at this her doing, but, repentant, he now effects a reconciliation with her. They celebrate a gloomy marriage feast under the new reign of Urizen, and the bride and bridegroom sit 'in discontent & scorn' while a terrible prophecy is sung about a desolate earth and ruined cities. Enion, blind and age-bent, the mother of this rebellious and incestuous pair, hovers near the golden feast, predicting hunger and suffering for all the earth's creatures. Albion grows very sick indeed: he has reached the point of inner crucifixion:

Now Man was come to the Palm Tree & to the Oak of Weeping
Which stands on the edge of Beulah, & he sunk down
From the supporting arms of the Eternal Saviour who dispos'd
The pale limbs of his Eternal Individuality
Upon the Rock of Ages, Watching over him with Love & Care.

Messengers from Beulah appear before Christ:

Saying, 'Shiloh is in ruins, our brother is sick: Albion, he
Whom thou lovest is sick; he wanders from his house of Eternity.'

Throughout the plates dealing with the marriage feast, Blake has sketched strange figures: a twisting snake body ending in the head of a sleeping man; three large heads with an identical expression of anguished dream; an impressive sweeping drawing of Urizen; strange floating figures that it is hard to interpret.

Blake's method of narrative is confusing when the plan is not understood, especially since the text is always accompanied by disturbing illustrations that may or may not have anything to do with the story, or may be enacting it on still another level. But his method in *The Four Zoas* is really quite simple. Generally we move from inside Albion where we have been watching his interior turmoil on one or more levels, to a brief over-all glimpse of his state of spiritual health or sickness and his relation with his bride. Often we see him stretched out in his death-like sleep. Then we become aware of still another plane of action, that of those watchful presences rather like guardian angels. These presences are always in touch with Christ, no matter how much Albion may stray, and they go to Christ with the simple poignant words—'He whom thou lovest is sick; he wanders from his house of eternity.'

Seen as Blake intended it to be seen, such a book as *The Four Zoas* has a simple, almost naïve, coherence which is lost in a too myopic examination of its intricacies. It has something in common with twentieth-century stream of consciousness writing, and certainly with the psychological novel. Such a mode of writing lends itself to those moments of heightened vision where many threads are joined together and an illuminating pattern revealed. Such moments James Joyce calls 'epiphanies', and Blake not only makes use of similar moments, but describes them: the Daughters of Beulah are responsible for these moments of insight:

> Then Eno, a daughter of Beulah, took a Moment of Time
> And drew it out to seven thousand years with much care &
> affliction
> And many tears, & in every year made windows into Eden.
> She also took an atom of space & open'd its centre
> Into Infinitude & ornamented it with wondrous art.

Meanwhile, Urizen is trying to strike a shady sort of bargain with Luvah who will have none of it. Secretly Urizen plans to wipe out Luvah, the passions altogether. He wants to provoke Luvah, for he wants 'the rage of Luvah to pour its fury on himself and on the Eternal Man.' That is to say, he believes that the passions, given full rein because of Vala's betrayal, will destroy themselves and leave the wounded Albion completely in his power. The success of this scheme is what produces the final crack-up in Albion. All of his faculties are thrown into dire confusion:

> Sudden down they fell all together into an unknown Space,
> Deep, horrible, without End, separated from Beulah, far beneath.
> The Man's exteriors are become indefinite, open'd to pain
> In a fierce hungry void, & none can visit his regions.

Jerusalem, his Emanation, is become a ruin,
Her little ones are slain on top of every street,
And she herself led captive & scatter'd into the indefinite.

The fearful loneliness and the gnawing but indefinite sensual
hunger that is a painful characteristic of breakdown, comes
across clearly in this passage, also Albion's sense of desolation
and separation from the watchful guardians of Beulah. Jerusalem,
too, is become a ruin. Blake uses the biblical imagery with
strong effect to suggest Jerusalem's sense of unfulfilment and
indefiniteness because her unborn children are murdered before
they are conceived. The breakdown within Albion and in his
marriage relationship has been caused by the warfare to the
death between his passions and his intellect, each fighting for
sole supremacy over him. And Urizen has won.

With the accession of Urizen begins a period, not of serene
intellect-guided clarity of vision, but one of extreme mental
illness for Albion. The destructive fantasies of Enitharmon play
a major role, and Jerusalem believes that Albion has preferred
Vala to her, and she refuses him imaginative sympathy and love
because she is hurt. And, following the guide of terrible Enitharmon, she shuts her husband out just when he needs her
most. But, unknown to Enitharmon, the Daughters of Beulah
prepare a couch where Jerusalem can sink into exhausted sleep
while the battle rages in Albion, which is better than having
her do active mischief under the direction of Enitharmon:

> The Daughters of Beulah beheld the Emanation; they pitied,
> They wept before the Inner gates of Enitharmon's bosom,
> And of her fine wrought brain, & of her bowels within her loins.
> These gates within, Glorious & bright, open into Beulah
> From Enitharmon's inward parts; but the bright female terror
> Refus'd to open the bright gates; she clos'd & barr'd them fast
> Lest Los should enter into Beulah thro' her beautiful gates.

> The Emanation stood before the gates of Enitharmon,
> Weeping; the Daughters of Beulah silent in the Porches
> Spread her a couch unknown to Enitharmon; here repos'd
> Jerusalem in slumbers soft, lull'd into silent rest.
> Terrific rag'd the Eternal wheels of intellect, terrific rag'd
> The living creatures of the wheels, in Wars of Eternal life.
> But perverse roll'd the wheels of Urizen & Luvah, back revers'd
> Downwards & outwards, consuming in the wars of Eternal Death.

The four living creatures of the wheels are the four Zoas or the faculties. The emanation stands for Albion's emotional sexual nature, of course, as well as for his bride. The mysterious Daughters of Beulah are the guardians of peace and love even when Albion and Jerusalem are separated in misunderstanding and strife, and they prepare places for them in Beulah which is the realm of sexual peace and harmony, for in Beulah 'contrarieties are equally true'.

There is a drawing of a woman who seems to be bound to a rock, a womb-like crevice above her, her head twisted to gaze at the figure of a child descending from above in swirling garments. This ends the first of the nine sections or 'Nights' of *The Four Zoas*.

Night the Second begins with Albion on his sickbed, 'turning his Eyes outward to Self, losing the Divine Vision'. There is a sketch of Albion's outstretched and sadly up-gazing figure. His face is the bearded face of Urizen, for Albion has summoned Urizen and made him the ruler of his soul and master over his other faculties. This is, of course, what had already happened on the subterranean levels of Albion's being causing the illness. Now it has become conscious. Now in the grip of his sickness Albion makes it his deliberate choice, feeling wholly virtuous in his action. He says to his Reason—'Take thou possession! take this Scepter! go forth in my might, for I am weary and must sleep the dark sleep of Death.'

Even Urizen, exultant in his triumph, is none the less horrified at Albion's state:

> First he beheld the body of Man, pale, cold; the horrors of death
> Beneath his feet shot thro' him as he stood in the Human Brain,
> And all its golden porches grew pale with his sickening light,
> No more exulting, for he saw Eternal Death beneath . . .
> Terrific Urizen strode above in fear & pale dismay.
> He saw the indefinite space beneath & his soul shrunk with horror,
> His feet upon the verge of Non Existence.

Upon accession, Urizen sets to work immediately to build the Mundane Shell around Albion, that is, the delusive appearance of a world upon which mind must impose the reality of its abstract laws. There follows one of those long lists that rightly irritate the critical reader because it is full of superfluous, dull, and wilfully eccentric detail that has nothing to do with poetry and little importance in the story. This list to which Blake gives so much space is simply of the workers who build the Mundane Shell and of whom we shall never hear again. The drawings on these plates are faintly obscene in the Hieronymus Bosch manner. We are shown flying creatures with human breasts and pronounced genitals, repulsive furry moth bodies topped by babies' heads, or headless bodies of children borne on bat wings. This is a nightmare world all out of touch with reality that Urizen is creating, not the clear brilliant light of intellectual gnosis.

The building of the Mundane Shell accomplished, Urizen then throws his deadly enemy, Luvah the passions, into the furnace that had been used in the building project. And Vala, Luvah's wife who betrayed him and fled to Albion's pillow although she is ostensibly looking for her lover, is in such a state of delusion that 'In joy she heard his howlings and forgot he was her Luvah with whom she walk'd in bliss in times of innocence and youth.' There is poignance in the cry of Luvah from the depths of the furnace, which Vala does not hear, of how he has always tried to protect Vala, but his loving care of her has been in vain:

> I brought her thro' the Wilderness, a dry & thirsty land,
> And I commanded springs to rise for her in the black desart,
> Till she became a Dragon, winged, bright & poisonous.
> I open'd all the floodgates of the heavens to quench her thirst,
> And I commanded the Great deep to hide her in his hand
> Till she became a little weeping Infant a span long.
> I carried her in my bosom as a man carries a lamb,
> I loved her, I gave her all my soul & my delight.

Luvah tries in vain to comfort the unhappy Vala, but she does not even recognize him:

> . . . she lamented day & night, compell'd to labour & sorrow.
> Luvah in vain her lamentations heard: in vain his love
> Brought him in various forms before her, still she knew him not,
> Still she despis'd him, calling on his name & knowing him not,
> Still hating, still professing love, still labouring in the smoke.

70

Blake gives us a drawing of a vast amorphous crouching Vala, in front of whom Luvah is standing, smiling sadly, but she will not look.

On the level of imagination, Los and Enitharmon are maliciously enjoying 'the sorrows of Luvah and the labour of Urizen'. And they concoct a new scheme which is 'to plant divisions in the soul of Urizen and Ahania'. The beginning of such a division is already there, for in the palace Urizen has built, which is a horrible travesty of the four-square city of Jerusalem, Urizen's wife, Ahania, 'His Shadowy Feminine Semblance', reposes on a white couch in jealousy and discontent:

> Two wills they had, two intellects, & not as in times of old.
> This Urizen perceiv'd, & silent brooded in dark'ning Clouds.
> To him his Labour was but Sorrow & his Kingdom was
> Repentance.
> He drave the Male Spirits all away from Ahania,
> And she drave the Females from him away.

But before Los and Enitharmon go on to deepen this discord we are allowed for a moment to have a God's-eye-view, and we find that, although it looks as if man's passions, Luvah, have been entirely destroyed by man's overweening intellect, this is not altogether the case. Christ has intervened, and himself put on the bloody robes of Luvah:

> The Divine Lamb, even Jesus, who is the Divine Vision,
> Permitted all, lest Man should fall into Eternal Death;
> For when Luvah sunk down, himself put on the robes of blood
> Lest the state call'd Luvah should cease; & the Divine Vision
> Walked in robes of blood till he who slept should awake.
> Thus were the stars of heaven created like a golden chain
> To bind the Body of Man to heaven from falling into the Abyss.

This is a profound commentary on the meaning of the Passion, and Blake's conclusions are very like those of D. H. Lawrence in *The Man Who Died*. It is man's own reason who destroys his passions as sinful, and Christ himself becomes these passions lest human love should be annihilated altogether before man awakes and sees it as holy rather than sinful. We must take

careful notice of the activities of Luvah from now on, knowing
that it is Christ who is dressed in Luvah's garments.

Meanwhile all is discord between Albion and Jerusalem on
their various levels. Luvah cries: 'O when will you return, Vala
the Wanderer?' There is a striking drawing that represents the
situation of all the faculties and their emanations. A bearded
male figure with stern countenance and emaciated body regards
his voluptuous emanation to whom he is still joined since their
trunks seem to merge. She is straining backwards in wanton
provocation and defiance with a laughing grimace of scorn.

Los and Enitharmon are behaving like a pair of mischievous
nature sprites, playing magical tricks to amuse themselves:

> For Los & Enitharmon walk'd forth on the dewy Earth
> Contracting or expanding all their flexible senses
> At will to murmur in the flowers small as the honey bee,
> At will to stretch across the heavens & step from star to star,
> Or standing on the earth erect, or on the stormy waves
> Driving the storms before them, or delighting in sunny beams,
> While round their heads the Elemental Gods kept harmony.

Yet for all their power they are not happy. Enitharmon cries
accusingly to Los: 'My spirit still pursues thy false love over
rocks and valleys', and he answers:

> 'Cold & repining Los
> Still dies for Enitharmon, nor a spirit springs from my dead
> corse;
> Then I am dead till thou revivest me with thy sweet song.
> Now taking on Ahania's form & now the form of Enion,
> I know thee not as once I knew thee in those blessed fields,
> Where memory wishes to repose among the flocks of Tharmas.'
> Enitharmon answer'd: 'Wherefore didst thou throw thine arms
> around
> Ahania's Image? I deceiv'd thee & will still deceive.
> Urizen saw thy sin & hid his beams in dark'ning clouds.
> I still keep watch altho' I tremble & wither across the heavens
> In strong vibrations of fierce jealousy; for thou art mine,
> Created for my will, my slave, tho' strong, tho' I am weak,
> Farewell, the God calls me away. I depart in my sweet bliss.'
> She fled, vanishing on the wind, And left a dead corse
> In Los's arms . . . he languish'd till dead he also fell.
> Night passed, & Enitharmon, e'er the dawn, return'd in bliss.
> She sang o'er Los reviving him to Life: his groans were terrible.

Enitharmon in this witching magical mood sings a song that is a part of her 'rapturous delusive trance', all about

> The joy of woman is the death of her most best beloved
> Who dies for Love of her
> In torments of fierce jealousy & pangs of adoration.

Oddly, her song contains one stanza that is not part of the delusion, but contains the very essence of Blake's affirmation of life:

> Arise, you little glancing wings & sing your infant joy!
> Arise & drink your bliss!
> For everything that lives is holy; for the source of life
> Descends to be a weeping babe;
> For the Earthworm renews the moisture of the sandy plain.

And her song contains also such a beautiful cry to the beloved as this:

> O I am weary! lay thine hand upon me or I faint,
> I faint beneath these beams of thine,
> For thou hast touched my five senses & they answer'd thee.
> Now I am nothing, & I sink
> And on the bed of silence sleep till thou awakest me.

This whole song of Enitharmon's is ambiguous, but it is an insert and may have really belonged elsewhere.

After this song we return to the plot of these two youthful terrors to separate Urizen and Ahania by planting divisions in their soul. Again, as in the fantasy of Vala flying to Albion's pillow, the mischief is done by means of a dream vision. They plan to conduct 'the voice of Enion to Ahania's midnight pillow'. Enion's lament does indeed reach Ahania's pillow, filling her with horror at what her husband, Urizen, has done. It is a very beautiful passage, containing the important lines about the desolate market which were discussed in the first chapter, and I would like here to quote it in full to reveal its psalm-like thought, its exotic phraseology and almost oriental splendour:

> I am made to sow the thistle for wheat, the nettle for a nourishing
>   dainty.
> I have planted a false oath in the earth: it has brought forth a
>   poison tree.

I have chosen the serpent for a councellor, & the dog
For a schoolmaster to my children.
I have blotted out from light & living the dove & nightingale,
And I have caused the earthworm to beg from door to door.

I have taught the thief a secret path into the house of the just.
I have taught pale artifice to spread his nets upon the morning.
My heavens are brass, my earth is iron, my moon a clod of clay,
My sun a pestilence burning at noon & a vapour of death in night.

What is the price of Experience? do men buy it for a song?
Or Wisdom for a dance in the street? No, it is bought with the
price
Of all that a man hath, his house, his wife, his children.
Wisdom is sold in the desolate market where none come to buy,
And in the wither'd field where the farmer plows for bread in
vain.

It is an easy thing to triumph in the summer's sun
And in the vintage & to sing on the waggon loaded with corn.
It is an easy thing to talk of patience to the afflicted,
To speak the laws of prudence to the houseless wanderer,
To listen to the hungry raven's cry in wintry season.
When the red blood is fill'd with wine & with the marrow of
lambs.

It is an easy thing to laugh at wrathful elements,
To hear the dog howl at the wintry door, the ox in the
slaughter-house moan;
To see a god on every wind & a blessing on every blast;
To hear the sounds of love in the thunder storm that destroys
our enemies' house;
To rejoice in the blight that covers his field, & the sickness that
cuts off his children,
While our olive & vine sing & laugh round our door, & our
children bring fruits & flowers.
Then the groan & the dolor are quite forgotten, & the slave
grinding at the mill,
And the captive in chains, & the poor in the prison, & the soldier
in the field
When the shatter'd bone hath laid him groaning among the
happier dead.
It is an easy thing to rejoice in the tents of prosperity:
Thus could I sing & thus rejoice: but it is not so with me.

And this remarkable Night the Second of *The Four Zoas* ends
with Ahania's reaction to Enion's lament which was conducted

to her pillow by Los and Enitharmon in order to alienate her
from Urizen. Jerusalem's mind and senses seek each other.

> Ahania heard the Lamentation, & a swift Vibration
> Spread thro' her Golden frame. She rose up e'er the dawn of day
> When Urizen slept on his couch: drawn thro' unbounded space
> On the margin of Non Entity the bright Female came.
> Then she beheld the Spectrous form of Enion in the Void,
> And never from that moment could she rest upon her pillow.

The drawing of Ahania descending, clutching her head, is a far
cry from the previous drawing, a lovely family group of rejoicing figures tilling a fruitful earth in illustration to Enion's
song.

Night the Third opens with the attempt of Ahania to persuade
Urizen to give up the false tyranny that is producing so much
misery. And Blake draws her bowing low before his feet. She
is in fact pleading with Lucifer to redress his sin of pride:

> O Prince, the Eternal One has set thee leader of his hosts,
> Raise then thy radiant eyes to him, raise thy obedient hands,
> And comforts shall descend from heaven into thy dark'ning
>   clouds.
> Leave all futurity to him. Resume thy fields of Light.

Ahania is full of foreboding about the future now that she
realizes what her husband has done. In telling her version of
Albion's downfall, she relates how he was 'smitten by Urizen's
power, and how, instead of his wife, Jerusalem, Vala 'walk'd
with him in dreams of soft deluding slumber'. Jerusalem as a
whole person could have warned Albion against seizing this
false power, but instead he consulted Vala, who, as sexual
woman, was bound only to admire any display of power on the
male's part. Ahania tells next how 'a Shadow rose from his
weary intellect' and how Albion prostrated himself before it, to
the momentary sincere consternation of herself and Urizen who
had not until then dreamt of being in such a position of power,
and did not originally want to be put on a throne that was not
theirs. But Urizen soon took his own superiority for granted,
and Ahania remembers how Urizen and Luvah fought for
possession of the body of Albion, and that head won over heart,

because it was Albion himself who chose, and 'put forth Luvah from his presence', even though Luvah is Christ. And Ahania cries in Cassandra-like despair:

> I can no longer hide
> The dismal vision of mine eyes. O love & life & light!
> Prophetic dreads urge me to speak; futurity is before me,
> Life a dark lamp. Eternal death haunts all my expectation.
> Rent from Eternal Brotherhood we die & are no more.

On these pages of the M.S. are partially erased drawings, one of a woman who has thrown herself on to the lifeless body of a man, another of two children gazing at the figure of a prostrate man, and a third showing a group of crouching figures with a boy in the background chasing a bat-like creature.

Urizen simply detests having his wife draw his attention to all the havoc that is resulting from his rule. But Ahania, who was once feminine wisdom, now that she has allowed the evidence of the senses and fact speak to her in the form of Enion, feels compelled to speak to her husband and try to make him see 'reason'! She tells him how Jerusalem, who has lost Christ just as Albion has, is actually turning into Vala, sexual woman seeking her lover like some terrible nature goddess bent on a union that will consume her beloved.

> Vala shrunk in like the dark sea that leaves its slimy banks,
> And from her bosom Luvah fell far as the east & west
> And the vast form of Nature, like a serpent, roll'd between.
> *Whether this is Jerusalem or Babylon we know not.*
> *All is Confusion. All is tumult, & we alone are escaped.*

She cries: 'O Urizen, why art thou pale at the vision of Ahania?' but she ends her prophecies hastily, 'for his wrathful throne burst forth the black hail storm'. Not only has Urizen been inattentive to her description of the confusion he has caused, but he interrupts her with blustering and threatening insistence that he is sole god, and he brings all the traditional machinery of godship with him to prove it: thunders and lightnings, clouds and ice and violence:

> 'Am I not God' said Urizen. 'Who is Equal to me?' . . .
> He spoke, mustering his heavy clouds around him, black, opake.
> Then thunders roll'd around & lightnings darted to & fro;

76

His visage chang'd to darkness, & his strong right hand came
　　forth
To cast Ahania to the Earth; he seiz'd her by the hair
And threw her from the steps of ice that froze around his throne,
Saying, 'Art thou also become like Vala? thus I cast thee out!
Shall the feminine indolent bliss, the indulgent self of weariness,
The passive idle sleep, the enormous night & darkness of Death
Set herself up to give her laws to the active masculine virtue?'

There is rueful humour in Blake's portrayal of Urizen's noisy
bluster, and his lack of subtlety in the way he simply produces
the signs and symbols of his power to prove that he has it. He is
diminished not only by this, but by the way he takes up Ahania's
tragic story of how Jerusalem is becoming Vala, only to turn it
against his wife and say that she, too, is behaving like Vala.
This is far from the case at this moment, as Ahania is in dead
earnest offering him his last chance to join forces once more with
his feminine counterpart, intuitive wisdom. But Urizen deliberately refuses this last chance to redeem his rule.

So loud in thunders spoke the king, folded in dark despair,
And threw Ahania from his bosom obdurate. She fell like
　　lightning . . .
A crash ran through the immense. The bounds of Destiny were
　　broken.
The bounds of Destiny crash'd direful, & the swelling sea
Burst from its bonds in whirlpools fierce, roaring with Human
　　voice,
Triumphing even to the stars at bright Ahania's fall.

Urizen has cast out the feminine side of wisdom which is one
side of himself, and by this perverts what had been destiny, the
basic bond of male and female. And he unlooses thereby the
dark waters of the unconscious sea that surge and cry with
human voice and triumph perversely in their own despair. For
Urizen does it deliberately, he separates himself from Ahania
knowing full well that despair lies therein, but stubbornly he
maintains the weak argument that it is 'intellectual suicide' to
the manly active virtues of intellect to accept wisdom that is
based upon fact and intuition rather than on abstract rational
ideas and proofs.

It is significant that Ahania is the only woman of the four

77

emanations within Jerusalem who is not in the position of Eve, tempting her husband. Rather, she tries in vain to wean Urizen from his overwhelming pride. The guilt she sees in him is real and precise, not vague and imaginary such as that which Enion accused Tharmas of. In this she is Sophia, Wisdom, but Urizen casts her out, calling her Vala without the slightest excuse to do so except that he wants to get rid of her embarrassing insight into what he has done.

Night the Third ends with Ahania's fall 'far into Non Entity', which means, of course, non-integration. Urizen, too, falls into this state when, too late, he rushes after her, possibly regretting what he has done. On this plate there is a finished pen drawing of Urizen holding a scroll covered with Hebrew lettering. Urizen falls precipitately into the abyss where Tharmas already wanders. Here there is a pencil sketch, full of fantastic humour, of Tharmas on the sea-shore, berating one of his own sea 'monsters Who sit mocking upon the little pebbles of the tide In all my rivers & on dried shells that the fish have quite forsaken.'

Tharmas, who is extremely myopic as befits the faculty of blind touch or instinct, sees Ahania's fall as the fall of his wife Enion. He strikes out at her, really in self-hatred and despair, until:

> no more remain'd of Enion in the dismal air,
> Only a voice eternal wailing in the elements.

There is a drawing of his terrible hoary figure threatening a shrinking female form under what looks like a cave. The words that are given to the lonely voice in the elements are some of the most tender in the poem:

> These are the words of Enion, heard from the cold waves of
>   despair:
> 'O Tharmas, I had lost thee, & when I hoped I had found thee,
> O Tharmas, do not destroy me quite, but let
> A little shadow, but a little showery form of Enion
> Be near thee, loved Terror; let me still remain, & then do thou
> Thy righteous doom upon me; only let me hear thy voice . . .
> *Make me not like the things forgotten as they had not been.*
> *Make me not the thing that loveth thee a tear wiped away.'*

78

Night the Fourth relates the struggle of Los, imagination, with his own father, Tharmas or instinct, for supremacy over Albion now that Urizen is no longer god. It is prefaced by a finished drawing of Albion, looking suspiciously like Blake, gazing beseechingly at the sun-chariot of imagination. His emanation reclines against him, and to the side, a large sun-flower springs exotically towards the sun, and a feminine figure within it raises her arms to the bright rays. Behind them, as always, lies the sea. Los cries in triumph:

> We have drunk up the Eternal Man by our unbounded power . . .
> And Los remains God over all.

There is ironic play on the name of Los here, for loss is truly all that remains of Albion after the warfare of his faculties for supremacy, and he gazes forlornly at the chariot of imagination, not knowing whether to follow it or to turn back to the instinctual life that leans heavily against him and springs glowing in its own right from the earth like a flower. But often, too, the instinctual life represented by the emanation, like Thel, flower-like turns away from him, cold and shuddering at the warmth and intensity of passion.

> Ah, Sun-flower! weary of time,
> Who countest the steps of the Sun,
> Seeking after that sweet golden clime
> Where the traveller's journey is done:
>
> Where the Youth pined away with desire
> And the pale Virgin shrouded in snow
> Arise from their graves, and aspire
> Where my Sun-flower wishes to go.

Once again, as with the 'Sick Rose', and the 'Tyger', we find that in the prophetic books Blake is simply expanding all that he had once been able to contain in the condensed implication of one incomparable image. And, as always, the lyric, less didactic in its explanation or implication, says much more.

Los challenged Tharmas, but Tharmas is not sure that he wants to fight his own son, who was once Urthona, creative imagination. Nor is he sure that he wants to be god.

79

Doubting stood Tharmas in the solemn darkness . . .
Now he resolv'd to destroy Los, & now his tears flowed down.

Finally Tharmas steels himself to fight Los for the kingship.
Once he has made up his mind, taking pleasure in the idea that
the laws of empirical fact will now succeed Urizen's rational
supremacy, he swells himself in pride and simply ignores Los.
And so the power comes automatically into his hands:

> Now all comes into the power of Tharmas, Urizen is fall'n,
> And Luvah hidden in the Elemental forms of Life & Death.
> Urthona is my son. O Los, thou art Urthona, & Tharmas
> Is God, the Eternal Man is seal'd, never to be deliver'd.

And yet Tharmas knows that he is miserable as sole god. He
misses Enion terribly:

> Yet tho' I rage God over all, A portion of my Life
> That in Eternal fields in comfort wander'd with my flocks
> At noon & laid her head upon my wearied bosom at night,
> She is divided. She is vanish'd, even like Luvah & Vala.
> O why did foul ambition seize thee, Urizen, Prince of Light?
> And thee, O Luvah, Prince of Love, till Tharmas was divided?
> And I, what can I now behold but an Eternal Death
> Before my Eyes, & an Eternal weary work to strive
> Against the monstrous forms that breed among my silent waves?
> Is this to be a God? far rather would I be a Man.

Tharmas,[1] blundering and clown-like as he is, never loses sight
altogether of the truth. He knows that he and Enion love one
another and should be together, and he doesn't like being god.
He departs into the unknown to look for Enion. Los remains, and,
looking into the abyss, 'terrified, Los beheld the ruins of Urizen
beneath'. In order to bind Urizen, Los sets about rebuilding the
ruined furnaces that had built up the Mundane Shell. And as
he works, Los blasphemes against Tharmas who is the present
God:

[1] It is interesting that Ahania (intellect) in Jerusalem, and Tharmas
(instinct) in Albion, keep sight of the truth, while their opposites, Vala
(passion) in Jerusalem and Urizen (Reason) in Albion, fight for supremacy and distortion. The first two hold the fort and the balance, as it
were, no matter how they are rejected.

And thus began the binding of Urizen; day & night in fear
Circling round the dark Demon, with howlings, dismay & Sharp
blightings,
The Prophet of Eternity beat on his iron links & links of brass;
And as he beat round the hurtling Demon, terrified at the shapes
Enslav'd humanity put on, he became what he beheld.
Raging against Tharmas his God, & uttering
Ambiguous words, blasphemous, fill'd with envy, firm resolv'd
On hate Eternal, in his vast disdain he labour'd beating
The Links of fate, link after link, an endless chain of sorrows.
The Eternal Mind, bounded, began to roll eddies of wrath
ceaseless . . .
Forgetfulness, dumbness, necessity, in chains of the mind
lock'd up.

In such manner begin the ages of torment for Urizen, which
we first witnessed in Blake's *Book of Urizen*. Paradoxically, the
fine intellect of man is bound and cannot know Eternity just
because it assumes and claims its own power to do so, to be
'unbounded'. Paradoxically, too, when Reason tries to be
supreme ruler of man, the intellect is not clear and beautifully
comprehending of eternal truths: it is rather, as Blake has shown
us, full of obscene creatures and murk. It is also forgetful and
vague, bound, but lacking 'the wirey bounding line' that makes
things clear. Had Reason remained in a working relation of
equality to the other faculties in Albion, it would have encom-
passed infinity in Christ, who would have ruled from the centre
of Albion's soul. But because of Urizen's excessive pride Albion
is sick, near to death.

And yet, even when Albion is in such a pitiful state, he is
watched over with love by divine presences. His sickness is
somehow identical with the crucifixion of Christ in his soul:

The Council of God on high watching over the body
Of Man cloth'd in Luvah's robes of blood, saw & wept.

The Daughters of Beulah see this Divine Vision and 'were
comforted'. For the moment they are identified with the sisters
of Lazarus, one of whom is Mary Magdalene:

Lord Saviour, if thou hadst been here our brother had not died,
And now we know that whatsoever thou wilt ask of God
He will give it thee; for we are weak women & dare not lift

81

Our eyes to the Divine pavilions; therefore in mercy thou
Appearest cloth'd in Luvah's garments that we may behold thee
And live. Behold Eternal Death is in Beulah. Behold
We perish & shall not be found unless thou grant a place
In which we may be hidden under the shadow of wings.
For if we, who are but for a time & who pass away in winter,
Behold these wonders of Eternity, we shall consume.

Again we have the theme of Eternity being too rigorous for the
weak female. But none the less, it is Jerusalem—for Blake says
specifically that the Daughters of Beulah who appear here as the
sisters of Lazarus, 'a double female form, loveliness & perfection
of beauty', are the 'Feminine Emanation'—who calls Eternity
down to heal the sick Albion.

The Saviour mild & gentle bent over the corse of Death,
Saying, 'If ye will Believe, your Brother shall rise again . . .'
Then wondrously the Starry Wheels felt the divine hand. Limit
Was put to Eternal Death.

There is a drawing that Blake places elsewhere on a blank page
of the MS. which is probably meant to illustrate this scene. It
shows Christ in flowing robes bending down to touch the heart
of the naked Albion.[1]

Night the Fifth is a strange and most important book.[2] It is
the story of what is happening in Albion's imagination while he
is in this state of death-like trance. For although we have been
inside Albion watching the four faculties fighting for supremacy
—his intellect, his imagination, his passions, and instinct—the
realm of imagination contains a whole and vitally important
world within it with key images of great significance. It is this
archetypal world of Albion's imagination that we enter in Night
the Fifth.

The archetypal history of Albion's illness that we have
already seen in terms of war among the faculties, is an astonish-

[1] There is another drawing, a man and a boy (father and son?) having
a friendly tug of war. The man pulls the boy to him. A finished pen
drawing shows a serene Christ to whom parents are bringing their
children.
[2] This section is prefaced by a full-page drawing of a demon and a
bristly dog watching gleefully as a smooth dog leaps at the throat of a
naked man.

ing feat of insight and ordering of unconscious material on Blake's part. It begins with the birth of 'a terrible child' named Orc to Los and Enitharmon who conceived him in a moment of almost mad terror at the threatened return of Christ to Albion's soul. And so we have Orc, not Christ, born within Albion. At Orc's birth, which should have been the birth of Christ,

> The Enormous Demons woke & howl'd around the new born
> King,
> Crying, 'Luvah, King of Love, thou art the King of rage & death.'

A drawing of Christ, pierced by nails and crowned with thorns, emerges from flames with a look of profound pity.

The trouble begins with Orc's embrace of his mother, Enitharmon, which, although innocent, is immediately condemned by his jealous father, Los. There are two pictures illustrating the text in the MS. of Night the Fifth that are tremendously significant. On one side of the page is a loving family group, the mother and father obviously doting on the joyful naked boy, smaller than his father's hand-span, which measures him in the cradle. On the other side of the page, the adolescent boy is lying naked on a rock, his sexual maturity very apparent, and his mother hugs herself with an expression of horror, and the father turns away in anger and dismay.

> when fourteen summers & winters had revolved over
> Their solemn habitation, Los beheld the ruddy boy
> Embracing his bright mother, & beheld malignant fires
> In his young eyes, discerning plain that Orc plotted his death.
> Grief rose upon his ruddy brows; a tightning girdle grew
> Around his bosom like a bloody cord; in secret sobs
> He burst it, but next morn another girdle succeeds
> Around his bosom. Every day he view'd the fiery youth
> With silent fear, & his immortal cheeks grew deadly pale.[1]

Enitharmon calls Los's fear and pain 'the chain of Jealousy' and is heart-broken when Los binds the boy upon a mountain-top with the 'accursed chain'. Los forces Enitharmon to come away from the mountain to which her son is chained,

[1] There is a drawing of a naked woman reclining, her head in her hands. A boy watches her thoughtfully.

83

Giving the Spectre sternest charge over the howling fiend,
Concenter'd into Love of Parent, Storgous Appetite, Craving.

There is another profound sketch. To the boy it must have appeared that his mother needed no urging to leave him, and that his father had won out in her love. For the pencil sketch shows us the bound boy watching his parents move away, entwined arm in arm closely and oblivious of his pain, gazing into each other's eyes with the engrossed eyes of love and whispering together.

Los and Enitharmon return home, and suddenly, Blake tells us with a certain irony:

> Felt all the sorrow Parents feel, they wept toward one another
> And Los repented that he had chain'd Orc upon the mountain.
> And Enitharmon's tears prevail'd; parental love return'd,
> Tho' terrible his dread of that infernal chain. They rose
> At midnight hasting to their much beloved care.

But they are too late. Blake observes with startling clarity of vision that irreparable harm has already been done to the boy. Orc has grown roots from the chain of jealousy and is rooted into the rock:

> Los, taking Enitharmon by the hand, led her along
> The dismal vales & up to the iron mountain's top where Orc
> Howl'd in the furious wind; he thought to give to Enitharmon
> Her son in tenfold joy, & to compensate for her tears
> Even if his own death resulted, so much pity him pain'd.
> But when they came to the dark rock & to the spectrous cave,
> Lo, the young limbs had strucken root into the rock, & strong
> Fibres had from the Chain of Jealousy inwove themselves
> In a swift vegetation round the rock & round the Cave
> And over the immortal limbs of the terrible fiery boy.
> In vain they strove now to unchain, in vain with bitter tears
> To melt the chain of Jealousy; not Enitharmon's death,
> Nor the Consummation of Los could ever melt the chain
> Nor unroot the infernal fibres from their rocky bed.

This sorry tale has, of course, a startling resemblance to the genesis of what today's psychologists call the Oedipus Complex. However, Blake slants it a little differently. The sense of guilt is produced wholly by the attitude of the father. A boy does not start life with a 'mother fixation'. He embraces his mother in all innocence at the time of puberty, as he did as a child. It is the father who sees evil where there is none. Seeing the boy's growing body, he distorts the boy's natural affection for his mother into something unnatural and horrible. He is jealous of the boy's approaching young manhood just when he himself is losing the vigour of youth. The consequences of the father's jealousy do irrevocable damage to the boy. By the time that the parents regret chaining the boy to the mountain, it is too late. The boy's very outlook is chained and distorted and rooted in anger. He has been forced into the pattern of an Oedipus relationship with his mother, and indeed with any woman that he may try to love. Neither the death of his actual mother will eradicate this effect, nor identification with his father and recognition of the sexual relationship between his parents. The damage that has been done under the name of parental love cannot be undone.

Blake is profound in placing the parental contribution to Albion's breakdown wholly on the level of distorted imagination or fantasy. We know nothing about Albion's actual parents or his relationship with them. Instead, we are given the history of Orc, who is Albion as he appears to himself in his sick fantasies, and his relation to his archetypal parents, Los and Enitharmon. That Blake was astonishingly aware of what we now call archetypes cannot be doubted. If he is not talking about those forces in the following passage from *A Descriptive Catalogue*, I do not know what he is talking about:

'Chaucer's characters are a description of the eternal principles that exist in all ages . . . visions of these eternal principles or characters of human life appear to poets, in all ages . . . These gods (of the Greeks) are visions of the eternal attributes, or divine names, which, when erected into gods, become destructive to humanity. They ought to be the servants, and not the masters of man, or of Society. They ought to be made to sacrifice to Man, and not man compelled to sacrifice to them; for when separated from man or humanity, who is Jesus the Saviour, the vine of Eternity, they are thieves and rebels, they are destroyers. KEYNES, Nonesuch, vol. III, p. 101.

Quite literally, we get the inside story of what Albion at his sickest *believed* his parents to have done to him, whatever they may have done or not done in actual fact. To be able to blame his archetypal parents for his sorry plight is, of course, one way Albion has of lifting the burden of guilt from his own shoulders concerning his failure in relationship with his wife.

This permanent chaining of Orc within Albion has dire effects on Jerusalem as well, and on Enitharmon, Orc's mother, within Jerusalem. In Enitharmon as in Jerusalem 'Vala began to reanimate in bursting sobs'. And soon Vala will join forces with Urizen to do further damage. But at the moment we find Urizen alone in a short-lived state of repentance, listening to the howls of Orc. He remembers his peaceful existence before his pride made him take advantage of Christ's mildness:

> O Fool! to think that I could hide from his all piercing eyes
> The gold & silver & costly stones, his holy workmanship!
> O Fool! could I forget the light that filled my bright spheres
> Was a reflection of his face who call'd me from the deep!

> I well remember, for I heard the mild & holy voice
> Saying, 'O light, spring up & shine,' & I sprang up from the deep.
> He gave me a silver sceptre, & crown'd me with a golden crown,
> And said, 'Go forth & guide my Son who wanders on the ocean.'

> I went not forth: I hid myself in black clouds of my wrath;
> I call'd the stars around my feet in the night of councils dark;
> The stars threw down their spears & fled naked away.
> We fell . . .

> I will arise, Explore these dens, & find that deep pulsation
> That shakes my cavern with strong shudders; perhaps this is the night
> Of Prophecy, & Luvah hath burst his way from Enitharmon.
> When Thought is clos'd in Caves Then Love shall shew its root
> in deepest Hell.

The last line, with its platonic image of the cave, is curiously like Kant's conclusion that thought without content is empty, just as emotion or empirical fact without thought is blind. The passage about the stars throwing down their spears casts light on the lyric that Blake called 'The Tyger'. We realize that it is Urizen's fall and tyranny which was the mysterious and beauti-

ful evil that stalked the forests of the night: the Tyger is the
terrible beauty of thought separated from Love:

> When the stars threw down their spears
> And water'd heaven with their tears,
> Did he smile his work to see?
> Did he who made the Lamb make thee?

Night the Fifth ends with Urizen's realization that thought
without love is nothing, and love without thought is hell.

Night the Sixth opens with Urizen gathering himself to
explore his den. He 'arose, & leaning on his spear explor'd his
dens.' He comes upon three mysterious women who are later
revealed as his daughters, Eleth, Uveth, and Ona, who were the
Moral Virtues in the *Everlasting Gospel*, and probably the Fates.
The whole scene is certainly reminiscent of Lear. Miss Kathleen
Raine maintained in a lecture[1] that the early crude poem,
Tiriel, is one of Blake's 'major works', and a profound criticism
of *King Lear*. Be this as it may, I cannot remember whether she
mentioned the startling resemblance of this scene in *The Four
Zoas* to Lear.

Urizen does not at first recognize his daughters:

> 'Who art thou, Eldest Woman, sitting in thy clouds? . . .
> Answerest thou not?' said Urizen, 'Then thou maist answer me,
> Thou terrible woman, clad in blue, whose strong attractive power
> Draws all into a fountain at the rock of thy attraction;
> With frowning brow thou sittest, mistress of these mighty
>   waters.'
> She answer'd not, but stretched her arms & threw her limbs
>   abroad.
> 'Or wilt thou answer, youngest Woman, clad in shining green?
> With labour & care thou dost divide the current into four.
> Queen of these dreadful rivers, speak, & let me hear thy voice.'

> They rear'd up a wall of rocks, & Urizen rais'd his spear.
> They gave a scream, they knew their father. Urizen knew his
>   daughters.
> They shrunk into their channels, dry the rocky strand beneath his
>   feet,
> Hiding themselves in rocky forms from the Eyes of Urizen.

[1] At Girton, 1954.

Urizen weeps in sorrow and fury that after all he has given them, they chose Tharmas as their God. That he has done so much for them we must take on faith, for we have not heard of the daughters before now except in *The Everlasting Gospel*:

> Am I not Lucifer the Great,
> And you my daughters in great state
> The fruit of my Mysterious Tree . . .
> The Moral Virtues in Great fear
> Formed the Cross & Nails & Spear.

And in the lyric 'A Little Girl Lost', the daughter who has loved, and confronts her stern father is named Ona. Urizen curses his ungrateful daughters like Lear, and Tharmas comes at their scream:

> Crying: 'What & Who art thou, Cold Demon? art thou Urizen?
> Art thou, like me, risen again from death? or art thou deathless?
> If thou art he, my desperate purpose hear, & give me death,
> For death to me is better far than life, death my desire
> That I in vain in various paths have sought, but still I live.
> The Body of Man is given to me. I seek in vain to destroy.'

Tharmas, longing for death, proposes that they should destroy one another and so end the misery of their fallen state. Tharmas says to Urizen:

> Withhold thy light from me for ever, & I will withhold
> From thee thy food; so shall we cease to be, & all our sorrows
> End, & the Eternal Man no more renew beneath our power.

In Albion in his fallen state the wish for death is dominant, at least on the level of instinct. But Urizen does not answer Tharmas' proposal of a death-pact, and makes his way through caverns which can only be the caves of the mind in mental sickness:

> For Urizen beheld the terrors of the Abyss wandering among
> The ruin'd Spirits, once his children & the children of Luvah.
> Scar'd at the sound of their own sigh that seems to shake the
>   immense
> They wander Moping, in their heart a sun, a dreary moon,
> A Universe of fiery constellations in their brain,
> An earth of wintry woe beneath their feet, & round their loins

Waters or winds or clouds or brooding lightnings & pestilential
    plagues.
Beyond the bounds of their own self their senses cannot penetrate:
As the tree knows not what is outside of its leaves & bark
And yet it drinks the summer joy & fears the winter sorrow,
So, in the regions of the grave, none knows his dark compeer
Tho' he partakes of his dire woes & mutual returns the pang,
The throb, the dolor, the convulsion, in soul-sickening woes.

Urizen finds that matters are much worse within the caverns of
Albion's mind than he alone had power to make them:

Here he had time enough to repent of his rashly threaten'd curse.
He saw them curs'd beyond his Curse: his soul melted with fear.
He could not take their fetters off, for they grew from the soul,
Nor could he quench the fires, for they flam'd out from the heart,
Nor could he calm the Elements, because himself was subject.

Urizen throws himself into the void in despair at what he sees,
and he falls even further into the abyss he is already in. And
once again, we get a sudden shift from this whirling chaos inside
of Albion, to the dizzying heights of divine guidance. Christ
sees Urizen's despair:

The ever pitying one who seeth all things, saw his fall,
And in the dark vacuity created a bosom of clay . . .
Endless had been his travel, but the Divine hand him led.

Urizen recognizes the tragedy he has caused in its full horror:

    O, thou poor ruin'd world!
Thou horrible ruin! Once like me thou wast all glorious,
And now like me partaking desolate thy master's lot.
Art thou, O ruin, the once glorious heaven? are these thy rocks
Where joy sang on the trees & pleasure sported in the rivers,
And laughter sat beneath the Oaks, & innocence sported round
Upon the green plains, & sweet friendship met in palaces,
And books & instruments of song & pictures of delight? . . .
I am regenerated, to fall or rise at will . . .

In an effort to rise again and to make some sense of the ruined
world, Urizen invents the sciences to explain and control nature:

So he began to form of gold, silver & iron
And brass, vast instruments to measure out the immense & fix
The whole into another world better suited to obey

His will, where none should dare oppose his will, himself being
    King,
Of All, & all futurity be bound in his vast chain.
And the Sciences were fix'd & the Vortexes began to operate
On all the sons of men, & every human soul terrified
At the living wheels of heaven shrunk away inward, with'ring
    away.

Urizen is up to his old tricks again. His moment of repentance
fades easily into new schemes for power. Tharmas tries his best
to kill Urizen by refusing him nourishment from his own
domain of nature and empirical fact, but Urizen goes inexorably
on, imposing an abstract tyranny of scientific law on that body of
experience which, Tharmas feels, should be learnt only through
the senses. This has a horrible effect on the world of imagination,
and, 'All these around the world of Los cast forth their monstrous births.'

Night the Seventh begins with Urizen banishing Tharmas. It
then takes us back to the story of Orc. This is both the most
difficult and the most important and subtle section of *The Four
Zoas*. It relates how Orc, after his Oedipus-like experience,
inevitably becomes entangled in Urizen's false religion.

Urizen descends to the cave where Orc is bound, and finds the
boy worshipping at the shrine of his own mother, Enitharmon:

Howling & rending his dark caves the awful Demon lay:
Pulse after pulse beat on his fetters, pulse after pulse his spirit
Darted & darted higher & higher to the shrine of Enitharmon.

This is the 'deep pulsation that shakes my cavern with strong
shudders' which Urizen had previously felt and feared might be
the birth of Luvah who is Christ. But it is only Orc born in
Albion's soul where Christ should be. And it is an Orc ripe for
and already conditioned for Urizen's father-god religion of
'Thou Shalt Not'. Orc is already worshipping the mother image
who is seen as holy and unattainable, and at the same time as
the terrible harlot, Nature or Vala, who lures him towards
destruction. For within Enitharmon in her pride at being
worshipped by her son, 'Vala began to reanimate'. Orc is
feeding himself 'with visions of sweet bliss far other than this
burning clime'. That is to say, he does not want any human love,

but is thirsting for the unattainable romantic ideal of womanhood that the mother represents. But, should this image seem
accessible, she is immediately condemned as a harlot.

Urizen sits down to watch this interesting phenomenon. But,
since he is the self-appointed father-god, he soon finds himself
feeling half jealous of Orc's worship of the mother image. He
finds himself aching to replace Orc's actual father, who is Los,
and himself be worshipped together with the mother. Blake
indicates with brilliant subtlety how Orc's sick relation to his
parents merges almost unnoticed into his sick religion on the
level of Albion's warped imagination.

It is a short step from Orc's fear and hatred of his own
father, Los, to confusing this father with a tyrannical god. And
a god has the unquestionable authority to condemn as guilty a
love that has already been made to seem guilty by the less
potent authority of a father.

The actual replacement of Los, the real father of Orc, by
Urizen, the father-god, in Albion's sick imagination, is bril-
liantly suggested. It is significant that after this replacement
occurs, Orc seems to himself less like the innocent sinner,
Oedipus, and more like Prometheus who deliberately stole fire
from the god: 'I stole thy light and it became fire consuming'
cries Orc in Promethean imagery, confessing to a deliberate
crime he did not commit. He is no longer simply the wronged
son who has been accused and chained although innocent. He
has become the chained creative imagination itself become
deliberately evil in the service of a false god. He now intends to
worship at the shrine of the mother whether the father-god is
jealous or not. Orc is a raging and terrified child, but he is also
a demon. He hides Christ, true imagination and love in Albion,
in whom the Father is implicit. Orc separates off from the father
and both hates and worships him as larger than life.

By now Orc is entangled not only in the simple worship and
fear of his own father, but in all the intricate branches of the
tree of mystery religion which Urizen brings with him when he
almost magically replaces Los. The fibres that grew from the
original chain of jealousy with which Los chained Orc to the
mountain, rooting Orc to sickness, have become irrevocably
entwined with the roots of the tree of mystery.

This tree of mystery is the tree of the knowledge of good and evil which divides life up into the opposites of good and bad on rational grounds. Blake suggests that this is a development that springs almost involuntarily from Albion's fallen state almost *despite* Urizen. Urizen simply sat down to watch Orc worshipping the mother, and is almost as surprised as anyone to find his mild wish to replace Los magically become fact:

> Urizen approach'd *not near* but took his seat on a rock
> And rang'd his books around him, brooding Envious over Orc . . .
> Los felt the Envy in his limbs like to a blighted tree,
> For Urizen fix'd in envy sat brooding . . . til underneath his heel
>   a deadly root
> Struck thro' the rock, the root of Mystery accursed shooting up
> Branches into the heaven of Los: they, pipe form'd, bending down
> Take root again wherever they touch, again branching forth
> In intricate labyrinths o'erspreading many a grizly deep.

The various gradations of tree imagery, from Los' feeling of Urizen's envy in his limbs like 'to a blighted tree' to the full branching of the tree of Mystery, hold together this incredible scene of illusions and replacements in Albion's sick fantasy.

Urizen, in his opaque understanding of his own motivation, is amazed to find himself confused with and already taking the place of Orc's father, Los:

> Amaz'd started Urizen when he found himself compass'd round
> And high rooted over with trees; he arose, but the stems
> Stood so thick he with difficulty & great pain brought
> His books out of the dismal shade, all but the book of iron.

Urizen, concerned only in rescuing his precious books from the encroaching undergrowth, is altogether surprised at finding himself in his new role. But he soon gets used to it, and persuades himself that it was a deliberate act of altruism that moved him to come. He tells Orc:

> Pity for thee mov'd me to break my dark & long repose,
> And to reveal myself before thee in a form of wisdom.

This is pure pompous nonsense. Urizen, fallen into the abyss, had out of sheer boredom and restlessness been exploring the caves of his prison. No profound repose has been disturbed by his coming. But none the less he sententiously holds forth in the manner of the bookish great man, acclaimed, assured, and generous with advice: it is a very funny parody of a type of man that Blake knew well:

> Read my books, explore my Constellations,
> Enquire of my Sons & they shall teach thee how to War.

Urizen says kindly to young Orc, who languishes consumed with the bothersome fires of youth.

Urizen decides to get rid of Los altogether and himself become the substitute father, forestalling rivalry from the real father who may make trouble as he is bewildered by what is happening. Urizen sits

> On a rock of iron frowning over the foaming fires of Orc.
> And Urizen hung over Orc & view'd his terrible wrath.

For Orc's wrath against his father is now given free rein within the mystery religion. Finally Urizen tells his three daughters, the Moral Virtues,

> To bring the Shadow of Enitharmon beneath our wondrous tree,
> That Los may evaporate like smoke & be no more.

And so, under protection of the Moral Virtues, the mother image is safely conveyed into her place in the religion of Mystery, and Orc's actual father, Los, is replaced once and for all by Urizen. Los disappears 'like smoke' in Orc's mind.

Blake shows us the bewilderment of Los who does not know at all what is happening. For he has no way of guessing that Orc has in imagination annihilated him, and now quite safely can worship the mother image under the authority of Urizen, who is also the supreme avenger should Orc dare to unite with the mother goddess.

All that Los is able to see is that his wife, Enitharmon, has withdrawn from him in spirit, and seems to find joy and nourishment in some invisible source. She is radiant, and goes through strange emotional crises that he cannot understand because he cannot see what is causing them:

> Silent he stood over Enitharmon watching her pale face ... nor
>   could his eyes perceive ...
> The cause of her dire anguish, for she lay the image of death ...
>   Now she was pale as snow
> When the mountains & hills are cover'd over & the paths of Men
>   shut up,
> But when her spirit return'd as ruddy as a morning when
> The ripe fruit blushes into joy in heaven's eternal halls,
> She secret joy'd to see; she fed herself on his Despair.
> She said, 'I am reveng'd for all my sufferings of old.'

Of course, this separation between Los and Enitharmon began long before Orc was born. From their own childhood days this pair was wayward and perverse, and Christ played no part in their union. The birth of Orc should have been the birth of Christ, had they not been so terrified at anything resembling true love. Their separation was effectively completed when Enitharmon interceded in vain for her son against Los's jealousy and anger. Now in retaliation for Los's cruelty, she becomes with a vengeance the mother goddess in Urizen's religion, content with the worship of her son because she no longer loves her husband. She does not pause for a moment to consider that she is destroying all chance that Orc may someday find his own female counterpart, by keeping him in this position of unsatisfied suppliant at her shrine.

This instalment of the mother in Urizen's religion completes the picture of Orc's illness, which is Albion's. From now on he is cut off from actual life, living in this world of looming parent images, for ever worshipping and desiring the mother, but forbidden to unite with her by the father god. It is really the two sides of himself, the opposites of father and mother within his own being that Urizen has forbidden Orc to unite. He has thus condemned Orc to impotent inaction. For it is only when we can manage by some imaginative re-creation to play out that part of our earthly existence of which we have no remembrance —the union of our parents and our conception and birth—that we wed together consciously the two sides of ourselves and are consciously brought to birth as a functioning human entity. Until then guilt makes the whole process of birth a monstrous thing and, like Albion, we die from day to day, which is one way of looking at life.

The successful setting up of Urizen's religion has completed Albion's division off from that half of himself which he feels is evil and taboo. The mother image becomes the desired and forbidden unattainable which he will project on to any woman who may attract him, and it is really his own feared emotional nature. This image, because of Urizen's false laws which surround it, seems at one and the same time, impossibly 'good', a terrible travesty of the Virgin Mary, and also a looming temptress, a belle dame sans merci who lures him to destruction like a harlot. Until he can unite with this image within his own imagination, he can have no real relationship with a woman, for he is seeking the unattainable mother to intercede for him with the angry father, not an equal partner in a marriage relationship.

Enitharmon as she is, is a horrible caricature of the Virgin Mary. Urizen fears that she will give birth to Christ, but he needn't have worried, for she can only give birth to Orc and new forms of Urizen in endless cycle. Urizen's spectre prepares her for this event, coming like some dark angel of annunciation:

The Spectre . . . saw the Shadow of Enitharmon
Beneath the Tree of Mystery . . . the demon strong prepar'd the
  poison of sweet Love . . .
'Loveliest delight of Men! Enitharmon . . . the next joy of thine
  shall be in sweet delusion
And its birth in fainting & sleep & sweet delusions of Vala.

Los, Enitharmon's husband, by this time realizes that his wife partakes no longer of Jerusalem, but wholly of Vala, Nature, and is worshipped as the mother goddess in Urizen's religion. He laments her departure into the realm of Mystery and the unattainable, knowing that for himself as well as for Orc, she must from now on be the luring belle dame sans merci with all of her powers of temptation that never intend to satisfy:

Why can I not Enjoy thy beauty, lovely Enitharmon?
When I return from clouds of Grief in the wand'ring Elements
Where thou in thrilling joy, in beaming summer loveliness,

Delectable reposest, ruddy in my absence, flaming with beauty,
Cold pale in sorrow at my approach, trembling at my terrific
Forehead & eyes, thy lips decay like roses in the spring.
How thou art shrunk! . . .
Thus Los lamented in the night, unheard by Enitharmon.
For the Shadow of Enitharmon descended down the Tree of
    Mystery.'

Orc very rightly suspects that this 'benevolent' move on Urizen's
part, gratifying his desire by bringing the mother image into his
religion and making her ever worshipful but mysteriously unattainable, is making his illness worse instead of better. It is a
granting of desire that means further tyranny. He has a momentary conviction that his god, Urizen, is really Lucifer:

Then Orc cried: 'Curse thy Cold hypocrisy! already round thy Tree
In scales that shine with gold & rubies, thou beginnest to weaken
My divided Spirit. Like a worm I rise in peace, unbound
From wrath. Now when I rage my fetters bind me more . . .
Give me example of thy mildness. King of furious hailstorms,
Art thou the cold attractive power that holds me in this chain? . . .
        Thou know'st me now, O Urizen, Prince of Light,
And I know thee.'

Urizen is terrified by this moment of insight and rebellion on
Orc's part. In a panic, Urizen is convinced that Orc has suddenly
become his old enemy, Luvah, who is Christ. There is something
both comical and profound in Blake's portrayal of the archetypal
tyrannical father, tottering in his power at the first moment of
insight on the part of the sick Orc. Urizen is afraid that he and
Enitharmon have inadvertently given birth to Christ: 'Terrified
Urizen heard Orc, now certain that he was Luvah.'
    Urizen needn't have feared. Orc has not become Christ, but
a sick caricature of Christ at the centre of Albion's soul. He is
impotence that passes for holiness, inhibition that passes for
morality, shame that is 'Pride's cloak' and passes for goodness.
In the same way, the mother image is a sick caricature of the
Virgin Mary within Jerusalem. She is become the sick rose and
Orc is the invisible worm who destroys her with his dark love

    ¹ Blake has drawn a swiftly running male figure, almost horizontal,
holding a circlet of stars before him as he runs. Many of the drawings in
the MS., like this one, have nothing to do with the immediate text.

in the strange nightmare fantasy of Urizen's howling storms. We have now in the religion of Mystery, a false father-god in Urizen, a false Son in Orc, a false Holy Ghost in the Spectre and a false virgin-mother in Enitharmon. In contrast to true Christianity, Orc's dualistic religion is that which Blake criticized in *The Marriage of Heaven and Hell*, saying:

'All Bibles or sacred codes have been the causes of the following Errors:

1. That Man has two real existing principles: Viz. a Body and a Soul.
2. That Energy, call'd Evil, is alone from the Body; and that Reason, call'd Good, is alone from the Soul.
3. That God will torment Man in Eternity for following his Energies.

But the following Contraries to these are True:

1. Man has no Body distinct from his Soul; for that call'd Body is a portion of the Soul discern'd by the five senses, the chief inlets of Soul in this age.
2. Energy is the only life, and is from the Body; and Reason is the bound, or outward circumference of Energy.
3. Energy is Eternal Delight.'

The nightmare repeats itself in various forms, each time adding some new horror to the basic conception of Orc's illness, which is, we must always remember, simply the core of Albion's sickness. Love, energy, power, inhibited, turn poisonous.

> Among the flowers of Beulah, walk'd the Eternal Man & saw
> Vala, the lilly of the desart melting in high noon.
> Upon her bosom in sweet bliss he fainted. Wonder seiz'd
> All heaven; they saw him dark; they built a golden wall
> Round Beulah. There he revel'd in delight among the Flowers.
> Vala was pregnant & brought forth Urizen, Prince of Light,
> First born of Generation. Then behold a wonder to the Eyes
> Of the now fallen Man; a double form Vala appear'd, a Male
> And female; shudd'ring pale the Fallen Man recoil'd
> From the Enormity & call'd them Luvah & Vala, turning down
> The vales to find his way back into Heaven, but found none.[1]

[1] Behind the text is a huge winged Hecate-like figure and in the river that runs by her feet float all sorts of heads—a child's head, a strong woman swimmer's, despairing heads, praying hands. A pale grave woman paces along the bank.

All this Enitharmon tells to the Spectre, asking him naïvely:

> Art thou, terrible Shade,
> Set over this sweet boy of mine to guard him lest he rend
> His mother to the winds of heaven?

And she ends piously:

> But thou, Spectre dark,
> Maist find a way to punish Vala in thy fiery south,
> To bring her down subjected to the rage of my fierce boy.

Enitharmon has no conception of what she is doing to her 'sweet' and 'fierce' boy. Even as she tells the story of his wandering in the delusive Beulah and succumbing to the Lilith-like Vala, she has no idea that Vala has divided into two, and that her son is now in the state where he could conceivably be lured by a masculine Vala, Luvah, who is no longer in him but appears as an outside entity, even though as yet he recoils from such a monstrous aberration. Urizen is born again, and his laws equate abstention from passion with piety. Thus the stage is set for some perversion of the passions.

Urizen himself does not realize the far-reaching effect that his own confusing of the impotently ascetic Orc with Christ will have. Orc, forced into 'a pale lecherous virginity' by his own difficulties with his archetypal parents, is far from the Christ-like figure he is mistaken for. But we find Albion at his sickest when he has entirely rejected Christ from his soul, looking in his passive withdrawn state of impotence, exactly like the popular idea of Christ. His bound inhibitions appear on the surface like pious and holy restraint, when in actual fact beneath the surface he is raging like a demon and full of hatred, and perverted desires.

It is a confusion that many have made, Christians and non-Christians alike. For Blake tells us that Orc *is* the monk, and that monkish asceticism based on impotence rather than holiness is the serpent that eats at the heart of Christianity. It postulates a life-hatred and feeble dividedness of the human being in the place of the energetic and joyful involvement in life that is the only health, and the only holiness: 'for everything that lives is holy'. The whole history of Orc has been building up to this view of him as the monk who is really the serpent. The bisexual nature of the serpent-monk appears later on.

Our realization that Orc is a monk and also the evil serpent dawns slowly. But when the shock comes, we realize, too, that the imagery has paved the way carefully. More than once the sick and ascetic Orc calls himself 'A Worm compell'd'. He bores away, causing further division in the divided heart of Albion, and soon, grown fat on this diet, he swells to serpent strength:

> Orc began to organize a Serpent body . . .
> A self consuming devourer rising into the heavens . . .
> Urizen envious brooding . . . made Orc,
> In serpent form compell'd, stretch up & out the mysterious tree.
> He suffer'd him to climb that he might draw all human forms
> Into submission to his will, nor knew the dread result.

Finally, this serpent is seen to be the priest, wearing a cowl. And more than this he is the perpetrator of war and of all conflicts. War and asceticism are the two sides of the same penny:

> The Prester Serpent runs
> Along the ranks, crying, 'Listen to the Priest of God, ye warriors;
> This Cowl upon my head he plac'd in times of Everlasting.'[1]

Blake's story of how the ascetic was born is impressive, although it leaves no room for any true form of asceticism within Christianity. All forms of monasticism, he would claim, are a kind of illness and impotence rather than piety. This claim he made in earlier poems, too, in gnomic form, namely that the life of abstinence and denial which is commonly thought of as Christianity, has nothing whatever to do with what Christ taught, which can be summed up in two phrases: 'Thy own Humanity learn to adore' and 'Everything that lives is holy'. The ascetic, Blake argues, is simply the man who, possibly through no fault of his own originally, has been so warped by experience that he has turned into a life-hater. He has cast life and humanity from his soul with Christ, substituting his own Reason and its flesh-subduing Mystery religion.

Blake has shown us very carefully the steps by which Albion sickened into Orc, the monk. This man who might delude us

[1] At the end of Night the Seventh is a drawing of a snake ending in the weak head of Orc.

into thinking him a holy man is as near to spiritual death as he can get. His state is near despair. 'If any could desire what he is incapable of possessing, despair must be his eternal lot.' He has not only cast Christ from him, but also his own emotional nature and the capacity for love of any sort. Blake sees the love between man and woman as the most vital part of Christianity, without which there can be no wholeness. His rehabilitation of woman from her position of Eve, the temptress, is as difficult as getting Albion well. But both of these things must be accomplished before Christ can return, and with Christ, energy.

Now that Orc is seen as the priest, Blake underscores the pagan anti-Christian nature of the mysteries he celebrates. Under guise of conflict with Vala, he unites over and over with the mother. As an individual he goes up in smoke, and only the abstraction of priesthood remains, masquerading as Christianity:

> No more remain'd of Orc but the serpent round the tree of
>   Mystery.
> The form of Orc was gone.

The imagery with which Blake surrounds Orc is complex, richer and more consistent in its variety than the symbols associated with any other character in the prophetic books. He has been Oedipus and Prometheus, and the image of Promethean fire remains with him throughout. He had been the 'Worm compell'd', and has grown to the serpent who is the cowled monk. He is a demon as his name implies. Above all, he is 'the invisible worm' that destroys the beauty of the rose into which it burrows with its angry impotent lust, making the rose seem more like a harlot on her crimson bed than like Mary, who is traditionally associated with the rose.

Orc is a frightened bound child who cannot grow up and free himself from parental bondage. But he is also the grown man, raging impotently against his chains, streaming with fire. The rage of the man is the adult expression of the child's fear, and the man in him rages against the father-god's tyranny, while the worm remains compelled: power strains against passivity.

> The Man shall rage, bound with this chain, the worm in silence
>   creep . . .
> I rage in the deep . . .

This seething rage, the other side of compulsive asceticism, explodes into conflict and war. Excess violence, like too great withdrawal, reveals bound immaturity. Both waste powerful life energies.

If Albion is ever to get well, he must grow up, against Orc's fierce resistance, that part of him that Orc stands for and which is still bound to archetypal parents. Orc is not the sensitive imaginative child of the *Songs of Innocence*, trusting the world and loving Christ. He is, rather, wizened and old, jealous, sullen, and hostile, a demon who fills Albion's 'troubled head with terrible visages & flaming hair'. Orc glories in self-pity. He is deceitful and selfish. He never gives love, but only clamours endlessly for that love and sympathy which was denied to him as a child, and which he cannot trust himself to deserve as an adult man. And he takes out his discontent on his wife, forcing her into the position of mother-virgin, and harlot, demanding love that he would have no need to beg for were he fourfold and adult.

One might, upon first glance, argue that the existence of the monkish child, Orc, within Albion is a carrying out of Christ's warning—'Except ye turn again and become as little children, ye shall not enter the kingdom of heaven'. But this is not so. Albion has never grown up, and until he has, he cannot 'turn again'. It is a case of first having to grow mature in order to become young for the first time, of having to become disillusioned in order to become wise, and of having to accept one's participation in error and guilt in order to become innocent.

Like the child having a tantrum, Orc is trying to appear very babyish, but his eyes glitter with ancient malice and he looks old and wizened. He is trying to appear impossibly 'good' to show that he has been terribly misjudged and misused, but his ascetic piety is only destructive inhibition. He is full of his own tragedy, but he has never taken a really calm look at the worst, and at his own part in creating it, and so has not emerged with that tranquil wisdom which Blake calls 'organized' or 'reorganized' innocence.

Unorganiz'd Innocence: An Impossibility.
Innocence dwells with Wisdom, but never with Ignorance.

Although Orc's original chaining to the mountain was indeed a tragedy in which he was the innocent victim, he now banks upon it too much to win him sympathy no matter how obnoxious he may be, and he counts on it to relieve him of all responsibility no matter what mischief he does to spite the world. A very hollow and false note is often struck by Orc in his howlings. And he often strikes the reader as irresistibly comic in his cosmic rages, appearing Thurberesque just when he is bewailing most passionately the wrongs that were done to him. He has none of the 'mirthful serenity' which comes when the worst has been faced and accepted, nor the accompanying almost light-hearted sense of still being a functioning and somehow less encumbered entity. Orc carries the whole dreary baggage of his miserable past with him wherever he goes.

Orc could, at a moment's notice, give way to Christ, should the moment of Albion's healing arrive. He, the monk, the life-hater and serpent, can disappear and reveal Christ in love's garments, as Urizen feared had already happened. 'Satan is the Spectre of Orc, & Orc is the generate Luvah.' Orc is the disguise that hides Christ and love, and his asceticism is only a compulsive chastity and inability to love stemming from emotional immaturity. The obverse side of his chastity is the fact that in imagination he pursues many women, or rather the mother image in them, which makes Jerusalem jealous. At the same time he sees her provocation as harlotry. He is chaste in fact because he is compelled to be, but he is promiscuous in imagination.

In *The Four Zoas* Blake gives a remarkable account of the genesis of asceticism within Christianity as a hangover of fear of the vengeful father-god of the old dispensation. It is born of a feeling that we must still scourge the flesh in order to pay for our original sin, when Christ came to forgive and to command 'Thy own Humanity learn to adore'. But we, with unconscious irony, make vengeful father-gods out of our own intellects rather than fulfil the law of love which is too difficult, having within it nothing to rebel against.

A glance at the views which Blake stated first in *The Everlasting Gospel* should help to clarify these observations:

If Moral Virtue was Christianity
Christ's pretensions were all vanity . . .
For what is Antichrist but those
Who against Sinners Heaven close
With Iron bars, in Virtuous State . . .
The vision of Christ that thou dost see
Is my vision's greatest Enemy . . .
Was Jesus Chaste? or did he
Give any Lessons of Chastity? . . .
Thou Angel of the Presence Divine
That didst create this Body of Mine,
Wherefore hast thou writ these laws
And created Hell's dark jaws?

To continue examining Night the Seventh: we find Enitharmon being persuaded by the sly Spectre that to become the
mother-goddess in Urizen's religion is the best way to bring
back Albion-Orc's health. This is a flashback, as it were, to
show how Enitharmon was deluded into accepting the role of
goddess that we have seen her playing to such devastating
effect. The Spectre is persuading Enitharmon to become the
mother goddess, and this is a delusion. He does, however, paint
a true picture and a nostalgic one of the days before Albion's
faculties fell into confusion.

The Spectre said: 'Thou lovely Vision, this delightful Tree
Is given us for a Shelter from the tempests of Void & Solid,
Till once again the morn of ages shall renew upon us,
To reunite in those mild fields of happy Eternity
Where thou & I in undivided essence walk'd about
Imbodied, thou my garden of delight & I the spirit in the garden;
Mutual there we dwelt in one another's joy, revolving
Days of Eternity, with Tharmas mild & Luvah sweet melodious
Upon our waters. This thou well rememberest; listen, I will tell
What thou forgettest. They in us & we in them alternate Liv'd,
Drinking the joys of Universal Manhood. One dread morn . . .

The manhood was divided, for the gentle passions, making way
Thro' the infinite labyrinths of the heart & thro' the nostrils
    issuing
In odorous stupefaction, stood before the Eyes of Man
A female bright . . . I sunk along
The goary tide even to the place of seed, & there dividing

I was divided in darkness & oblivion; thou an infant woe,
And I an infant terror in the womb of Enion.
My masculine spirit scorning the frail body, issued forth
From Enion's brain . . .'

Notice particularly in the last lines of this passage, how the too looming passions combined with the spectrous intellect, keep Albion from getting himself born psychologically. The Spectre prevents the inner marriage of the 'maternal' passions and the 'masculine' intellect that would make Albion an integrated functioning entity, by carrying his sense of guilt and dividedness 'even to the place of seed'. Any attempts to reconstruct and so accept his own conception and birth must be abortive because his so-called 'masculine' intellect cannot bear to incarnate or be born through the earthy flesh of the mother, while the 'feminine' emotions try to scorn the intellect altogether and be pure earthly 'motherness'. That is to say, Albion cannot accept being both male and female, both intellect and emotions, both father and mother. Yet his trying to be all masculine intellect does not make him more male, but, paradoxically, less: 'In terror of losing the male in the female it had in fact lost both.'[1] This 'difficulty in allowing the internal male and female to interact'[2] is Albion's whole trouble, and why there is breakdown in his relation with himself, his wife, and his universe. He does not realize that, in the words of Lao-Tze: 'He who, being a man, remains a woman, will become a universal channel.'[3]

The Spectre knows his own horrible nature, and, in one sense, truly wants Albion to be whole again, but he goes about it the wrong way. He thinks that he can unite with Enitharmon who is now almost one with Vala, the nature goddess. He is right in seeking union, but it is of the wrong things. It is of the false delusive appearance of Albion and Jerusalem, rather than of two real lovers.

> . . . but listen thou my vision.
> I view futurity in thee. I will bring down soft Vala
> To the embraces of this terror, & I will destroy
> That body I created; then shall we unite again in bliss;

[1] *A Life of One's Own*, Joanna Field, Pelican Books, 1952, p. 215.
[2] *Ibid.*, p. 217.
[3] *Ibid.*, p. 213.

For til these terrors planted round the Gates of Eternal life
Are driven away & annihilated, we never can repass the Gates.
Thou knowest that the Spectre is in every Man, insane, brutish,
Deform'd, that I am thus a ravening devouring lust continually
Craving & devouring.

Enitharmon in false hope does embrace the Spectre of Los, but as
they are both only delusive shadows, her resulting pregnancy
brings to birth only a 'wonder horrible', a shadowy rebirth of
Orc. And in sympathy,

Many of the Dead burst forth from the bottoms of their tombs
In male forms without female counterparts or Emanations.

Los, pitying, is reconciled with his own Spectre who has thus
tried in lust alone to unite with Enitharmon:

Los embrac'd the Spectre, first as a brother,
Then as another Self, astonish'd, humanizing & in tears,
In Self abasement Giving up his Domineering lust.

The Spectre, unassimilated, is the ghostly messenger of Urizen,
the brutish, guilt-ridden puritan conscience who condemns lust
and yet is lustful in direct proportion to his condemnations. But
when Los unites with his own Spectre, then it becomes the
delicately tuned conscience that responds to good and evil as
truly as a weathervane. The Spectre knows this and speaks to
Los:

Thou canst never embrace sweet Enitharmon, terrible Demon,
Till
Thou art united with thy Spectre . . . & by Self annihilation back
returning
To Life Eternal; be assur'd I am thy real self,
Tho' thus divided from thee & the slave of Every passion
Of thy fierce Soul . . .
If we unite in one, another better world will be
Open'd within your heart & loins & wondrous brain,
Threefold, as it was in Eternity, & this, the fourth Universe,
Will be renew'd by the three & consummated in Mental fires;
But if thou dost refuse, Another body will be prepar'd
For me, & thou, annihilate, evaporate & be no more.
For thou art but a form & organ of life, & of thyself
Art nothing, being Created Continually by Mercy & Love divine.

Los is convinced that he can be reunited with his wife, if only he can be really one with his Spectre, although he knows that he is still 'furious, controllable by Reason's power'. Enitharmon has been lost to him ever since she became the mother goddess in Urizen's mystery religion, worshipped by their son, Orc. Hopefully Los answers the Spectre:

> '. . . Spectre horrible, thy words astound my Ear
> With irresistible conviction . . . Even I already feel a World
> within
> Opening its gates, & in it all the real substances
> Of which these in the outward World are shadows which pass
> away.
> Come then into my Bosom, & in thy shadowy arms bring with
> thee
> My lovely Enitharmon. I will quell my fury & teach
> Peace to the soul of dark revenge, & repentance to Cruelty.'
>
> So spoke Los & Embracing Enitharmon & the Spectre,
> Clouds would have folded round in Extacy & Love uniting,
> But Enitharmon trembling, fled & hid beneath Urizen's tree . . .[1]

And so fades the momentary hope that on the level of imagination, at least, Albion and Jerusalem could reunite in love and understanding when Los and Enitharmon embraced. Just as this is about to take place, Enitharmon panics. She is not ready to take back her husband in terms of comparatively unglamorous marriage, with all of its concrete demands. Within the sick Albion she has been in the position of mother goddess in Urizen's mystery religion, and she cannot all in a moment get free of its illusions and taboos. Nor is she altogether sure she wants to give up the status and the mysterious power that she has possessed in her role of the unattainable mother. It is almost a magical power that she has wielded, and it seems very tame to become an ordinary wife again. She prefers living in an atmosphere of danger and abstraction and witch-like powers.

And so she flees back to the tree of Mystery, and, to gain time, she claims that she is afraid of death as punishment for her sin, and that Los must fetch her some assurance that this is not so. 'Give me proof of life Eternal or I die,' she cries. Los would

[1] Here there is a graceful female figure, kneeling, holding her breasts.

have succumbed to this temptation to seek forbidden knowledge,
had the Spectre not intervened: she is only confusing the issue.

> Then Los plucked the fruit & Eat & sat down in Despair,
> And must have given himself to death Eternal. But
> Urthona's spectre in part mingling with him, comforted him,
> Being a medium between him & Enitharmon. But this Union
> Was not to be Effected without Cares & Sorrows & Troubles
> Of Six thousand Years of self denial & of bitter Contrition.

Although Blake is vehement about denouncing anything that
looks like a deliberate asceticism and scourging of the sinful
flesh, he does recognize that when mistakes have been made in
a relationship there is usually a long and difficult period of
sorrow and self-denial before things can be made right again.
This phase of experience is what Los and Enitharmon must now
face before their union is possible.

Despite Enitharmon's retreat back to the mystery religion,
Los and his Spectre are reunited at any rate. And Los: 'wondering beheld the Centre open'd; by Divine Mercy inspir'd . . .
was open'd new heavens & a new earth beneath & within,
Threefold, within the brain, within the heart, within the loins
. . . but yet having a limit.'

The Spectre recognizes that it was he who began the division
within Albion, and he repents bitterly, saying:

> I am the cause
> That this dire state commences. I began the dreadful state
> Of Separation, & on my dark head the curse & punishment
> Must fall unless a way be found to Ransom & Redeem.

The Spectre who, following Urizen, did everything to make
Albion scorn the body and the flesh, sees now that 'without a
created body the Spectre is Eternal Death.'

Los, in his new state of wholeness, comforts Enitharmon who
is still fearful. He tells her that Christ will come in the guise of
Luvah to redeem the passions:

> Turn inwardly thine Eyes & there behold the Lamb of God
> Cloth'd in Luvah's robes of blood descending to redeem . . .
> O Enitharmon!

107

Couldst thou but cease from terror & trembling & affright
When I appear before thee in forgiveness of ancient injuries,
Why shouldst thou remember & be afraid? I surely have died in
    pain
Often enough to convince thy jealousy & fear & terror.
Come hither; be patient; let us converse together, because
I also tremble at myself & at all my former life.

But Enitharmon is unable to free herself from the fear of revenge.
She is afraid that Christ will come to punish her like the father
god, Urizen. She is full of abstract fears that prevent concrete
reunion.

Enitharmon answer'd: 'I behold the Lamb of God descending
To meet these Spectres of the Dead. I therefore fear that he
Will give us to Eternal Death, fit punishment for such
Hideous offenders: uttermost extinction in eternal pain:
An ever dying life of stifling & obstruction: shut out
Of existence to be a sign & terror to all who behold,
Lest any in futurity do as we have done in heaven.
Such is our state; nor will the Son of God redeem us, but destroy.'
So Enitharmon spoke trembling & in torrents of tears.

Enitharmon, refusing to be comforted, none the less has a
feminine afterthought. She thinks she just might manage to free
herself from Urizen's religion if Los cares enough for her to
labour in creating 'bodies' or images for the poor disembodied
spectres of the dead 'to assimilate themselves into'. And with
Los's ready compliance we are given a rather charming domestic
scene that must have been a familiar one in Blake's own home.
For we know that Blake with infinite patience not only taught
his wife to colour his drawings, but also to see visions. And
here we find Los, who is imagination, busily drawing while
Enitharmon colours what he produces:

And first he drew a line upon the walls of shining heaven,
And Enitharmon tinctur'd it with beams of blushing love.
It remain'd permanent, a lovely form, inspir'd, divinely human
Dividing into just proportions. Los unwearied labour'd
The immortal lines upon the heavens.

Just as before, when Albion was at his sickest, imagination as
irresponsible fantasy created destructive monstrous images, so

now that there is hope of his recovery, imagination labours with good will to create images that correspond to actual fact. These attempts to create healing images are wholly successful. 'Orc was comforted in the deeps; his soul reviv'd.' The father god fades from Orc's mind as he recognizes his real father in Los. Urizen becomes Rintrah, the mild reason which, applied to particular situations, is a valid guide, working in harmony with the evidence produced by the other faculties rather than issuing general laws that have little bearing on fact. And though Orc is still bound, there are healing factors at work, for:

> Los loved . . .
> And Enitharmon's smiles & tears prevail'd over self protection.
> They rather chose to meet Eternal Death than to destroy
> The offspring of their Care & Pity.

The first part of Night the Seventh ends on this hopeful note:

> Startled was Los; he found his enemy Urizen now
> In his hands; he wonder'd that he felt love & not hate.
> His whole soul lov'd him; he beheld him an infant
> Lovely, breath'd from Enitharmon; he trembled within himself.

There is a second part to Night the Seventh, and it shows in more detail the last throes of Urizen's tyranny over Albion. In an effort to maintain his hold on the Universal Man, Urizen, as we have seen:

> Builded a temple in the image of the human heart . . .
>   hid in chambers dark the nightly harlot
> Plays in Disguise in whispered hymn & mumbling prayer: The
>   Priests
> He ordain'd & Priestesses, cloth'd in disguises bestial . . .
> The day for war, the night for secret religion in his temple.

We saw earlier on that while one side of Orc's subjugation to Urizen manifested itself in an ascetic religion, the other side erupted in rage and war. Now it becomes apparent that Urizen deliberately built his temple in the human heart for the exercising of these two activities. In the daytime war rages, and it is war against the bestial harlot, Vala. In the night the same Vala is worshipped as the mother goddess, Nature. But Urizen's scheme for maintaining this perpetual doubleness is defeated by itself. For as Orc wars against Vala in an effort to destroy her, in actual fact he mingles with her and is himself destroyed.

This means that, although Albion is still very weak, the way is clear for Christ to return to his soul and heal him, for Orc has been purged from it. The necessary destructive and forbidden union with the mother has taken place as in a pagan ritual and Orc disappears, even though the consummation took place in fear and rage and jealousy where it could have been effected in understanding love had Jerusalem herself been integrated enough to comprehend what was necessary.

Vala does not immediately realize what has happened. She does not understand that Orc is no more, and the warfare ended. 'All day she riots in Excess,' Blake tells us, and he comments sadly, 'the Battle rages still round thy tender limbs, O Vala.' And Vala plays to the full her role of rampaging mother goddess.

When he wished to use it, Blake could command a novelist's power of characterization. It is a gift that is largely wasted on mythological figures, but occasionally it manifests itself, as, for instance, in the meeting between Tharmas and Vala. The forces of regeneration are at work within Albion, bringing about the necessary destruction of Orc, as well as the reunion of Los and Enitharmon.

Now another important step towards Albion's recovery is taken when Vala, who is the terrible shadowy female that the sick Albion sees instead of his wife, suddenly makes friends with Tharmas, who is the blind and lost fact of Albion's instinctual love for Jerusalem. The disappearance of the impotent Orc allows this meeting to take place. Instead of rampaging in hurt and angry pride and a mood of 'If that's what he wants, I'll show him', Vala within Jerusalem, that is, the passions, drops into good-humoured helpfulness when she realizes that in actual fact Albion's instinct is seeking, with innocent and myopic and despairing persistence, the wife he has lost and wants again.

The encounter with Tharmas takes place just when Vala, engaged in the warfare of Urizen's temple, is noisily rushing about, going all out to play her part, and rather enjoying and wallowing in her own outrageous power:

> The Shadowy Female Varied in the War in her delight,
> Howling in discontent, black & heavy, uttering brute sounds,
> Wading thro' fires among the slimy weeds, making Lamentations
> To deceive . . .

She is nonplussed when Tharmas, old and naïve with watery short-sighted eyes, blunders on to the scene and mistakes her for his mild wife, Enion. 'Art thou bright Enion? is the shadow of hope return'd?' he wistfully asks this melodramatic harlot. And she, taken aback and interested, makes an abrupt descent into good-natured and honest helpfulness. She becomes the novelist's harlot with the heart of gold. Dimly Jerusalem comprehends that whatever Albion has turned her into on the level of his sick imagination, in actual fact on the instinctual level he is longing for the return of his true wife, as Tharmas longs for Enion's return.

Vala is touched that Tharmas should mistake her for Enion, and she replies helpfully:

> Tharmas, I am Vala, bless thy innocent face!
> Doth Enion avoid the sight of thy blue wat'ry eyes?
> Be not perswaded that the air knows this, or the falling dew.

Tharmas immediately settles down trustfully and tells Vala all of his troubles from the very beginning, and she listens patiently:

> Tharmas repli'd: 'O Vala, once I liv'd in a garden of delight;
> I waken'd Enion in the morning & she turn'd away
> Among the apple trees, & all the garden of delight
> Swam like a dream before my eyes. I went to seek the steps
> Of Enion in the gardens, & the shadows compass'd me
> And clos'd me in a watery world of woe when Enion stood
> Trembling before me like a shadow, like a mist, like air.
> And she is gone, & here alone I war with darkness & death . . .
> And life appear & vanish, mocking me with shadows of false
>   hope.'

This is a moving description of the unreality which overtook Tharmas from the moment that he doubted the goodness and validity of sensory experience. When Enion fled from him, there was set into motion all the shadowy machinery of breakdown within Albion.

This getting together of Tharmas and Vala is a great step towards Albion's healing. Jerusalem sees that she must stop being Vala alone, and must become fourfold, allowing Tharmas to find Enion within her before all the other faculties can be reunited. In a kind of apology she tells Tharmas why she became altogether Vala. She was trying to force her lover (Luvah) to return to her, frightened that he was hidden by the ascetic, Orc, who calls her sinful:

> Lo, him whom I love
> Is hidden from me, & I never in all Eternity
> Shall see him. Enitharmon . . .
> Hid him in that outrageous form of Orc, which torments me for
> Sin.

What Jerusalem should have done, and knows she should have done, was to remain fourfold and Christ-centred even if Albion was no longer her lover, rather than becoming all Vala in order to provoke his waning passion. The reason that she did not remain strongly and firmly herself was because she had not consciously effected her own inner marriage of passion and intellect, mother and father. Although she has not so many difficulties as has Albion before this union can be achieved, she is none the less unsure of herself and what she feels about sex and her husband, and this causes her reactions to be uncertain and confusing just when she should be very sure of what she is and feels in order to help Albion. As it is, she is sometimes Thel and sometimes Vala which only makes Albion more confused.

Her inability to achieve the interior marriage is a kind of immature vacillation rather than a real chaining such as has bound Orc within Albion. She must reach the point where she knows consciously, all the time, that she is Jerusalem, Albion's wife, rather than Vala, the mother goddess and femme fatale, although this is a very attractive part of her personality which she must not, on the other hand, fear and hide altogether. 'And I heard the Name of their Emanations, they are named Jerusalem' is the quiet ending of the final prophetic book, *The Song of Jerusalem*. And these words are accompanied by the lovely engraving of Jerusalem being gathered to the bosom of God the Father. It is only when this happens that Albion is really healed, but this is to anticipate. Already in *The Four Zoas* we see the beginnings of Albion's recovery, and Orc does not appear again which means that the central core of the diseased personality which governed Albion like a demon is destroyed. The healing process continues throughout *Milton* and *Jerusalem*, although at times Albion is still pictured as very weak indeed.

Night the Eighth of *The Four Zoas* tells of the awakening of Albion from the sleep of death as his faculties feebly begin to work in harmony once more:

> Then All in Great Eternity Met in the Council of God
> As one Man, even Jesus . . . to create the Fallen Man.
> The Fallen Man stretch'd like a corse upon the oozy Rock,
> Wash'd with the tides, pale, overgrown with weeds
> That mov'd with horrible dreams.

All Beulah watches over him with Christ. And the realm of Beulah which is the realm of art and marital harmony appears like two guardian angels:

>   hovering high over his head
> Two winged immortal shapes, one standing at his feet
> Toward the East, one standing at his head toward the west,
> Their wings join'd in the Zenith over head; but other wings
> They had which cloth'd their bodies like a garment of soft down,
> Silvery white, shining upon the dark blue sky in silver.
> Their wings touch'd the heavens; their fair feet hover'd above
> The swelling tides; they bent over the dead corse like an arch,
> Pointed at top in highest heavens, of precious stones & pearl.
> Such is a Vision of All Beulah hov'ring over the Sleeper.

Albion wakens from the sleep of death, sneezing seven times. 'He repos'd in the Saviour's arms, in the arms of tender mercy & loving kindness.'

Imagination, that is, Los and Enitharmon, after their long distortion, see with wonder the astonishing simplicity and rightness of divine mercy:

> Then Los said: 'I behold the Divine Vision thro' the broken Gates
> Of thy poor broken heart, astonish'd, melted into Compassion &
>   Love.'

113

And Enitharmon said: 'I see the Lamb of God upon Mount Zion.'
Wondering with love & Awe they felt the divine hand upon them.

Through Enitharmon's broken and compassionate heart, no longer filled with pride at being the mother goddess in the mystery religion, the guardian angels are able to enter Urizen's temple in the human heart. And Los once more is allowed to see the secret heart of his wife.

> Los could enter into Enitharmon's bosom & explore
> Its intricate Labyrinths now the Obdurate heart was broken . . .
> The Divine Hand was upon him
> And upon Enitharmon, & the Divine Countenance shone . . .
> Looking down, the Daughters of Beulah saw
> With joy the bright Light, & in it a Human form,
> And knew he was the Saviour, Even Jesus; & they worshipped.

> Astonish'd, comforted, Delighted, in notes of Rapturous Extacy
> All Beulah stood astonish'd, looking down to Eternal Death.
> They saw the Saviour beyond the Pit of death & destruction;
> For whether they look'd upward they saw the Divine Vision,
> Or whether they look'd downward they still saw the Divine
> Vision
> Surrounding them on all sides beyond sin & death & hell.

Next comes a very significant passage. We remember that when Orc was first born in Albion's soul, Urizen was terribly afraid that it was really Christ being born. Now that Albion is getting well, Christ does appear quite openly as Luvah, love, in the place formerly occupied by Orc. Urizen is totally confused:

> When Urizen saw the Lamb of God cloth'd in Luvah's robes
> Perplex'd & terrifi'd he stood, tho' well he knew that Orc
> Was Luvah. But now he beheld a new Luvah, or Orc
> Who assum'd Luvah's form & stood before him opposite.

Blake gives the reader an aside piece of advice while Urizen stands perplexed, trying to take in what has happened:

> learn distinct to know . . .
> The difference between States & Individuals of those states.
> That state call'd Satan never can be redeem'd in all Eternity;
> But when Luvah in Orc became a serpent, he descended into
> That state call'd Satan.

114

That is, although the satanic state that Albion was in emotionally when he was Orc instead of Christ-centred, is unredeemable, the individual can be redeemed when he emerges from the state of mind he had descended into. And Christ as Luvah descends into this hellish state of mind to redeem the individual. Urizen cannot take all of this in. In his mind's eye he still sees Orc within Albion,

> Orc a serpent form augmenting time on times
> In the fierce battle . . . Stretching to serpent length
> His human bulk, while the dark shadowy female, brooding over,
> Measur'd his food morning & evening in cups & baskets of
>   iron . . .
> Gath'ring the food of that mysterious tree, circling its root
> She spread herself thro' all the branches in the power of Orc.

This should have warned Urizen of what was about to follow. For even in his mind's eye the serpent has become bisexual, and Vala, the brooding mother-goddess inhabits the serpent form of Orc as well as the impotent ascetic himself. But 'Urizen in self deceit his warlike preparations fabricated'; that is, even when Albion is getting back his power of love, Urizen still causes the passion between men and women to seem sinful. Only one thing can result, a perverting of the newly released love in Albion away from its proper object which is his wife:

> Terrified & astonish'd Urizen beheld the battle take a form
> *Which he intended not*: a Shadowy hermaphrodite, black & opake.
> The soldiers nam'd it Satan, but he was yet unform'd & vast.
> Hermaphroditic it at length became, hiding the Male
> Within as in a Tabernacle, Abominable, Deadly.

Long before the subject could be openly discussed, Blake pursues ruthlessly to its inevitable homosexual conclusions the tyranny of Urizen's rule, within the individual soul as within religion based on a hatred of natural sexual love between male and female.

Blake, with an enormously modern insight, realizes that the two tendencies, a compulsive asceticism and homosexuality, can easily follow one another in the strange logic of breakdown, and that both are a result of Urizen's terrible perfectionism, even though Urizen does not foresee or want the perversion of the natural love he terms sinful. Such a perversion takes place, not at the very worst period of Albion's illness which is completely dominated by the impotent monk, Orc, but, paradoxically, just when there is every chance for Albion's recovery because Orc has disappeared and the passions are released from bondage. The stage was set for the reunion of Albion and his bride, Jerusalem. But Urizen, with blind muddle-headedness, is bent on continuing the warfare between intellect and the passions, and so he creates the new fear within Albion, whose passions, directed towards reunion with his wife, now swerve aside into homosexual channels just when this reunion should have taken place.

> The war roar'd round Jerusalem's Gates; it took a hideous form
> Seen in the aggregate, a Vast Hermaphroditic form
> Heav'd like an Earthquake lab'ring with convulsive groans
> Intolerable; at length an awful wonder burst
> From the Hermaphroditic bosom. Satan he was nam'd,
> Son of Perdition, terrible his form, dishumanis'd, monstrous,
> A male without a female counterpart, a howling fiend
> Forlorn of Eden & repugnant to the forms of life,
> Yet hiding the shadowy female Vala as in an ark & Curtains,
> Abhorr'd, accursed, ever dying an Eternal death,
> Being multitudes of tyrant Men in union blasphemous
> Against the Divine Image, Congregated assemblies of wicked
> men.

Urizen goes altogether mad, wholeheartedly furthering this perversion which will end all life, rather than risk his own downfall in the return of love and Christ: he tries to

> pervert all the faculties of sense
> Into their own destruction, if perhaps he might avert
> His own despair even at the cost of everything that breathes.

Vala tries to stop this mad Urizen who has gone completely off the rails in a final attempt to destroy rather than be destroyed. In the phrasing of her plea there is a rich depth of suggestion reminiscent of the many earth-goddesses of myth and legend who have gone seeking the lost lover, who is also the dying god:

Where hast thou hid him whom I love; in what remote Abyss
Resides that God of my delight? O might my eyes behold
My Luvah, then could I deliver all the sons of God
From Bondage of these terrors . . .
The Eternal Man is seal'd by thee, never to be deliver'd.
We are all servants to thy will. O King of light, relent
Thy furious power; to be our father & our loved King.
But if my Luvah is no more, If thou hast smitten him
And laid him in the Sepulcher . . . Silent I bow with dread.
But happiness can never (come) to thee.

Urizen realizes that he has been caught in the web of falsehood
that he himself has spun when Vala, the mother goddess in his
own religion, turns against him:

Sitting within his temple, furious, felt the numbing stupor,
Himself tangled in his own net, in sorrow, lust, repentance.

Meanwhile, imagination has been busy creating anew Jerusalem who has been hidden in the guise of Vala:

And Enitharmon nam'd the Female, Jerusalem the holy.
Wond'ring she saw the Lamb of God within Jerusalem's Veil;
The Divine Vision seen within the inmost deep recess
Of fair Jerusalem's bosom in a gently beaming fire.

Once Jerusalem is again herself, Christ can be born through her
and through her resurrect the fallen Albion. Once more she
partakes of the nature of Mary who has control of the Eve-Vala
within her:

Pitying, the Lamb of God descended thro' Jerusalem's Gates
To put off Mystery time after time; & as a Man
Is born on Earth, so he was born of Fair Jerusalem
In mystery's woven mantle, & in the Robes of Luvah.
He stood in fair Jerusalem to awake up into Eden
The fallen Man.

But Urizen will not yet admit defeat. He brings about the
crucifixion of Christ within Albion.

Urizen call'd together the Synagogue of Satan . . .
To judge the Lamb of God to Death as a murderer & robber.

And by means of 'devilish arts, abominable, unlawful, unutterable', Urizen forces Vala to appear in his religion again as the harlot writ large, Babylon, the Church of Mystery:

> A False Feminine Counterpart, of Lovely Delusive Beauty
> Dividing & Uniting at will in the cruelties of Holiness,
> Vala, drawn down into a Vegetated body, now triumphant.
> The Synagogue of Satan Clothed her with Scarlet robes & Gems,
> And on her forehead was her name written in blood,
>   'Mystery'.

And so the crucifixion of Christ is accomplished:

> Thus was the Lamb of God condemn'd to Death.
> They nail'd him upon the tree of Mystery, weeping over him
> And then mocking & then worshipping, calling him Lord & King.
> Sometimes as twelve daughters lovely, sometimes as five
> They stood in beaming beauty, & sometimes as one, even Rahab
> Who is Mystery, Babylon the Great, the Mother of Harlots.

The rest of Night the Eighth is a confused panorama of the historical growth of Urizen's power after the crucifixion, and of the bondage of Jerusalem. We are given a lurid picture of the awful pride of the mother goddess who must be redeemed 'time after time by the Divine Lamb' re-entering Jerusalem.

With dire foreboding, Ahania, Urizen's true wife whom he has long since cast into the abyss, sees her husband's increasing preoccupation with Babylon. She cries out in Cassandra-like despair, for she had predicted this catastrophic state of affairs from the beginning, but Urizen had not listened. Enion, the wife of Tharmas, is more hopeful, and looks towards the Second Coming.

> And Los & Enitharmon took the Body of the Lamb
> Down from the Cross & plac'd it in a sepulcher . . . trembling &
>   in despair
> Jerusalem wept over the Sepulcher two thousand years.

> Rahab triumphs over all; she took Jerusalem
> Captive, a Willian Captive; by delusive arts impell'd
> To worship Urizen's Dragon form . . .

118

The Ashes of Mystery began to animate; they call'd it Deism
And Natural Religion; as of old, so now anew began
Babylon again in Infancy, call'd Natural Religion.[1]

The final section of *The Four Zoas*, Night the Ninth, is called
'The Last Judgement'.[2] It contains much chaotic and confusing
description which Blake undoubtedly felt was necessary to convey the atmosphere proper to this occasion. Since it is of little
relevance to the progression of the story, I will skip over most of
it. There are, however, fine bits of isolated description such as
the following lines which tell of two spectres,

> their bodies lost, they stood
> Trembling & weak, a faint embrace, a fierce desire, as when
> Two shadows mingle on a wall.

And all the while the trumpet is sounding for the Last Judgement, and 'the tree of Mystery went up in folding flames' and
'All Tyranny was cut off from the face of the Earth.' To all
eyes Albion still lies stretched out in death:

> Beyond this Universal Confusion . . . there stands
> A Horrible rock far in the South . . .
> On this rock lay the faded head of the Eternal Man
> Enwrapped round with weeds of death, pale cold in sorrow & woe.
> He lifts the blue lamps of his Eyes & cries with heavenly voice:
> Bowing his head over the consuming Universe, he cried:
> 'O weakness & O weariness! O war within my members! . . .
> My birds are silent on my hills, flocks die beneath my branches.'

As we have seen, although Albion still seems very ill,
regeneration has actually been taking place within him on
several levels. But because Albion has not consciously and in so
many words repudiated Urizen's tyranny within him, he is still
more in the power of death than of life. There is in Albion a
creative power and energy in direct proportion to the power of
his inhibiting fear and fantasy which, if it can be released, will
make his life a tremendous thing. But until he can consciously

[1] Then is a drawing all by itself, a sketch, full of life, of a marital fight.
He with pity holds her lightly as she tears her hair in rage.
[2] A rather lovely sketch shows Christ pushing aside the walls of the
tomb.

put Urizen, the father god, into his proper place, his energy cannot be released to the life of Christ, the Son. Albion feels and half sees the way out of his sickness. He must affirm his own life positively, consciously excluding the forces of life-hatred. Until he can do this he will remain listless and indolent, all of his creative powers unused, even though he is no longer torn by interior warfare.

> When shall the Man of future times become as in the days of old?
> O weary life! Why sit I here & give up all my powers
> To indolence, to the night of death, when indolence & mourning
> Sit hovering over my dark threshold? tho' I arise, look out
> And scorn the war within my members, yet my heart is weak
> And my head faint. Yet will I look again into the morning.

The simple and touching willingness of Albion to 'look again into the morning' gives him just that minimum of strength needed to take a positive stand. He summons Urizen in order to reduce him to his proper status:

> The Eternal Man sat on the Rocks & cried with awful voice:
> 'O Prince of Light, where art thou? I behold thee not as once
> In those Eternal fields, in clouds of morning stepping forth
> With harps & songs when bright Ahania sang before thy face . . .
> See you not all this wracking furious confusion?
> Come forth from slumbers of thy cold abstraction! Come forth,
> Arise to Eternal births! Shake off thy cold repose,
> Schoolmaster of souls, great opposer of change, arise!
> That the Eternal worlds may see thy face in peace & joy.'

Urizen refuses to answer or appear. Albion gets very angry and threatens to throw him out of the fourfold harmony altogether unless he repents and returns to his original place of equality with the other faculties. This is, of course, a threat that Albion uses only for effect:

> O how couldst thou deform those beautiful proportions
> Of life & person; for as the Person, so is his life proportion'd . . .
> But if thou darest obstinate refuse my stern behest,
> Thy crown & scepter I will seize . . . cast thee out into the
>   indefinite
> Where nothing lives . . . I will steel my heart
> Against thee to Eternity . . . thy religion,

The first author of this war & the distracting of honest minds
Into confused perturbation & strife & horror & pride,
Is a deceit so detestable that I will cast thee out
If thou repentest not, & leave thee as a rotten branch to be
    burn'd
With Mystery the Harlot & with Satan for Ever & Ever.

The mock threat works. Urizen weeps, 'anxious his scaly form to reassume the human'. He repents of his tyrannical ways and gives up his power, admitting that he has had no joy of it.[1] Immediately he is reborn,

> he shook the snows from off his shoulders & arose
> As on a Pyramid of mist . . . glorious, bright, Exulting in his joy
> He sounding rose into the heavens in naked majesty,
> In radiant Youth.

Ahania, his wife, rushes to meet him, but drops dead in excess of pure joy. Albion warns Urizen that it is not good to have the accomplishment of a truth follow immediately upon its perception, and that a period of labour and purgation is necessary first, else the burden of truth is too great to be borne. Such a period must elapse before Urizen can be reunited with Ahania or Albion with Jerusalem.

And the Eternal Man said: 'Hear my words, O Prince of Light.
Behold Jerusalem in whose bosom the Lamb of God
Is seen: tho' slain before her Gates, he self-renew'd remains
Eternal, & I thro' him awake from death's dark vale.
The times revolve; the time is coming when all these delights
Shall be renew'd, & all these Elements that now consume
Shall reflourish. Then bright Ahania shall awake from death,
A glorious Vision to thine Eyes, a self-renewing Vision:
The spring, the summer, to be thine . . .
The winter thou shalt plow & lay thine stores into thy barns
Expecting to receive Ahania in the spring with joy.'

It is interesting that in *The Four Zoas* Blake uses the future tense about the reunion of Albion and Jerusalem. It has not yet taken place, but he is certain that it will happen.

[1] Albion is pictured on his couch, angels swooping down.

> Because the Lamb of God creates himself a bride & wife
> That we his children evermore may live in Jerusalem
> Which now descendeth out of heaven, a City, yet a Woman,
> Mother of myriads redeem'd & born in her spiritual palaces,
> By a New Spiritual birth Regenerated from Death.

Jerusalem is both the bride of God and, partaking of Mary, the mother of Christ, both a city and Albion's wife.

Once Albion has reduced Urizen to his station in the fourfold harmony, then wonderful things begin to happen. Albion sees clearly the possibility of being whole and well again, but both he and Urizen know that they cannot be reunited with their emanations until the period of labour is past:

> And the Fall'n Man Who was arisen upon the Rock of Ages
> Beheld the Vision of God, & he arose up from the Rock,
> And Urizen arose up with him, walking thro' the flames
> To meet the Lord coming to Judgment; but the flames repell'd
>   them
> Still to the Rock; in vain they strove to Enter the Consummation
> Together, for the Redeem'd Man could not enter the Consumma-
>   tion.

Albion and Urizen work with a good will, and when they rest, 'in joy they view the human harvest springing up'. Ahania arises from the dead in the spring as was promised and joyfully takes her place beside Urizen. Albion, participating in this, is tempted once more to feel that intellectual union with the beloved is all that matters, but he is not allowed to lapse into a belittling of the body: he is driven back to the state of marital union.

> The Eternal Man sat down . . .
> Sorrowful that he could not put off his new risen body
> In Mental flames: the flames refus'd, they drove him back to
>   Beulah.
> His body was redeem'd to be permanent thro' Mercy Divine.

But Orc, within Albion, is allowed to enter the flames and consume away:

> And now fierce Orc had quite consum'd himself in Mental flames,
> Expending all his energy against the fuel of fire.

Next, Albion summons Luvah and Vala, the passions, and
sends them to their rightful place in the fourfold harmony:

> Luvah & Vala, henceforth you are Servants; obey & live.
> You shall forget your former state; return, & Love in peace,
> Into your place, the place of seed, not in the brain or heart . . .
> Servants to the infinite & Eternal of the Human form.

That is, the passions are at one and the same time the most and
the least important part of the marriage. They are the attractive
power and are concerned with making eternal the human form
in children, but they are not to be elevated into the brain as an
idealistic romantic love, nor are they to be confused within the
heart with tenderness for the whole person.

And so Albion and Jerusalem are reunited not only on the
levels of imagination and of intellect, but also on the level of
passionate love. This is a most lyrical reunion. Now all that
remains is that Tharmas should find his lost Enion, that is, that
Albion should find Jerusalem again on the level of actual sensory
touch. Vala, the passions within Jerusalem, is the instrument of
this reunion, which is, of course, the function of her place within
the fourfold personality, to pave the way for physical union
instead of fleeing it. Luvah cries to her:

> 'Come forth, O Vala, from the grass & from the silent dew,
> Rise from the dews of death, for the Eternal Man is Risen'. . .
> She answer'd thus: 'Whose voice is this? . . .
> Where dost thou dwell? for it is thee I seek, & but for thee
> I must have slept Eternally, nor have felt the dew of thy morning.

Going back to her conversation with Tharmas, Vala works to
bring Tharmas and Enion together again in the same garden
where they lost each other:

> Why weep'st thou, Tharmas . . . in the bright house of joy?
> Doth Enion avoid the sight of thy blue heavenly Eyes?

She urges him to go to Enion, but Tharmas replies:

> O Vala, I am sick, & all this garden of Pleasure
> Swims like a dream before my eyes . . . I fade, even as a water lilly
> In the sun's heat, till in the night on the couch of Enion
> I drink new life & feel the breath of sleeping Enion.

> But in the morning she arises to avoid my Eyes,
> Then my loins fade & in the house I sit me down & weep.

On the level of sexual union there is still this pathetic barrier between Albion and Jerusalem, a psychological hangover of sexual shame from Urizen's religion of taboos, even though on every other level they are now reunited. Enion, too, is still mistrustful, but says:

> Soon renew'd, a Golden Moth,
> I shall cast off my death clothes & Embrace Tharmas again.
> For Lo, the winter melted away upon the distant hills,
> And all the black mould sings.

And soon this lovely renewal does indeed come to pass, and Tharmas, her husband, understands that this is so:

> Joy thrill'd thro' all the Furious forms of Tharmas harmonizing.
> Mild he Embrac'd her whom he sought; he rais'd her thro' the
>   heavens,
> Sounding his trumpet to awake the dead . . .
> The Eternal Man arose. He welcom'd them to the Feast.

There follows a magnificent feast to celebrate the reunion of Albion and his bride. All of the faculties and their emanations are the guests. They get wonderfully drunk and voice eternal truths somewhat pompously:

> 'Attempting to be more than Man We become less,' said Luvah
> As he arose from the bright feast, drunk with the wine of ages.

And as the Eternal Man finally walks forth from the fires of his marriage consummation, in wonder all the creatures of the earth ask him why it is that they have not perished in the fire of love, but are instead transformed:

> How is it we have walk'd thro' fires & yet are not consum'd?
> How is it that all things are chang'd, even as in ancient times?

The answer is possibly what Blake wrote on the margin of the MS. of this poem:

> Unorganiz'd Innocence: an Impossibility.
> Innocence dwells with Wisdom, but never with Ignorance.

The last plate is illustrated with a joyous figure dancing over the top of the world.

Part Three

MILTON

MILTON

OF the three prophetic books proper—*The Four Zoas, Milton,* and *Jerusalem*—*Milton* is the least successful. Although the poem does indeed contain lovely passages, mostly about Felpham, it is on the whole eccentric, shrill, and defiant of its audience. Its comparatively superficial tone and level of attack seem almost to disown the profound psychological insight arrived at so painfully in *The Four Zoas. Milton* is full of uneasily maintained, rather than inevitable, tensions. It contains to an annoying degree long lists of unexplained characters and place names, and mischievous nonsense names. Its wilful obscurity seems to me much more indicative of a disturbed state of mind in its author than does the painful but sincere struggle for clear vision of the first prophetic book. *The Four Zoas* is an ordering of hurtful experience directed towards reintegration. Its difficulty and obscurity arise from what Blake was trying to say, and to say for the first time without any of the short-cuts of terminology or of accepted knowledge that we have today. The vision itself, no matter how awkwardly expressed, is coherent and positive, and it strives towards healing and truth. There is something grand about the conception of *The Four Zoas. Milton,* in contrast, seems in many ways petty and idiosyncratic, a kind of bitter and agitated reaction or aftermath to the perception of a truth too far from present reality to endure. *Milton* is concerned largely with Blake's private quarrel with Hayley, which widens out to embrace his quarrel with all of the forces that hinder true art.

Blake had two sets of terms for his prophetic vision, and although they are supposed to merge, they more often give the effect of alternation. The first is the symbolism connected with places and with politico-historical events seen in cosmic distortion. This is the terminology of *America* and *The French Revolution*, and it carries over into *Milton*. *Milton* follows on logically to these two early prophecies, just as *The Four Zoas* and *Jerusalem* connect in sequence with *The Book of Thel*, *The Visions of the Daughters of Albion*, and, of course, *The Marriage of Heaven and Hell*.

The second, and more successful way in which Blake presents his vision is in terms of human relationships and spiritual states of being, the story, in short, of Albion and Jerusalem as everyman and everywoman, and as man and the church. This is, of course, what we saw in *The Four Zoas*. The implications of the names as place names are left to take care of themselves, and the reader does not fail to notice and draw the appropriate conclusions. Little or no attention is paid to elaborating the significance of England and the holy city becoming one. Blake's interest is concentrated wholly on the spiritual and psychological condition of the lovers in *The Four Zoas*. The geographical theme is almost non-existent except in the names themselves.

Milton is largely an attempt to merge the two sets of terms for the first time. Blake tones down the psychological drama until it takes second place to another story that plays up the historical, social, and geographical aspects of the Albion–Jerusalem alliance and gives rise to interminable lists of English counties and towns meticulously corresponding to various points of Albion's anatomy, and to the compass points where stand the Four Zoas, constituting Albion's soul-anatomy. It is as if Blake suddenly recalled that he had intended Albion to stand for England as well as for the Universal Man, and that Jerusalem was not only the eternal feminine but the holy city. It is not surprising that this sudden reversal of interest in *Milton* strikes a slightly hollow note.

The one or two passages that carry forward the theme of the married lovers seem almost out of context in *Milton* which presents us with an altogether new surface story, and one that is much less universal as it is based, not on any experience that Blake found in his marriage situation, but on the much more idiosyncratic role he found himself playing at Felpham as misunderstood poet. This tragi-comic, or rather, pathetic-comic situation he found himself in with Hayley, Blake tries unsuccessfully to elevate into a cosmic lining up of the forces of good and evil behind himself, who, as an improved reincarnation of Milton, represents true English poetry, and Hayley who, as Satan, represents all that is false and misguided in English verse. The love story of Albion and Jerusalem does not coincide with this new story at all, but is introduced from time to time all the same, largely, one suspects, to act as a springboard for the schoolboy game Blake plays of equating the points of Albion's trance-bound body with towns and cities of England. Blake goes so far as to make Hayley–Satan and Milton's God responsible not only for bad poetry, but for the pernicious class system in England, and for the industrial revolution and its concomitant ills. Blake himself, as the new Milton, appears querulously in the midst of all this wondrous confusion to complain that no one recognizes him as the poet-prophet who is to set right all of these ills.

Needless to say, this new story does not touch on any of the real problems that Blake's deep concern with Albion and Jerusalem always probes whenever he turns to their story, leaving his game of equation and spiteful identification. The two passages in *Milton* that do pertain to Albion and Jerusalem directly are very fine indeed and cannot be left out of consideration as they throw much light on the relationship between the lovers. But one is none the less almost tempted to abstract these passages and attach them to *The Four Zoas* or *Jerusalem* where they would be much more in context.

The thin connection between the story of Albion and Jerusalem and the story Blake tells in *Milton*, is simply that in *Milton* Blake gives a picture of an England sick and dying, a victim of the industrial revolution and class system, and upholding a satanic art and religion because it is under the tyranny of Milton's God who is Urizen.

Blake's whole procedure is negative. His purpose is to prove not only Hayley, but Milton himself wrong, and to present himself as the new bard of England who will put right the errors of belief that weaken Albion. Blake appears in this poem. First as Palamabron, and then as himself, with the spirits of Los and

Milton entering into him, he upholds imagination and true vision against the satanic forces. He guards in himself that which was good in Milton, and corrects that part of Milton's thinking that was false. It is quite certain that poor Hayley, the successful man of letters and patron of the arts, sat, all unwittingly, for Blake's portrait of Satan.

Such a personal, arbitrary and quixotic plan for a poem that claims to be a prophecy obscures the very vision that Blake purports to offer, and brings *Milton* down to something much closer to an attack on those who do not understand William Blake, no matter how this fact is obscured by cosmic machinery. In a sense, *Milton* is easier to understand than *The Four Zoas*, simply because it is less profound. Its surface difficulties once mastered, and its bitter tone detected, there is little else to trouble the understanding. I cannot agree with those critics who, finding *Milton* comparatively easy to decipher, conclude that it is a more valuable poem than *The Four Zoas*.

Milton is a tirade against many things, but none of these things strike the reader as being the real cause of the author's unease. It is as if Blake, frightened and disturbed by the lack of an audience, took time out to attack all of the things that stand in the way of true art. The precipitating event may well have been Hayley's reading and condemnation of the MS. of *The Four Zoas*. It is perhaps significant that *The Four Zoas* never got beyond the manuscript stage, although Blake engraved both of the later prophetic books. Hayley's lack of sympathy for the poem into which Blake had put his deepest psychological insight may well have brought home to Blake his loneliness as a poet, alarming him into writing the defiant and egocentric poem, *Milton*. The poem *Milton* is Blake's almost hysterical over-insistence that he possesses vision, coming between two poems that actually embody the vision he claims. None the less, there are lovely passages of poetry hidden within the vast incoherent bulk of the poem, lyrical outbursts that seem to break out of the airless room of Blake's preoccupied defiance. One must remember that Blake was determined to find renewed inspiration at Felpham, and *Milton* was written in the disillusionment following Blake's realization that Hayley's patronage was not going to end all of his troubles as he had dared to hope.

Blake was, of course, as familiar with Milton's writings as he was with the Bible. He admired Milton tremendously, although he never hesitated to point out what he considered Milton's grave errors. A very interesting study might be made of Milton's stylistic influence on Blake's prophetic books, and also of the similarity in the plans of the prophetic books to *Paradise Lost*. Even the themes are similar, for Blake starts in *The Four Zoas* with the fall of man, within himself, and *Jerusalem* tells of a paradise regained in the reunion of Albion and Jerusalem. These are aspects of the relation between Milton and Blake not covered by Denis Saurat. It is, however, too large a subject to attempt in the present study, as is the question of Blake's unique usage of biblical language and imagery.

At the beginning of *Milton* is the famous lyric known as 'Jerusalem'. This lyric stands as one of Blake's most successful fusions of Jerusalem and Albion as significant places, with the idea of Jerusalem and Albion as people. However, the lyric is generally taken simply as a plea to rebuild the holy city in England.

Little of *Milton* lives up to the promise of this lyric. The body of the poem is more concerned with crediting the 'dark Satanic mills' to Milton's God, than with bringing Jerusalem and Albion together in either sense. There is no glorious fourfold vision at the end of *Milton* as there is at the end of *The Four Zoas* and of *Jerusalem*, but only a wistful hint that such glory may be possible after many errors are abolished.

Blake, like Milton, writes his poem 'to Justify the Ways of God to Men'. Paralleling Milton's introduction, Blake has a prose preface to his poem, and in it he cries out against the influence of those classical writers who 'infected' both Milton and Shakespeare. Blake concludes that 'we do not want either Greek or Roman Models if we are but just and true to our own Imaginations, those Worlds of Eternity in which we shall live for ever in Jesus our Lord.' After this preface comes the lyric, 'Jerusalem'.

> And did those feet in ancient time
> Walk upon England's mountains green?
> And was the holy Lamb of God
> On England's pleasant pastures seen?

And did the Countenance Divine
Shine forth upon our clouded hills?
And was Jerusalem builded here
Among these dark Satanic mills?

Bring me my Bow of burning gold:
Bring me my Arrows of desire:
Bring me my Spear: O clouds unfold!
Bring me my Chariot of fire.

I will not cease from Mental Fight,
Nor shall my Sword sleep in my hand
Till we have built Jerusalem
In England's green and pleasant Land.

The question in the lyric refers, of course, to the Glastonbury legends, which Blake knew and which allege that Christ was brought to England as a young boy by his uncle, Joseph of Arimathea, who was a tin merchant. For some years before his ministry began, Christ is reputed to have been living quietly at Glastonbury in a wattle hut. Glastonbury was the centre of the Druid religion which Christ overcame.

The much-discussed 'dark Satanic mills' refer, I think, to anything that has to do with natural religion and the rational laws of Urizen rather than with Christ's rule of love. This would include both the religion of the Druids, which is said to have been both magical and highly intellectual, and the abuses of the industrial age beginning in Blake's own time, including mill slavery.

The image of the mill which Blake uses fairly frequently has always to do with the naturalistic 'laws' which seem to be imposed by reason, whether these laws occur in religion, in art, or in practical life. We remember that in *The Marriage of Heaven and Hell* the false 'Angel' had to go through a mill before he could impose his magical delusion on the honest 'Devil'. The so-called 'laws' of Urizen are akin to magical delusion, whether they are found in the druid religion or in the modern slavery of the mills that we are told is for 'the common good'. For such abstract laws pay no attention to particularity and fact, but simply put into motion all the supposedly infallible and mill-like machinery of 'Your Reason', arriving at something

that is far from the truth, but almost magically persuades us
that it must be true. Such was the masterful illusion, or series
of illusions, by which Urizen replaced Orc's real father and
created the mystery religion in *The Four Zoas*. Mystery and
magic and the false imposition of ideas and will and slavery, can
always be traced back to a satanic misuse of reason, which,
proud of being the most 'god-like' faculty, tries to be God, and
falls far short.

The illustration that accompanies the first page of the text
proper of *Milton* is one of lovely colours—rose, blue and yellow,
a yellow star streaming with red light in which a man and
woman swim as if under water, surrounded by weeds and water-
tendrils. On the title-page Blake drew a naked man, his back to
us, and his hand outstretched into the thundery distance.

The body of the poem opens clearly enough. The curiously
'neural' imagery that characterizes the final prophetic books is
apparent in the first section:

> Daughters of Beulah! Muses who inspire the Poet's Song,
> Record the journey of immortal Milton thro' your Realms
> Of terror & mild moony lustre in soft sexual delusions
> Of varied beauty, to delight the wanderer & repose
> His burning thirst & freezing hunger! Come into my hand,
> By your mild power descending down the Nerves of my right arm
> From out the portals of my Brain, where by your ministry
> The Eternal Great Humanity Divine planted his Paradise . . .
>   Tell also of the False Tongue! vegetated
> Beneath your land of shadows, of its sacrifices and
> Its offerings: even till Jesus, the image of the Invisible God,
> Became its prey, a curse, an offering & an atonement
> For Death Eternal in the heavens of Albion & before the Gates
> Of Jerusalem, his Emanation, in the heavens beneath Beulah.
> Say first! what mov'd Milton, who walk'd about in Eternity
> One hundred years, pond'ring the intricate mazes of Providence,
> Unhappy tho' in heav'n—he obey'd, he murmur'd not, he was
>   silent
> Viewing his Sixfold Emanation scatter'd thro' the deep
> In torment—To go into the deep her to redeem & himself
>   perish?
> That cause at length mov'd Milton to this unexampled deed.
> A Bard's prophetic Song! for sitting at eternal tables,
> Terrific among the Sons of Albion, in chorus solemn & loud
> A Bard broke forth: all sat attentive to the awful man.

All this is to say that Milton wandered around heaven for one hundred years, unable to settle down happily because he knows that a part of his poetry was inspired by the 'False Tongue'. Chief among his errors were his mistaken ideas about God and about Christ, and the resulting mistaken idea about women's place in creation. His sixfold emanation, that is, his three wives and three daughters, wanders below, unredeemed. To redeem her he is moved to an unprecedented action. After his hundred years of restlessness, at last there appears on earth a poet worthy for him to enter into, leaving heaven in order to redeem his poetry and his emanation. The earthly poet is, of course, none other than Blake! Crabb Robinson records what Blake told him in conversation: 'I saw Milton in imagination, and he told me to beware of being misled by his *Paradise Lost*.'

Blake is, of course, following closely Milton's opening in *Paradise Lost*, almost parodying Milton's 'Say first what Moved our Grand Parents', with his 'Say first! what mov'd Milton'. What actually does move Milton to return to earth is the 'Bard's prophetic Song'. And the song sung by this bard who is Blake is a kind of parable all about true and false poetry. The Bard himself seems to merge with the figure of Palamabron who stands for true poetry.

The Bard tells of the terrible situation on earth in England. 'Albion was slain', and Urizen lies 'in darkness & solitude, in chains of the mind lock'd up'. This passage parallels Milton's description of the fallen Satan. Ages of woe pass over Urizen, and Los watches in terror as in *The Four Zoas*. In fact, we get a hasty summary of what has already happened in *The Four Zoas*. In the sick Albion 'First Orc was born, then the shadowy Female'. Now Blake tells us that another son was born to Los and Enitharmon, distorted imagination, and this son's name is Satan. He is 'the Miller of Eternity', Urizen's henchman. In *The Four Zoas* Orc and Satan were one and the same, and Blake splits them up and effects this second birth for the purposes of the parable. Los in his distorted state speaks to Satan, his youngest born, and reminds him that 'Thy work is Eternal Death with Mills & Ovens & Cauldrons', and orders him to 'Get to thy Labours at the Mills & leave me to my wrath'. The symbolism of places makes itself felt here, for at this command of Los's, in Albion's capitol,

> Between South Molton Street & Stratford Place, Calvary's foot,
> Where the Victims were preparing for Sacrifice their Cherubim.

There is a beautiful illustration of a druidic arch through which tiny figures move in a deep blue starry night with a crescent moon and white racing clouds.

The new character of Palamabron, who stands for true art and imagination over against Satan's false rational art, now appears in the parable. Palamabron cultivates the living earth in contrast to Satan's mills:

> Palambron with the fiery Harrow in morning returning
> From breathing fields, Satan fainted beneath the artillery.

In *Milton* Blake is concerned with the three classes of men. On the one hand these classes correspond to Blake's own mythological scheme, but on the other, they refer quite directly to lower, middle and upper classes. Poor Blake at Felpham, perhaps for the first time, had much cause to ponder this phenomenon of society. Blake is particularly incensed by the plight of the working classes who have been forced to turn from cultivation of the breathing earth, which is, after all, a kind of art, to slavery in dark ugly mills or mines, to be shut away from air and light, and for ever warped in their response to nature's beauty, and unable to live life as it is meant to be lived. The following remarkable passage speaks of this situation in no uncertain terms, and comes in the poem as a parallel to Milton's 'farewell happy Fields where Joy for ever dwells: Hail horrours . . .':

> Ah weak & wide astray! Ah shut in narrow doleful form,
> Creeping in reptile flesh upon the narrow bosom of the ground!
> The Eye of Man a little narrow orb, clos'd up & dark,
> Scarcely beholding the great light, conversing with the Void;
> The Ear a little shell, in small volutions shutting out
> All melodies & comprehending only Discord & Harmony;
> The Tongue a little moisture fills, a little food it cloys,
> A little sound it utters & its cries are faintly heard,
> Then brings forth Moral Virtue the cruel Virgin Babylon.

Can such an Eye judge of the stars? & looking thro' its tubes
Measure the sunny rays that point their spears on Udan-adan?
Can such an Ear, fill'd with the vapours of the yawning pit,
Judge of the pure melodious harp struck by a hand divine?
Can such closed Nostrils feel a joy? or tell of autumn fruits
When grapes & figs burst their covering to the joyful air?
Can such a Tongue boast of the living waters? or take in
Ought but the Vegetable Ratio & loathe the faint delight?
Can such gross Lips perceive? alas, folded within themselves
They touch not ought, but pallid turn & tremble at every wind.[1]

This could be real poetry of the Thel variety save for certain carelessnesses and the irritating intrusion of Udanadan. 'Thus they sing,' Blake goes on, 'Creating the Three Classes among Druid Rocks,' once more allying the modern results of Urizen's rule with all such errors in England, back to the Druids. They are all part of the same mainstream of delusion.

Blake gives us a catalogue of the extent of destruction in England because of such delusive assumptions:

Thro' Albion's four Forests which overspread all the Earth
From London Stone to Blackheath east: to Hounslow west:
To Finchley north: to Norwood south . . .
The Surrey hills glow like the clinkers of the furnace; Lambeth's
  Vale
Where Jerusalem's foundations began, where they were laid in
  ruins,
Where they were laid in ruins from every Nation . . .
When shall Jerusalem return & overspread all the Nations?
Return, return to Lambeth's Vale, O building of human souls!
Thence stony Druid Temples overspread the Island white,
And thence from Jerusalem's ruins, from her walls of salvation
And praise, thro' the whole Earth were rear'd from Ireland
To Mexico & Peru west, & east to China & Japan, till Babel
The Spectre of Albion frown'd over the Nations in glory & war.
All things begin & end in Albion's ancient Druid rocky shore:
But now the Starry Heavens are fled from the mighty limbs of
  Albion.

Blake has more to say about the three classes of men in relation to the most recent cultural errors perpetrated by Urizen. Here he undoubtedly means upper, middle and lower

[1] There is only one copy of this plate which begins with the line 'Palamabron with the fiery harrow in morning returning.'

class England. Satan, with his arrogance hidden under a mild persuasive charm, belongs to the 'first class', and this is almost surely a portrait of Hayley. Blake, of course, is Palamabron, the true artist who works in living fields. Satan tries to take Palamabron's place without having the talent to do so, and Palamabron is afraid of being accused of ingratitude if he does not yield it:

> Loud sounds the Hammer of Los, loud turn the Wheels of
> Enitharmon:
> Her looms vibrate with soft affections, weaving the Web of Life,
> Out from the ashes of the Dead; Los lifts his iron Ladles
> With molten ore: he heaves the iron cliffs in his rattling chains
> From Hyde Park to the Alms-houses of Mile-end & old Bow.
> Here the Three Classes of Mortal Men take their fix'd
> destinations,
> And hence they overspread the Nations of the Whole Earth, &
> hence
> The Web of Life is woven & the tender sinews of life created
> And the Three Classes of Men . . .
> The first, the Elect from before the foundation of the World:
> The second, The Redeem'd: The Third, The Reprobate &
> form'd
> To destruction from the mother's womb . . .
> Of the first class was Satan: with incomparable mildness,
> His primitive tyrannical attempts on Los, with most endearing
> love
> He soft entreated Los to give him Palamabron's station,
> For Palamabron return'd with labour wearied every evening.
> Palamabron oft refus'd, & as often Satan offer'd
> His service, till by repeated offers & repeated intreaties
> Los gave to him the Harrow of the Almighty; alas, blamable,
> Palamabron fear'd to be angry lest Satan should accuse him of
> Ingratitude & Los believe the accusation thro' Satan's extreme
> Mildness.

It must have been galling to Blake who knew himself an intellectual prince to hear continually, perhaps for the first time at Felpham, the intimation that somehow the lower classes were doomed from before birth, and that the middle class just achieved redemption barely recognized by the upper class fortunates who had never had a moment's insecurity.

No matter how genuinely grateful Blake often felt to Hayley, it must still have been maddening to be in the position of being patronized by this upper class man of letters with his easy charm who was also the acclaimed literary figure of the day. It is perhaps significant that Hayley wrote a biography of Milton. Most annoying of all must have been to see Hayley's effusions passing for true poetry while Blake's own went neglected. We can hardly blame Blake altogether for transmuting such feelings of annoyance and anger, of which he was undoubtedly ashamed, into a cosmic myth concerning the warfare between true and false art. And yet, the myth in which he does this has no comparison with the infinitely more moving picture he gives in *The Four Zoas* of his much more profound inner struggle to keep his own vision intact. In *Milton* Blake tries to build a myth out of external events and projected emotions, whereas in *The Four Zoas* he relates events that take place within the psyche which is the true stage for mythological happenings.

Blake suggests in *Milton* that the tyranny of false art over true art occurs when Urizen's rules are the only accepted measures for art and life. This was, of course, the main tenor of the eighteenth century which was called the Age of Reason, although it was a century that contained more variety in its experiments in art and life than perhaps any other comparable period, and even though this variety tends to be lost in the overall picture of a time of reason and sensibility.

Blake feels that the class system is all a part of Urizen's tyranny, as it forces the true artist to be beholden to the dilettante class who would not recognize true art if they saw it. Thus the man of genius is forced to do tasks unworthy of him for his living. Blake, deploring class snobbery, possessed that type of artistic or intellectual snobbery that felt that the world owed him a living. For such an attitude, patronage is the only solution, and it is a time-honoured one, but Blake wanted complete freedom as well.

Satan–Hayley is unable to control and drive the horses of Palamabron's Harrow, which is to say that he has no capacity to control and shape imagination. His attempt angers Palamabron who at last speaks his mind, risking the appearance of ingratitude:

> Next morning Palamabron rose; the horses of the Harrow
> Were madden'd with tormenting fury . . .
> Then Palamabron, reddening like the Moon in an Eclipse,

138

Spoke, saying: 'You know Satan's mildness & his self-imposition,
Seeming a brother, being a tyrant, even thinking himself a
    brother
While he is murdering the just: prophetic I behold
His future course thro' darkness & despair to eternal death.
But we must not be tyrants also: he hath assum'd my place
For one whole day under pretense of pity & love to me.
My horses has he madden'd & my fellow servants injur'd.
How should he, he, know the duties of another? O foolish
    forbearance!
Would I had told Los all my heart! but patience, O my friends,
All may be well: silent remain while I call Los & Satan.

The 'How should he, he, know the duties of another?' has close relation to Blake's letters of this time, relating how Hayley sets him to do work that keeps him from his true duties which are to lay up treasures in heaven. In *Milton* Blake has an excuse to let off steam against Hayley on a grand scale, an excuse he seemed badly to need. And he lets off steam about many other matters as well. He cries out, no more with the impersonal concern of 'I wandered through each chartered street', but in a hurt defiant tone, as if now mortally wounded by the many social abuses he could once see so clearly when untouched by direct pain. Now he laments in different terms the wrongs that society inflicts in the class system, the system of labour, mistaken ideas about art and God, and above all about life. Most of all he cries out against an audience so deluded by all of these devices of Urizen to obscure the truth, that they cannot even recognize true art when they have it before them. *Milton* is in many ways a negative poem, frightened and didactic out of defiance and self-doubt, the poem of a man fighting as he backs away from life rather than struggling to go forward with love as in *The Four Zoas*. It is clear that the more Blake felt the lack of an audience, the more hortatory became his tone, and the less convincing even to himself.

I have tried to indicate in an earlier chapter how difficult is the question of Blake's relation to his patron, Hayley, even though Hayley never meant to be anything but helpful. It is interesting to note that Blake always insists that Satan *meant* well, and it is certain that it was the close proximity to a patron who had what Blake felt was his rightful place in the world of art, that set off the sparks. For when the Blakes returned to London we find an affectionate correspondence going on which is surprising considering Blake's epigrams and accusations, and the picture of Hayley as Satan. It is almost certain that this cheerful and insensitive versifier never recognized himself in Satan, for he was, after all, the popular poet of his day, and he took this position very seriously.

From a distance the suppressed rage that Blake built up as regards Hayley looks more like a mild persecution phobia than fact. For Blake, given trivial tasks that made him feel all the more inferior, in doubting his worth as an artist, also had doubts concerning his ability to hold his wife, and suspected Hayley of trying to seduce Catherine. This is a natural and psychologically 'logical' train of thought. For if Blake had failed as an artist it meant that he had failed in his very being, and what woman would stand by a failure if such a charming paragon as Hayley were interested in her? This is undoubtedly what went on in a part of Blake's mind, while the other part knew perfectly well that Hayley only meant to be kind.

To return to *Milton*: with his soft-spoken blandishments Satan almost succeeds in persuading Los, imagination itself, that it would be the best for all concerned if he were to take over Palamabron's horses and Harrow. Even when Palamabron proves that all Satan can do is to madden the horses without hope of controlling them, Satan still uses his persuasive powers to win over Los despite the evidence:

> Palamabron call'd, & Los & Satan came before him,
> And Palamabron shew'd the horses & the servants. Satan wept
> And mildly cursing Palamabron, him accus'd of crimes
> Himself had wrought. Los trembled: Satan's blandishments almost
> Perswaded the Prophet of Eternity that Palamabron
> Was Satan's enemy . . .
> What could Los do? how could he judge, when Satan's self believ'd
> That he had not oppres'd the horses of the Harrow nor the servants.
> So Los said: 'Henceforth, Palamabron, let each his own station
> Keep: nor in pity false, nor in officious brotherhood, where
> None needs, be active.' Meantime Palamabron's horses
> Rag'd.

There is something rather poignant in Los's rebuke to Palamabron: 'Henceforth, Palamabron, let each his own station keep.' That Blake was made to feel tremendously class-conscious at Felpham for the first time is all too apparent. Palamabron is rebuked, too, kindly but firmly, for the misdeeds of Satan:

> Meanwhile wept Satan before Los accusing Palamabron
> Himself exculpating with mildest speech, for himself believ'd
> That he had not oppress'd nor injur'd the refractory servants.
> But Satan returning to his Mills (for Palamabron had serv'd
> The Mills of Satan as the easier task) found all confusion,
> And back return'd to Los, not fill'd with vengeance but with
>   tears,
> Himself convinc'd of Palamabron's turpitude. Los beheld
> The servants of the Mills drunken with wine & dancing wild
> With shouts & Palamabron's songs, rending the forests green
> With echoing confusion.

Palamabron is the true Bard, Orpheus himself, who disrupts the tidy orderliness of the Mills and instead causes joyful dancing and singing that echo through the forests, freeing life instead of binding it to the Mills. His crime is to shirk the business of making a living that has replaced life itself. Again, this hits close to Blake's own situation at Felpham. Los, imagination, who is himself confused and distorted under Urizen's rule, is not sure whether Palamabron is right or whether he should uphold Satan's neat reasonable way of life. But he is convinced by Satan that this disorderly scene at the Mills is a very bad sign indeed, and so—

> Los took off his left sandal, placing it on his head,
> Signal of solemn mourning . . .

Los decides to view the whole event as a disgraceful exhibition on Palamabron's part. What is even worse, he takes part of the blame upon himself, making Palamabron feel doubly guilty:

> And Los said: 'Ye Genii of the Mills! the Sun is on high,
> Your labours call you: Palamabron is also in sad dilemma:
> His horses are mad, his Harrow confounded, his companions
>   enrag'd.

> Mine is the fault! I should have remember'd that pity divides the
>   soul
> And man unmans: follow me with my Plow: this mournful day
> Must be a blank in Nature.'

Los believes that this shameful event has disgraced even nature, totally confusing Urizen's laws of slavery with the laws of nature that teach survival, but also allow for the disturbing and spontaneous miracle of art and the joy of life itself that comes irrespective of routine and earning power. Palamabron is in deep disgrace.

> Satan wept over Palamabron.
> Theotormon & Bromion contended on the side of Satan
> Pitying his youth & beauty, trembling at eternal death.

Even the characters of Blake's earlier prophecies are against Palamabron in this case. But he has on his side the archangel Michael who 'contended against Satan in the rolling thunder'. That is to say, although Palamabron the true artist has against him the whole world of sweet reasonableness, he has the world of supernature on his side, and he invokes its aid:

> But Palamabron call'd down a Great Solemn Assembly,
> That he who will not defend Truth, may be compell'd to
> Defend a lie, that he may be snared & caught & taken.

And at Palamabron's summoning, Eternity descends to sick England:

> And all Eden descended into Palamabron's tent
> Among Albion's Druids & Bards in the caves beneath Albion's
> Death Couch, in the caverns of death, in the corner of the
>   Atlantic.
> And in the midst of the Great Assembly Palamabron pray'd:
> O God, protect me from my friends.

This again has similarities to some of Blake's epigrams, especially the one to Hayley:

> Thy Friendship oft has made my heart to ake:
> Do by my Enemy for Friendship's sake.

Los is so angry at this unauthorized action of Palamabron's that he causes the realm of imagination within Albion to lose touch entirely with fact. He is, however, afraid to let his wife know that he is doing this!

> Los in his wrath curs'd heaven & earth; he rent up Nations,
> Standing on Albion's rocks among high-rear'd Druid temples
> Which reach the stars of heaven & stretch from pole to pole.
> He displac'd continents, the oceans fled before his face:
> He alter'd the poles of the world, east, west & north & south,
> But he clos'd up Enitharmon from the sight of all these things.

Satan, to counteract Palamabron's action, asserts himself as deputy-god for Urizen, 'drawing out his infernal scroll of Moral laws & cruel punishments upon the clouds of Jehovah'. And 'Thus Satan rag'd amidst the assembly, and his bosom grew opake against the Divine Wisdom.' The vast abyss opening into this state of Satan is what Blake calls Ulro. It becomes even more clear to Los and Enitharmon that Satan is none other than the spectrous puritan conscience of Urizen, continually reborn within the sick Albion who is Orc.

There is next a passage which really follows on to the story of *The Four Zoas* and tells of how Enitharmon, when she deserted her husband in spirit to become the goddess in the mystery religion, is seen in nightmare as a raging old woman and not a goddess at all:

> Then Los & Enitharmon knew that Satan is Urizen,
> Drawn by Orc & the Shadowy Female into Generation.
> Oft Enitharmon enter'd weeping into the Space, there appearing
> An aged Woman raging along the Streets (the Space is nam'd
> Canaan): then she return'd to Los, weary, frightened as from
>   dreams.

Los weeps incoherently over Satan 'who triumphant divided the Nations'. Yet perversely Los himself 'set his face against Jerusalem to divide the eon of Albion'. He is determined, in his

---

[1] Plate 8, in the British Museum copy, has an illustration of two figures, a man's and a woman's, probably Los and Enitharmon, standing, she in back of him so that they seem one. Sadly they watch a figure in flames, probably Orc.

distorted state, to destroy Jerusalem. It is significant that Blake here uses the gnostic term 'eon' for emanation, since it designates a lesser order of creation. Los is, in setting his face against Jerusalem, setting his face against his own wife, and so he does not let her know what he is doing.

Once again health and the possibility of reunion with Jerusalem is denied to Albion. And this is so because the same sort of error that existed in England in the time of the Druids still exists in different terms. This error is fundamentally the gnostic heresy which Urizen inculcates:

> And the Mills of Satan were separated into a moony Space
> Among the rocks of Albion's Temples, & Satan's Druid Sons
> Offer the Human Victims throughout all the Earth, & Albion's
> Dread Tomb, immortal on his Rock, overshadow'd the whole
> Earth,
> Where Satan, making to himself Laws from his own identity,
> Compell'd others to serve him in moral gratitude & submission,
> Being call'd God, setting himself above all that is called God;
> And all the Spectres of the Dead, calling themselves Sons of God,
> In his synagogues worship Satan under the Unutterable Name.

The real tragedy of Satan's moral law falls not so much upon Blake–Palamabron who has inner spiritual resources, but upon the working class labourers shut up in the Mills. This is the problem debated in the great assembly in eternity:

> And it was enquired Why in a Great Solemn Assembly
> The Innocent should be condemn'd for the Guilty.

One cannot be sure that Blake is not poking fun at governmental procedure with his solemn great assembly. An Eternal rises to his feet and offers a theory:

> Saying: 'If the Guilty should be condemn'd he must be an
> Eternal Death,
> And one must die for another throughout all Eternity.
> Satan is fall'n from his station & never can be redeemed,
> And must be new Created continually moment by moment.
> And therefore the Class of Satan shall be call'd the Elect, & those
> Of Rintrah the Reprobate, & those of Palamabron, the Redeem'd:
> For he is redeem'd from Satan's Law, the wrath falling on
> Rintrah.'

144

All of this discussion in the Assembly may be Blake's attempt to parallel the council of the fallen angels in *Paradise Lost*. The next part of the parable is very obscure indeed. An unexplained character named Leutha, the only other occurrence of this name being in *The Visions of the Daughters of Albion* when Oothoon says 'I plucked Leutha's flower', wants to take upon herself the burden of Satan's sin and so redeem him. Actually, she only brings about in Satan the 'feminine' delusion of pride. 'Offering herself a Ransom for Satan, taking on her his Sin' is a satanic parody of the Cross. Leutha tells how,

> entering the doors of Satan's brain night after night
> Like sweet perfumes, I stupefied the masculine perceptions
> And kept only the feminine awake: hence rose his soft
> Delusory love to Palamabron, admiration join'd with envy.

This seems to be also a satanic interpretation of the necessary interior marriage, the union with the feminine side of oneself. For Satan, instead of joining with Leutha who seems to be his emanation, is taken over by her, and is ridden by the feminine principle which should have, once accepted, freed his masculinity. It is difficult to say exactly what Blake is accusing Satan–Hayley of here. The implication that Hayley was somehow dominated by the feminine principle comes out again in a jingle written in Blake's notebook:

> Of H(ayley)'s birth this was the happy lot,
> His Mother on his Father him begot.

If Blake is accusing Hayley of effeminacy, further complications ensue when we remember that Blake also thought Hayley a seducer of women. However, the plight of Orc reminds us that being a frustrated and potentially homosexual ascetic is only one side of the penny. The other side is Orc's libertine imagination. Be this as it may, it is interesting that Blake at one time or another accused poor Hayley of every crime in the book, and seemed not in the least perturbed by apparent inconsistencies.

Satan has his Leutha, and Palamabron has a wife too, named Elynittra, whom we have not met until now. This is, of course, quite separate from the Albion–Jerusalem story. Elynittra knows

how to control her husband's horses and the Harrow. Leutha
tries to usurp her place just as Satan tries to take Palamabron's.
But Leutha at least has the grace to confess that it did not work:

> I sprang out of the breast of Satan, over the Harrow beaming
> In all my beauty, that I might unloose the flaming steeds
> As Elynittra used to do; but too well those living creatures
> Knew that I was not Elynittra & they brake the traces.

Leutha with her 'moth-like elegance' sees that she and Satan are
at fault and will get into trouble in the world of art if they
persist in such folly. She speaks of,

> A Hell of our own making; see! its flames still gird me round.
> Jehovah thunder'd above; Satan in pride of heart
> Drove the fierce Harrow among the constellations of Jehovah,
> Drawing a third part in the fires as stubble north & south
> To devour Albion & Jerusalem, the Emanation of Albion.

If Leutha is meant to be Eliza Hayley, the following lines make
sense, for Leutha speaks of her exile from Satan just as unstable
Eliza was exiled from Hayley. Hayley's marriage failed and
was childless and he had a son by a servant. According to
Blake the failure was Satan–Hayley's fault. And, according to
these lines, too, Satan–Hayley was intoxicated by the vitality of
Elynittra, Palamabron's wife: Leutha speaks:

> For Elynittra met Satan with all her singing women,
> Terrific in their joy & pouring wine of wildest power.
> They gave Satan their wine; indignant at the burning wrath,
> Wild with prophetic fury, his former life became like a dream.
> Cloth'd in the Serpent's folds, in selfish holiness demanding
>   purity,
> Being most impure, self-condemn'd to eternal tears, he drove
> Me from his inmost Brain & the doors clos'd with thunder's
>   sound.

Leutha realizes that this separation is similar to the separation
going on within Albion and Jerusalem, keeping them apart and
producing in their place Orc and Vala. This is the division begun
in the Garden of Eden and will not be healed until Albion and
Jerusalem are united and 'two Eternities meet together'.

All is my fault! We are the Spectre of Luvah, the murderer
Of Albion. O Vala! O Luvah! O Albion! O lovely Jerusalem!
The Sin was begun in Eternity & will not rest to Eternity
Till two Eternities meet together. Ah! lost, lost, lost forever.

The fullest implications of this passage are made clear when we
place beside it the short poem in Blake's notebook called
'Merlin's Prophecy'. It is perhaps significant that Satan, with
all his arts of mild persuasion and illusion, is like an enchanter.

The harvest shall flourish in wintry weather
When two virginities meet together:

The King & the Priest must be tied in a tether
Before two virgins shall meet together.

Everything that has happened up until now in *Milton* has
been part of the parable sung by the Bard about the woes taking
place on earth. Milton listens carefully, about to leave Eternity
and travel to earth to redeem his emanation. Now the Bard
comes to the end of his tale:

The Bard ceas'd. All consider'd & a loud resounding murmur
Continu'd round the Halls; & much they question'd the immortal
Loud voic'd Bard . . .
Then there was great murmuring in the Heavens of Albion
Concerning Generation & the Vegetative power & concerning
The Lamb the Saviour. Albion trembled to Italy, Greece & Egypt
To Tartary & Hindostan & China & to Great America,
Shaking the roots & fast foundations of the Earth in doubtfulness.
The loud voic'd Bard terrify'd took refuge in Milton's bosom.

And at the instigation of the Bard, Milton arises and prepares
to go to Earth again to try to set right the mistaken ideas that
he more than anyone else has fixed in the English imagination.
He confesses that he himself in his puritanical moral righteousness has been the Satan of the Bard's parable. He cries out in
anguish:

When will the Resurrection come to deliver the sleeping body
From corruptibility? O when, Lord Jesus, wilt thou come?
Tarry no longer, for my soul lies at the gates of death.
I will arise & look forth for the morning of the grave:
I will go down to the sepulcher to see if morning breaks:

I will go down to self-annihilation & eternal death,
Lest the Last Judgement come & find me unannihilate . . .
What do I here before the Judgement? without my Emanation?
With the daughters of memory & not with the daughters of
  inspiration?
I in my Selfhood am that Satan: I am that Evil One!
He is my Spectre.

Milton, because he lacks his emanation, must enter into his
horrible hermaphroditic Shadow for his journey back to Earth.
And 'to himself he seem'd a wanderer lost in dreary night', but
Blake reassures the reader by saying that 'His real & immortal
Self' appeared to those in Eternity 'as one sleeping on a couch
of gold'.[1] Journeying through space in the shadow of his once
mortal body, Milton leaves his immortal body in eternity, and
it is as if this journey is a dream of the sleeping body in eternity.
Into the shadow body there enter 'the Spirits of the Seven Angels
of the Presence', and the shadow becomes a kind of 'polypus
that vegetates beneath the deep' and finally attaches itself
beneath the death couch of Albion. Milton's journey back to
Earth is a perilous one, but he goes 'guarded within', 'A mournful form double hermaphroditic, male and female in one
wonderful body.'

The nature of infinity is this: That every thing has its
Own Vortex, & when once a traveller thro' Eternity
Has pass'd that Vortex, he perceives it roll backward behind
His path, into a globe itself infolding like a sun,
Or like a moon, or like a universe of starry majesty,
While he keeps onwards in his wondrous journey on the earth
Or like a human form, a friend with whom he liv'd benevolent.
As the eye of man views both the east & west encompassing
Its vortex, & the north & south with all their starry host,
Also the rising sun & setting moon he views surrounding
His corn-fields & his valleys of five hundred acres square,
Thus is the earth one infinite plane, & not as apparent
To the weak traveller confin'd beneath the moony shade.
Thus is the heaven a vortex pass'd already, & the earth
A vortex not yet pass'd by the traveller thro' Eternity.

[1] Plate 13, British Museum copy, shows Milton rising over the rim of
the world, the sun behind him. He is naked and haloed, dripping from the
sea, a garment in one hand, and a look of dedication on his face. The
colours are sombre.

'First Milton saw Albion upon the Rock of Ages, deadly pale
outstretch'd . . . in solemn death', and, coming near, 'Milton's
shadow fell precipitant, loud thund'ring into the Sea of Time
& Space.'

Blake admits that this is the first he actually saw with his own
eyes of Milton's descent, for he was standing in his garden at
Felpham and saw Milton's fall into time and space. Milton spots
Blake in his garden and loses no time in entering into this poet
as his earthly vehicle:

> Then first I saw him in the Zenith as a falling star
> Descending perpendicular, swift as the swallow or swift:
> And on my left foot falling on the tarsus, enter'd there:
> But from my left foot a black cloud redounding spread over
> Europe.[1]

Milton must now redeem himself in relation to 'those three
females whom his wives, & those three whom his Daughters
had represented & contain'd, that they might be resum'd by
giving up Selfhood.' These six women seen in the aggregate
constitute what Blake calls the 'Six-fold Miltonic female' who
has been very much in the unredeemed state of Vala. The Six-
fold Miltonic female is called Ololon, and, since Blake and
Milton are now one, we can assume that Ololon is also related
to Blake's wife.

The view of women as unredeemed and naturally sinful is due,
of course, to Milton's false concept of God as a vengeful
perfectionist deity who is none other than Urizen. That Milton
was really against this God and staunchly on the side of Adam
and Eve, Blake realizes, and tells us that Milton was really 'of
the Devil's party' without knowing it. Milton's God has also
created the illusion that the earth is a Mundane Shell. On this
illusory earth the Covering Cherub masks as the true Church:

> The Mundane Shell is a vast Concave Earth, an immense
> Harden'd shadow of all things upon our Vegetated Earth,
> Enlarg'd into dimension & deform'd into indefinite space,

[1] Plate 15 pictures the sons of God playing in a lovely yellow spring
light. Below them is an area of darkness and here sits the blind God of
laws and tablets, a naked figure stepping up to choke him. Written below
in green are the words: 'To Annihilate the Selfhood of Deceit, and false
Forgiveness.'

In Twenty-seven Heavens & all their Hells, with Chaos
And Ancient Night & Purgatory. It is a cavernous Earth
Of labyrinthine intricacy, twenty-seven-folds of opakeness,
And finishes where the lark mounts.

And, Blake adds,

> travellers from Eternity pass outward to Satan's seat,
> But travellers to Eternity pass inward to Golgonooza.[1]

Vala, the shadowy female, sees Milton's descent, and thinks he
has come to spread the same doctrines as before in the churches,
and that as before she will be condemned. It is clear that in the
lament Blake gives her he is speaking of actual social conditions
such as mill slavery as much as of symbolic events:

> And thus the Shadowy Female howls in articulate howlings:
> 'I will lament over Milton in the lamentations of the afflicted:
> My Garments shall be woven of sighs & heart broken lamenta-
>   tions:
> The misery of unhappy Families shall be drawn out into its
>   border,
> Wrought with the needle with dire sufferings, poverty, pain &
>   woe
> Along the rocky Island & thence throughout the whole Earth;
> There shall be the sick Father & his starving Family, there
> The Prisoner in the stone dungeon & the Slave at the Mill.
> I will have writings written all over it in Human Words
> That every Infant that is born upon the Earth shall read
> And get by rote as a hard task of a life of sixty years.
> I will have kings inwoven upon it & Councellors & Mighty Men:
> The Famine shall clasp it together with buckles & Clasps,
> And the Pestilence shall be its fringe & the War its girdle,
> To divide into Rahab & Tirzah that Milton may come to our
>   tents.
> For I will put on the Human Form & take the Image of God,
> Even Pity & Humanity, but my Clothing shall be Cruelty:
> And I will put on Holiness as a breastplate & as a helmet,
> And all my ornaments shall be of the gold of broken hearts,
> And the precious stones of anxiety & care & desperation &
>   death
> And repentance for sin & sorrow & punishment & fear,
> To defend me from thy terrors, O Orc, my only beloved.'

[1] Above in this plate are three grey women seated and looking into
darkness while three, clothed in pastels, make gestures of dismay. Below,
a man halts in fear, as a tree with man's body reaches out to grasp him in
its branches. A hoary head watches from the mossy ground.

With this final line of Vala's lament we move back into the situation of *The Four Zoas* as into another room or dimension. There is another passage later on which takes us back to the earlier poem in exactly the same way, and which follows on to this passage in meaning. I will therefore take the liberty of commenting on both together.

Blake tells us specifically that Orc is here Luvah or Christ despite his appearance of the sick monk. But Vala can only see him as the ascetic who condemns love because she herself is in a delusory state. And therefore she must hide from the terror of this strange beloved who was once her Luvah. She who should be a vital part of Jerusalem, Albion's bride, has become the Whore of Babylon instead. Just as Orc is the sick Christian, she is the sick Mother Church, and their relation is one of separation and warfare rather than of love and unity.

But 'Orc who is Luvah' although he is sick unto death can still speak when necessary with the voice of Christ although his disguise as the pious ascetic has almost silenced this voice of the true Christ within him. Thus he now speaks to Vala who is the false mother church, warning her against her own destructive tendency to be the Shadowy Female instead of Jerusalem. He begs her to stand firm as Jerusalem, if only for self-protection so that she may not be destroyed no matter how hurtful his sick actions are, and no matter how much he seems to want her to be the mother image, lusted after jealously and destructively and cruelly unattainable. For if, in her hurt and confusion, she were to become as sick as he is, then indeed all is lost. He speaks to her with tenderness from the depths of his own illness, and his sure touch, his seeing what she must do against almost insuperable difficulties, is indeed the voice of Christ coming as if from far off:

> Orc answer'd: 'Take not the Human Form, O loveliest, Take not
> Terror upon thee! Behold how I am & tremble lest thou also
> Consume in my Consummation; but thou maist take a Form
> Female & lovely, that cannot consume in Man's consummation.
> Wherefore dost thou Create & weave this Satan for a Covering?
> When thou attemptest to put on the Human Form, my wrath
> Burns to the top of heaven against thee in Jealousy & Fear;
> Then I rend thee asunder, then I howl over thy clay & ashes.
> When wilt thou put on the Female Form as in times of old,
> With a Garment of Pity & Compassion like the Garment of God?

His Garments are long sufferings for the children of Men;
Jerusalem is his Garment, & not thy Covering Cherub, O lovely
Shadow of my delight who wanderest seeking for the prey.'

'Human' in this passage, oddly for Blake, applies to the mother-
image of natural religion, Vala in all of her too human jealousy
and hurt behaviour. 'Female' is here used to describe Jerusalem's state of fourfold detached caring and not caring, when she
is capable of detecting those hurts which are caused by illness
and those which are intentional and perverse, and of acting
accordingly. Hers must be a calm detached sureness of touch in
love that is never thrown off balance by personal hurts. Her
anger must be just and wise.

In Blake's unique vision of Christianity the emphasis lies on
the Christian marriage. He insists that the love between man
and woman must be redeemed from the sense of sin that is still
attached to it, and freed from the feeling that marriage is a state
somehow inferior to celibacy. The whole teaching of the Church
on marriage is unsatisfactory and causes much confusion and
misery, more by what it omits to say than by what it actually
says. Blake sets out to tell us those things that the Church has
never articulated about the sanctity of the marriage relationship,
and how it can and indeed must achieve full union in God as
much as any mystic's consummation. The Church still manages
to imply that asceticism is a higher calling than marriage, that
the higher states of spiritual life are open only to the ascetic,
and that sex in any form is somehow polluting: if, it implies, one
is weak enough to have to give into natural desires, then one
must marry simply for the utilitarian purpose of bringing up a
family, without reference to the possibilities of a love relationship that can go as high and deep in union with God as the
experience of any mystic. Blake sets out to show the infinite
possibilities of a marriage ever expanding in Christ, but he
also shows with complete honesty the difficulties that stand in
the way, difficulties largely created by the false sense of guilt
fostered, however unwittingly, by the Church itself.

The feeling of guilt is, of course, projected on to Woman who
is seen as the Temptress by the male. This is a necessary
illusion, as a stage, and goes back to the Fall. But our faulty
interpretation of Christianity, Blake cannot insist often enough,

instead of curing the illness we have fallen into, is in fact pushing us ever nearer to spiritual death. Before the sick rose can begin to be healed, and before we can begin to recover we must learn to regard the love of woman for man in an altogether different light. Otherwise she will behave just as she is expected to behave, becoming Vala the temptress, or, if she is sensitive, fleeing in horror from the whole idea like Thel who is falsely nun-like, Orc's feminine equivalent. Most often she vacillates pathetically and confusingly between the two extremes, thrown by horror of the one to the other, not standing firm as she ought to as a whole person, Jerusalem. Love seen simply as sex can be highly destructive, for sexual attraction is only one aspect, at once the most and the least important part of a Christian marriage which must be the love between whole Christ-centred people. The perfect mystical union of man and woman together in God is possible, but only after an inner marriage or integration has first taken place within the man and within the woman, each until then self-divided.

This is what Christ hidden in Orc's disguise is trying to say to Jerusalem. There is something very poignant in his effort to help her from out of the depths of his own illness. Out of the love that Albion bears for his bride and which has not been altogether destroyed, Orc can speak to Jerusalem with momentary insight, seeing what is right for her and wanting her to stop being the destructive mother-goddess that he seems, when he is ill, to be clamouring for her to be. For although he is fascinated by Vala and craves her, at those moments when he can stand clear of his illness he realizes that Vala will destroy himself and Jerusalem just as surely as Jerusalem's standing firm as herself will cure him. She must realize that she must neither become Vala in response to the needs of the sick Orc, or, on the other hand, try to escape the whole problem by fleeing as Thel. Only to remain Jerusalem can help, to be fully herself at all times.

This is very difficult to achieve, for it means that she must be impervious to all the hurts caused by Albion's attitude when he is sick. It is doubly difficult because not only is she deprived of her Luvah, but she is paradoxically seen as the harlot, and the more she tries to get her lover back the more she seems the temptress. To make matters worse she tries to gain a semblance of purity by becoming the unattainable mother in Urizen's religion. As Vala she is as one-sided as Albion when he is Orc. As Vala she is the sick rose: as Jerusalem she is the rose of peace. A few months before his death Blake wrote the following curious lines which would seem to indicate that he thought that Orc and Vala had the final word: 'Flaxman is Gone, and we must All soon follow, every one to his Own Eternal House, Leaving the delusive Goddess mother and her Laws, to get into Freedom from all Laws of the Members, into The Mind, in which every one is king and Priest in his own House. God send it so on Earth, as it is in Heaven.'

Jerusalem's refusal to be Vala would steady Albion and almost force him to see things more clearly. Her temptation is always to give in to his sick fantasy and play her appointed role in it because he seems to want this. And in this way she so confuses herself as well as him that neither knows dream from reality. In terms of the Church, Blake is saying that if only the mother Church would be Jerusalem instead of Babylon, then the true Christ would emerge from behind the mask of Orc, the sick ascetic. For 'Jerusalem is his Garment, & not thy Covering Cherub O lovely Shadow'.

Orc explains all this to Jerusalem who stands hesitating in the guise of Vala–Babylon, not knowing whether to heed him for this is not Christ speaking in a dazzling form she could be sure of, but only her sick husband who too often deludes her, being sometimes a monk, sometimes a demon, sometimes a child, and all too seldom her lover. Christ can speak no more plainly if he chooses to speak from within Albion, for he must be bound to the extent that Albion is bound. Thus Jerusalem is very mistrustful, not knowing whether she should remain Vala and try to force her lover to return, or take his advice and become herself again. As she listens to this strangely hidden Christ, the thought of all her wrongs makes her go off the deep end again in the most Vala-ish way, and the tender wooing of Christ from within Orc is in vain: she chooses to be Vala:

> So spoke Orc . . . in the darkness
> Opening interiorly into Jerusalem & Babylon, shining glorious
> In the Shadowy Female's bosom. Jealous her darkness grew:
> Howlings fill'd all the desolate places in accusations of Sin,

In Female beauty shining in the unform'd void; & Orc in vain
Stretch'd out his hands of fire & wooed . . .
Thus darken'd the Shadowy Female tenfold, & Orc tenfold
Glow'd on his rocky Couch against the darkness: loud thunder
Told of the enormous conflict.

This is a very fine passage conveying with great beauty a
psychological situation difficult to describe. We are shown the
conflict between the two possibilities within Jerusalem, and
Orc's ability to see them. We get the momentary gleam of
Jerusalem's wavering on the brink of choosing to be herself,
and then the sudden darkening as she thinks of her past jealousies
and desolations and her present fears and doubts, and of how she
has unjustly been accused of Sin. She dwells on these wrongs
done to her by the person she loves most and trusts least, and
his tender wooing of her is in vain, and we are shown, instead
of their reunion, the battle of their gigantic wills as she becomes
Vala again, and he becomes more Orc than ever.

The reason that Jerusalem cannot stand firm as herself while
Albion is sick, is that she has never consciously worked out
where she stood, and what constituted being herself. She herself
is afraid that her own feminine nature is sinful, and believes
that either she must flee it as Thel, or give in to it wholesale as
Vala. She is afraid of life, of men and her attractiveness to them,
and above all, of herself. She is afraid that she is Eve-ill. She
cannot be Jerusalem until she fully accepts her own femininity
and responsibility for it, knowing it controllable by the values
of Christ and not fearing it as a force of nature that must either
sweep one away with it, or be suppressed altogether. As
Jerusalem she would understand that Vala is an essential part of
her nature, and a very delightful one when it does not try to be
the whole, just as the withdrawals of the nun-like Thel within
her also serve their purpose within the total personality. What
is confusing, both to herself and to her husband, is the attempt
of first one and then the other side of her immature self to
stand for the whole that is Jerusalem. What has to be achieved,
within her as within Albion, is the inner union of the earth-
mother of the passions with the controlling values of the father,
the Logos. Only then is stability and reality achieved, and an
external marriage possible.

The picture that Blake gives us of Jerusalem as Thel and as Vala, is almost as interesting as the one he gives of Orc, but he is not nearly so clear about its origins as he is about the genesis of Orc's predicament. He sees Jerusalem only in her relation to her sick husband, and not in relation to her own archetypal situation. It is only in the poem called *Jerusalem* that Blake sees that she has been in as complex a relation to archetypal parents as Orc has been, and that she, too, is struggling to achieve an inner marriage of the two sides of herself, and this is why she loses grip of herself whenever things go wrong. In Thel Blake seemed to be feeling his way towards such an understanding, but in the horror of seeing what is happening to Albion because he has lost touch with his emanation, he loses for a time sympathy with her struggle, and can only picture her as fallen from what she should be. If Thel is taken as the first evidence in Blake's writings of the sex-revulsion, it may indeed be that Albion's illness was provoked by Jerusalem's insecurity instead of the other way around. This would be most difficult to deduce in any case.

In the state that we now find Albion and Jerusalem, he mistakes the sickly asceticism of Orc for love of God, just as she mistakes her stormy emotions as Vala for true love. Each seems to offer to the other a kind of death. This, too, is the state of Christianity. Orc, impotently ascetic, ravaged by incestuous desires and life-hatred, is the true picture of what we imagine is the holy man. Jerusalem, as the unattainable mother in this false religion is 'pure', but if she descends from the pedestal, is condemned as a harlot. Just as Orc is the serpent at the heart of Christianity, so Vala is Babylon, the 'Covering Cherub' that hides the true Church and the true Virgin Mary. To see Christianity in this light is to escape its meaning altogether and to build it on the same kind of parental authority that is the basis of natural religion, with its taboos and guilts, and the desire for punishment that prevents men and women from growing up and being filled with the love and authority of the Christ within them.

Albion has reason to be disappointed with Jerusalem. When Albion first married her she gave every appearance of being fully herself, stable, serene and enduring. And so she was in appearance and potentially at every level. But her strength and quality had not yet been tested and confirmed. The same is true of Albion: he, too, appeared to be in every respect a man and sure of himself, but like her, he fell apart at the first test. She cries to him:

> Once thou wast to Me the loveliest son of heaven—But now
> Why art thou Terrible?

and he laments to her:

> When I first Married you, I gave you all my whole Soul.
> I thought that you would love my loves & joy in my delights.
> Seeking for pleasure in my pleasures, O Daughter of Babylon.
> Then thou wast lovely, mild & gentle; now thou art terrible
> In jealousy & unlovely in my sight, because thou hast cruelly
> Cut off my loves in fury till I have no love left for thee.
> Thy loves depend on him thou lovest, & on his dear loves
> Depend thy pleasures, which thou hast cut off by jealousy.
> Therefore I shew my Jealousy & set before you Death.[1]

His pride is intellectual as hers is sexual. Any doubt concerning her sexual attractiveness, even when she is making herself thoroughly unattractive, prevents her from loving spiritually, and she is full of such doubts because she has not come to terms with her own femininity. Any hurt to his intellectual pride and suggestion that he cannot be a god in reason, comes out in physical impotence, and there are many such hurts for he has not yet learned the bounds to the 'masculine' intellect. Each gives full attention to proving him or herself unequalled in what should have only half energy and half interest. Consequently, the other side of human nature is neglected, and she is spiritually impotent, just as he is physically.

And all this is because neither has accepted the main fact of the human condition which is its essential duality in that no man can be all 'masculine' force and intellect, nor can any woman be pure earthy attraction without thereby destroying

---

[1] An illustration shows Blake's brother, Robert, with Milton entering into his foot as a star. In the text Albion says to Jerusalem:

> Behold Milton descended to redeem the Female Shade
> From Death Eternal; such your lot, to be continually Redeem'd
> By death and misery of those you love and by Annihilation.

humanity. And this is for the simple reason that no man or woman is all male or female, just as no one is all spirit or all flesh or all mother or all father, but compounded of both in an infinitely delightful variation. Gods like Urizen are boring as are goddesses like Vala, but people are not. This is what Albion and Jerusalem do not realize when she puts all of her energies into being a rampaging earth-goddess as he puts all of his into serving Urizen. The irony of the situation is that she is not very attractive or feminine when she behaves like Vala, and he is certainly not masculine or brilliant as Orc. There is much waste.

But the divine voice speaking for a moment from within Orc tells Jerusalem in no uncertain terms that as Vala she is not lovable, and that he does not love her in this state although as Jerusalem he did love her. Painful as it is to be told this, just when she is rampaging because she feels unloved, this is exactly the jolt that Jerusalem needed. She listens this time. He tells her that she should have remained Jerusalem even when, due to illness, he could not be her lover. The temporary eclipse of passion has nothing to do with their basic love for each other and she should have known this instead of reacting in hurt pride and jealousy. By so acting she has made matters much worse than they would have been otherwise, whereas, had she remained herself she could have helped, seeing what was Albion's illness and what was not. This would be to care and not to care at the same time which is the only true way of loving, and, although it seems to sacrifice something in being much less intense than Vala's stormy love, it gains more than it loses in the diamond-like hardness that can endure, and the delicate sureness of response that can note the false notes both in herself and in Albion. Most of all, it keeps the touchstone of humorous serenity that can good-naturedly see through weakness and childishness and not allow it to rule, almost laughing it out of countenance. Had Jerusalem loved Albion maturely in this way she would never have allowed herself to be made into the mother-goddess in Urizen's religion, and would have detected in herself the hurt pride that made her welcome the glamour and power of this role. Nor would she have been unduly disturbed by any of Albion's aberrations because of an inner freedom which can place the cause and real meaning of such behaviour, and a love of humanity in all its weakness and lovability which makes it easier to forgive than to condemn. The keynote of such love is 'organiz'd innocence' which is both hard and soft, both charged with energy and peaceful, both strong and pliant, both luminous and solid, rather than the fearful uncertain withdrawal of Thel or the over-active intensity of Vala. This kind of love could have cured Albion and also redeemed woman from the 'accusation of sin'.

But in order to achieve such love Jerusalem must accept Vala in herself instead of simply giving into her and then being horrified. Instead of fearing her, she must become one with her and redeem the mother, her own earthy passionate nature, just as Albion must become at one with the father, his own intellect, in order to control and put in their proper place these faculties which loom large all out of proportion. To become one with the faculty that 'proves' one's masculinity or femininity is to become sure of oneself as a man or woman for the first time, and until this is somehow accomplished a woman will have an 'earth-wish' just as a man has a 'death-wish' in needing to become one with the father-logos.

As things are, however, neither Albion nor Jerusalem has achieved such a state of 'reorganiz'd innocence' and so neither can distinguish fact from fantasy. Neither is at all sure that Albion's ridiculous accusations are not true and that Jerusalem is not his wife but a sinful harlot, or potentially one. This is where, had Jerusalem herself not been afraid of her own passionate nature, she would have firmly and humorously declared herself Albion's wife and not a harlot, instead of herself feeling guilty and overwhelmed by Vala's lugubrious rampages. Because she has not come to terms with the Vala in herself, understanding that Vala is a necessary part of her personality that can be lived with only when controlled properly and not allowed to rampage, she thinks that she *must* behave like unredeemed Eve in order to get the love Albion denies her, and she loathes herself the whole time she is behaving this way, even though her power excites her. She sees, too, that Albion is in part a perverse and frightened child, and, as Vala, she sees nothing wrong in 'mothering' him when this is the case. She perceives that as the monk, Orc, he puts her on a pedestal, and so she plays the goddess as well, rather flattered. And thus it is impossible for Albion in his sick state to know whether Jerusalem is in fact his wife, or whether she is not really a harlot, a goddess or his mother. As Vala she is trying to provoke Albion into that very intensity and violence of love that, as Thel and Enion, she fled from because it seemed sinful. Now, seeing Albion as Orc repressing all of this violence and trying to be intellect alone, she realizes that in a lover there *must* be a core of crudity, vulgarity even, and humour. It is this, too late, that she tries to revive in Albion-Orc, by the wrong tactics, knowing that it was such energy above all that she loved and was ashamed of loving.

Neither knows himself or the other, unable as each is to distinguish fact from fantasy. The question 'Who am I?', so laughable in itself, becomes the essence of breakdown, or perhaps 'What am I?' What might in a healthy marriage have been imaginative make-believe—a momentary assumption by Jerusalem of the role of goddess, mother, or provocative temptress, or by Albion of the role of frowning god, father, or child to her mother—has become no longer a game but a terrifying nightmare in which the role played swallows up the whole identity. Vala, the earth mother, has swallowed up Jerusalem, just as Orc hides Albion and Christ. This is no magical play between grown-ups, but a frightening regression to a prolonged parent–child relationship. It is both terrifying and grotesque. The delicate gauge of what is reality is altogether out of gear, although, had Jerusalem remained herself, what now seems nightmare would have seemed too ridiculous to accept.

When Orc tells Jerusalem that he does not love her when she is Vala, and she still remains suspicious and jealous of him, he assures her that it is only because she has become Vala that he 'leaves her . . . intirely abstracting himself from Female loves'. He tells her that in order to save her own womanhood, if not his sanity, she must relent and stop being Vala:

> (when) intirely abstracting himself from Female loves,
> She shall relent in fear of death; she shall begin to give
> Her maidens to her husband, delighting in his delight.
> And then & then alone begins the happy Female joy
> As it is done in Beulah, & thou, O Virgin Babylon, Mother of
>   Whoredoms,

Shalt bring Jerusalem in thine arms in the night watches, and
No longer turning her a wandering Harlot in the streets
Shalt give her into the arms of God your Lord & Husband.

It is the mother and harlot-virgin, Vala herself, who will relent
and bring Jerusalem to her husband instead of making her a
harlot wandering the streets. That is, Vala will do this when
Jerusalem is reconciled with her and assimilates her as a part of
her personality instead of being dominated by her, and swallowed.
So ends that part of *Milton* which continues the story of
Albion and Jerusalem begun in *The Four Zoas*. Albion's reunion
with his bride is not yet to be realized, for 'Urizen emerged
from his Rocky Form & from his snows'. As I have said, this
section about Albion and Jerusalem seems out of context in
Milton which presents us with an altogether different story.
We return once more to Milton's journey through infinity to
earth. He comes to an England which is ruled by Urizen and
which is therefore unable to become one with the holy city of
Jerusalem. This was the jumping-off point for Blake's interpola-
tion of the psychological situation between Albion, the man, and
his bride. Milton is determined to fight against the false God,
the same deity that had so deluded him in his previous existence
on earth. 'Silent they met & silent strove . . . The Man &
Demon strove many periods.'
The four faculties or Zoas are now made to coincide with the
four points of the compass in England. They are in chaos
because Albion is still in chaos:

Four Universes round the Mundane Egg remain Chaotic,
One to the North, named Urthona: One to the South, named
    Urizen:
One to the East, named Luvah: One to the West, named Tharmas;
They are the Four Zoas that stood around the Throne Divine.
But when Luvah assum'd the World of Urizen to the South
And Albion was slain upon his mountains & in his tent,
All fell towards the Center in dire ruin sinking down.
And in the South remains a burning fire: in the East, a void;
In the West, a world of raging waters: in the North, a solid,
Unfathomable, without end. But in the midst of these
Is built eternally the Universe of Los & Enitharmon,
Towards which Milton went, but Urizen oppos'd his path.

Milton is tempted by various delusions of Urizen who tries to win him back to the false religion:

The Twofold form Hermaphroditic & the Double-sexed,
The Female–male & the Male–Female, self-dividing stood
Before him in their beauty & in cruelties of holiness,
Shining in darkness, glorious upon the deeps of Entuthon,
Saying: 'Come thou to Ephraim! behold the kings of Canaan!
The beautiful Amalekites behold the fires of youth
Bound with the Chain of Jealousy by Los & Enitharmon.
The banks of Cam, cold learning's stream, London's dark
   frowning towers
Lament upon the winds of Europe in Rephaim's Vale,
Because Ahania, rent apart into a desolate night,
Laments, & Enion wanders like a weeping inarticulate voice,
And Vala labours for her bread & water among the Furnaces . . .
Come, bring with thee Jerusalem with songs on the Grecian
   Lyre!
In Natural Religion, in experiments on Men
Let her be offer'd up to Holiness! . . .
Where is the Lamb of God? where is the promise of his
   coming? . . .
His Images are born for War, for Sacrifice to Tirzah,
To Natural Religion, to Tirzah, the Daughter of Rahab the
   Holy . . .
Within her bosom Albion lies enbalm'd, never to awake.'

These temptations offered to Milton are of that bisexual nature which, Blake feels, is the outcome of such a religion as Urizen's. Jerusalem is sacrificed to this religion. Blake was before his time in being aware of and articulating the fact that man is both male and female. No one so much as he realized that both components are necessary to the whole man or woman. It is only when Urizen in the man, or Vala in the woman, divides off from the whole that trouble is the result. Urizen can cause such a separation to seem natural and an end in itself, instead of a necessary breaking up before the validity of the whole is accepted. Paradoxically, the moment that a man accepts and unites with the female principle in himself, the more masculine he immediately becomes. 'O how can I with my gross tongue that cleaveth to the dust Tell of the Four-fold Man in starry numbers fitly order'd,' cries Blake. It is only when the presence of factors of the opposite sex in one are *not* accepted that they are likely to begin to lead a life of their own. Then the bisexual nature of man becomes all too apparent. This is obvious in the devotees of Urizen's religion, whether monk or scholar.

It has often been noted that there is a startling likeness between Blake's fourfold schema of the psyche and Jung's division. Blake differs, however, in saying that no one faculty should dominate the others, that the core of personality is something different and more to do with Christ's being at its centre than with anything else, for Christ is imagination. Jung says that the dominance of one or two of the faculties in combination cause all type differences, although he does not, of course, claim that such a theory solves completely the mystery of personality.

Milton strives valiantly with all the temptations of Urizen. To strengthen himself he has entered into Blake,[1] and Blake prays: 'O Lord, do with me as thou wilt! for I am nothing, & vanity. If thou chuse to elect a worm, it shall remove the mountains.' And this faith begins to work:

> Now Albion's sleeping Humanity began to turn upon
> his Couch,
> Feeling the electric flame of Milton's awful precipitate descent.
> Seest thou this little winged fly, smaller than a grain of sand?
> It has a heart like thee, a brain open to heaven & hell,
> Withinside wondrous & expansive: its gates are not clos'd:
> I hope thine are not: hence it clothes itself in rich array:
> Hence thou art cloth'd with human beauty, O thou mortal man . . .
> Thus Milton fell thro' Albion's heart, travelling outside of
> Humanity
> Beyond the Stars in Chaos, in Caverns of the Mundane Shell.

Los, imagination, who has been distorted by Urizen's rule like the rest of Albion's faculties, has not seen the point of Milton's descent into Blake at Felpham. Suddenly it dawns upon him. He understands that Blake is going to set Orc, the sick core of Albion, free from the father-god:

> At last when desperation almost tore his heart in twain
> He recollected an old Prophecy in Eden recorded
> And often sung to the loud harp at the immortal feasts:
> That Milton of the land of Albion should up ascend
> Forward from Ulro from the Vale of Felpham, & set free
> Orc from his Chain of Jealousy: he started at the thought.

[1] Plate 29 shows Milton entering 'William' as a star.

163

Milton is falling through the various faculties of Albion as he falls through Blake. This would lead one to believe that Blake's identification of himself with Albion is fairly straightforward even though he also appears in this poem in his own person. This backs up the biographical evidence I have already cited for this equation. Up until now I have leaned over backwards in my exegesis of the prophetic books not to indicate any identification between Blake and Albion where it was tempting to do so. However, since Blake himself makes the connection, it seems fairly safe to do so. Catherine Blake also appears in *Milton*, and she is referred to by Blake as 'my sweet Shadow of Delight', the same phrase that he often uses to describe Vala-Jerusalem.

> But Milton entering my Foot, I saw in the nether
> Regions of the Imagination—also all men on Earth
> And all in Heaven saw in the nether regions of the Imagination
> In Ulro beneath Beulah—the vast breach of Milton's descent.
> But I knew not that it was Milton, for man cannot know
> What passes in his members till periods of Space & Time
> Reveal the secrets of Eternity: far more extensive
> Than any other earthly things are Man's lineaments.
> And all this Vegetable World appear'd on my left Foot
> As a bright sandal form'd immortal of precious stones & gold.
> I stoop'd down & bound it on to walk forward thro' Eternity.

This is, of course, the same sandal that Los had placed on his head as a symbol of solemn mourning after Palamabron's disgrace in Satan's Mills. Palamabron as well as Milton is now to be redeemed in Blake. And Los, even though his realm of imagination is still in a highly distorted state, now sides with Blake and enters into him as the spirit of prophecy. But Blake is not really sure that Los means to be friendly after what happened to Palamabron:

> While Los heard indistinct in fear, what time I bound my sandals
> On to walk forward thro' Eternity, Los descended to me:
> And Los behind me stood, a terrible flaming Sun, just close
> Behind my back. I turned round in terror, & behold!
> Los stood in that fierce glowing fire, & he also stoop'd down
> And bound my sandals on in Udan-Adan; trembling I stood
> Exceedingly with fear & terror, standing in the Vale

Of Lambeth; but he kiss'd me & wish'd me health,
And I became One Man with him arising in my strength.
'Twas too late now to recede. Los had enter'd into my Soul . . .
I am that Shadowy Prophet . . .

Palamabron and Rintrah do not trust this return of Milton.
They fear that his followers will 'weave a new Religion from
new Jealousy of Theotormon. Milton's religion is the cause:
there is no end to destruction.' They are afraid that Milton comes,

To destroy Jerusalem as a Harlot, & her Sons as Reprobates,
To raise up Mystery the Virgin Harlot, Mother of War,
Babylon the Great, the Abomination of Desolation.[1]

Los speaks to them:

O noble Sons, be patient yet a little!
I have embrac'd the falling Death, he is become One with me.
O Sons, we live not by wrath, by mercy alone we live!
I recollect an old prophecy in Eden recorded in gold & oft
Sung to the harp, That Milton of the land of Albion
Should up ascend forward from Felpham's Vale & break the Chain
Of Jealousy from all its roots . . .
But how this is as yet we know not, & we cannot know
Till Albion is arisen: then patient wait a little while.

Los pleads for understanding as well as for patience. Los
equates Albion with Lazarus whom Christ raised from the dead.
Such a miracle was possible only in the days before the Covering
Cherub hid the true Church, and Christ's true power was hidden
behind sickly piety such as Orc's:

Pity then your Father's tears.
When Jesus rais'd Lazarus from the Grave I stood & saw
Lazarus, who is the Vehicular Body of Albion the Redeem'd,
Arise into the Covering Cherub, who is the Spectre of Albion, . . .
Upon his Rock beneath his Tomb. I saw the Covering Cherub
Divide Four-fold into Four Churches, when Lazarus arose,
Paul, Constantine, Charlemaine, Luther; behold, they stand
before us
Stretch'd over Europe & Asia! . . .
So Los spoke. Furious they descended to Bowlahoola &
Allamanda,
Indignant, unconvinc'd by Los's arguments . . .

[1] Plate 21 shows a male figure in a flaming sun, a female crouched
before him, looking back.

Part of Blake's eccentricity in *Milton* lies in the fact that in this poem he is playing games to hoodwink the same audience he is pleading with to give him a hearing. This is annoyingly evident in the over-frequent use of nonsense-names which have no vital connection with anything important, but simply appear once or twice to send the reader hunting all over for a profound meaning, and then disappear as casually. As well as demanding that we keep in mind the symbolic usages of real place names, Blake asks us to remember that Ulro is the space named Satan; that 'Bowlahoola is name'd Law by mortals'; and Golgonoora is the 'spiritual fourfold London in the loins of Albion'. We are expected to know at any momentary reference to them what Luban and the Lake of Udan-Adan and the Forests of Entuthon Benython stand for, as well as to recognize each of the minor characters who wander in from earlier prophetic books. The reader is not even convinced that all of these names are really important to Blake himself. The names strike falsely on the mind's ear as if Blake were deliberately and defiantly going too far into meaningless eccentricity to annoy the audience which pays no attention to him and which ignored the things he *was* profoundly concerned with. The theme and story of *Milton* are thin, childish, and unimportant compared to anything else Blake ever wrote, and Blake drifts passively in the idle current of his narrative, pulling in any straws of nonsense that float by, seeing what he can get away with. Blake as the author of *Milton* seems much like a bored child telling more and more fantastic tales in the hope that someone will pay attention if only to contradict. Only in the passages which carry on the story of Albion and Jerusalem begun in *The Four Zoas* do we get any feeling of a deep and necessary psychological drama playing itself out.

In vain Los announces that Milton has come to redeem his errors through Blake. No one listens to his extravagant claims:

> The Awakener is come outstretch'd over Europe: the Vision of
>   God is fulfill'd:
> The Ancient Man upon the Rock of Albion Awakes,
> He listens to the sounds of War astonish'd & asham'd,
> He sees his Children mock at Faith & deny Providence . . .
> But the time of your refreshing cometh: only a little moment

Still abstain from pleasure & rest in the labours of eternity . . .
Wait till the Judgement is past, till the Creation is consumed,
And then rush forward with me into the glorious spiritual
Vegetation, the Supper of the Lamb & his Bride, & the
Awaking of Albion our friend & ancient companion.
So Los spoke. But lightnings of discontent broke on all sides
  round . . .

Yet, despite all opposition Blake–Milton together with Los and
his sons labour to create the fourfold man and the fourfold city of
Jerusalem, even though Nature is recalcitrant. For,

           every Natural Effect has a Spiritual Cause, & Not
A Natural; for a Natural Cause only seems: it is a Delusion
Of Ulro & a ratio of the perishing Vegetable Memory.

The sons of Los who are the true artists set themselves all sorts
of tasks in the rebuilding of Jerusalem, the bride of Christ, the
holy city, the house of eternity:

Some Sons of Los surround the Passions with porches of iron
  and silver,
Creating form & beauty around the dark regions of sorrow,
Giving to airy nothing a name & habitation
Delightful, with bounds to the Infinite putting off the
  Indefinite
Into most holy forms of Thought; such is the power of
  inspiration.
They labour incessant with many tears & afflictions,
Creating the beautiful House for the piteous sufferer.
Others Cabinets richly fabricate of gold & ivory
For Doubts & fears unform'd & wretched & melancholy.
The little weeping Spectre stands on the threshold of Death
Eternal . . .

Again the emphasis is on the bounding line that must limit all
true and 'holy forms of thought'. Even if these bounds stretch
to Eternity, they are never indefinite. It is a delusion of Urizen
to make Albion think he can push his thought beyond all
bounds. It only makes Albion's sickness worse, and he suffers
from vague and indefinite fears. It is to house such fears that the
sons of Los labour to build rich cabinets: to embody airy
nothing imagination builds forms and dwellings. The only

way to grasp infinity is through Minute Particulars and the wirey bounding line. In a letter written a few months before his death, Blake comments: 'I know too well that the great majority of Englishmen are fond of the indefinite, which they measure by Newton's doctrine of the fluxions of an atom, a thing that does not exist. These are politicians and think that republican art is inimical to their atom, for a line or lineament is not formed by chance. A line is a line in its minutest subdivisions, strait or crooked. It is itself and not intermeasurable with or by anything else.'

When Albion tries to be god-like and encompass infinity with the mind alone, what he actually becomes is Orc, the weeping spectrous child full of fear and on the threshold of spiritual death and madness because reason is strained so far that it has no contact with his emotional nature. And mind stretched in this way, far from being God-like, reaches only the vague, the opaque and indefinite. This is not to say that reason in its right place cannot help Albion to know infinity. When reason is applied to a particular situation it reveals the eternal truth or form behind the minute particular, so that one may see the world in a grain of sand.

It is ironic that while Albion is convinced that by reason alone he can possess all knowledge, he is living in the constant vague but agonizing fear of utter extinction, because he is trying to equal the angry father-god. He cannot even enter the house of life, let alone eternity. He suffers piteously and is defeated by the too high standards of perfection set by his own reason. He is forbidden to live, but is none the less completely terrified by death. And all this started when Albion first doubted the goodness of sensory experience.

Blake, far from being the airy visionary and anti-rationalist that he is thought to be, is always struggling to control in himself a too rational bias. It is not the same thing as being anti-rational to recognize and try to put into its rightful place an overweening pride of reason in oneself, keeping it from getting the upper hand. Hence we have Blake's insistence on the validity of empirical fact and the evidence of the passions and emotions. Here, too, we have Blake's plea for minute particularity and the wirey bounding line in life as in art. And all too often his own analysing intellect keeps him from following his own advice. The measure of his rationality is indicated by the failure of the prophetic books to achieve this particularity and proportion. Pushed to such an extreme as Albion has pushed it, Blake sees that rationality becomes almost the same as complete irrationality, that is, madness. Without bounds the reason is nothing, and its possessor is at the mercy of Ideas become raging archetypes as much as any animal is at the mercy of instinct. He becomes Nebuchadnezzar in fact.

And so imagination, in the form of the sons of Los, is continually busy building forms for these empty ideas to find a home in. This is the house of eternity that is Jerusalem. They build windows into eternity, the timeless moments and creative periods:

> But others of the Sons of Los build Moments & Minutes & Hours
> And Days & Months & Years & Ages & Periods, wondrous
> buildings;
> And every Moment has a Couch of gold for soft repose,
> (A Moment equals a pulsation of the artery)
> And between every two Moments stands a Daughter of Beulah
> To feed the Sleepers on their Couches with maternal care.
> And every Minute has an azure Tent with silken Veils:
> And every Hour has a bright golden Gate carved with skill:
> And every Day & Night has Walls of brass & Gates of adamant,
> Shining like precious Stones & ornamented with appropriate signs:
> And every Month a silver paved Terrace builded high:
> And every Year invulnerable Barriers with high Towers:
> And every Age is Moated deep with Bridges of silver & gold:
> And every Seven Ages is Incircled with a Flaming Fire . . .
> Every Time less than a pulsation of the artery
> Is equal in its period & value to Six Thousand Years,
> For in this Period the Poet's Work is done, & all the Great
> Events of Time start forth & are conceiv'd in such a period,
> Within a Moment, a Pulsation of the Artery.

Book the First of *Milton* ends with these and other activities of the Sons of Los to rebuild Jerusalem.

The Second Book[1] opens with the description of the realm of

---

[1] There is a lovely illustration of three joyous floating and handspringing male figures; two female figures rush towards them in wonder. Mirror writing proclaims: 'How wide the Gulf unpassable between Simplicity and Insipidity' and 'Contraries are Positives—A Negation is not a Contrary.'

169

Beulah which I have quoted in an earlier chapter. The realm of
Beulah is that of threefold vision, the realm of the poet and of
marital peace and love. It is a place of repose from the dazzling
visions of eternity which cannot be sustained for too long.
From Beulah one can make brief excursions into eternity. In
Beulah there is no warfare or sexual strife. It is where Albion
and Jerusalem watch over each other in love and yet love in
freedom. Beulah should be the daily climate of marriage existing
around the full union with God that is Eternity. I suggested
when I quoted this passage that the single word 'unbounded' is
the giveaway that Blake does not really want to leave the
happiness of Beulah even for what he thinks is a higher realm of
truth where he can 'talk man to man' with God. This is not to
say that it is not good to at least postulate a higher realm of
what seem more eternal truths. The idea of such a realm can
well become, as it did for Keats and Yeats, an avenue of escape
when the 'fury and mire' of human life seems too impure. But
as Mr. Daiches has pointed out, both Keats and Yeats knew that
such a realm of platonic perfection is too cold and artificial to hold
the artist for long, even though he may speak of it longingly.
He must return to the warm living imperfection out of which art
springs, in itself a kind of transcendent and perfect flower.

Blake had less excuse than most poets to postulate such a
realm of escape. Blake professed to know Christ, the perfect
Humanity. Keats and Yeats do not claim such knowledge, but
seek in the pure forms of imagination and thought something
that is eternal. But Yeats knew that his tower was 'dead at the
top' and Keats knew that something warm and spontaneous was
lost in the beautiful figures on the urn.[1] Blake, on the other
hand, found in the realm of Beulah, not only art and marital
bliss, but Christ himself to raise his art and love to something
beyond the fury and the mire. And yet he tries to have his cake
and eat it in longing both for this incarnate truth of Christ, and
for a realm beyond it, the impersonal and inhuman truth of the
platonist. This is perhaps why we begrudge Blake his lifeless
'Eternity' and why it rings false in its insistence on pure disembodied gnosis after we have been shown the soft radiance of
Beulah.

[1] Daiches.

I have suggested that it is in the richness and tenderness of the poetry describing Beulah and in the thinness of that concerning Eternity that Blake reveals his true sympathies. It is interesting that he uses the giveaway word 'unbounded' to describe the vision of Eternity without realizing that he has just finished telling us that unbounded thought is madness. But the most convincing indication that something is wrong with Blake's thinking when he insists that the vision of Eternity is higher than that of Beulah, is that the female must be excluded from the higher vision. This from Blake whose whole doctrine is based on the belief that man cannot be spiritually whole without his emanation! He is, in effect, saying now that although woman can be weaned away from a Thel-like fear of life, and although she can be persuaded to control her Vala-like behaviour, it seems as if she cannot in the final analysis stand the vision of Eternity. She must wither away like a flower while her husband enters Eternity alone. This is to say that she cannot become Jerusalem, but must remain spiritually virgin, like Ololon a bride of 'twelve years'. It seems to Blake as if he had patiently followed this woman in her spiritual progress from Thel to Vala, and now when she ought to become Jerusalem, he must conclude that she is too weak to do so. She is a perfect wife in sympathy and love, but she is not a companion of the intellect, meaning, we note, that she doesn't agree with him intellectually!

If Blake keeps his view of Eternity and the need to 'prove' vision, it means that he must admit defeat in the whole doctrine of Albion and Jerusalem's male and female completeness in Christ, for it is clear that woman will not follow him in this venture of 'proving'. I cannot help feeling that the emanation is right this time, that the true fourfold vision, which is, after all, the vision of the whole man whose faculties are in harmony and in touch with those of his wife—is to be found in Beulah which is the realm of art and love and Christ, and not in the thin abstraction of Eternity, a redundancy incurred by Urizen.

The quarrel with Hayley goes deeper, then, than appears on the agitated surface of *Milton*. Because of the need to prove to rational Hayley and those like him his own artistic vision,

Blake has lost touch not only with this vision but with his wife as well, since unity with her is an essential part of the vision. All that they stood for together has to be put to the test of reason, and she will not have this, claiming that it needs no proof, only expression. Had woman been able to follow him into Eternity while he did his 'duty' of intellectual proof, the lack of any other audience would not have seemed so terrible a thing. But she will not follow, and in fact heartily disapproves of the venture, and leaves him to go alone. And although he lets her off from the heights of abstraction, that are too difficult for her, with a very great tenderness, he is still greatly disappointed and disillusioned, or so he *says*. In actual fact he enters with more poetic sympathy into the vision he professes to despise as inferior than into the allurements of Eternity to which he returns with almost audible sighs and lagging footsteps. The need to *prove* himself fourfold seems an almost subtler temptation of pride in reason than the out and out crude desire to be equal to Urizen. It is the temptation that ruins the prophetic books, and nowhere is it more apparent than in *Milton*. In the Songs Blake had no need to prove himself and his vision—they just were, for all to see, but the trouble was that no one saw what a small miracle Blake's Songs were. This, the human vision of the Songs and of Beulah, is Blake's real achievement, and all of his rather tired efforts to prove that he conversed with God and Ezekiel and Milton, are, in short, a temptation of Urizen to make himself appear in the rather crude but sensational light of clairvoyant and visionary that the popular mind can accept as marvellous. What he saw in the Songs was much more marvellous, although few understood this.

I think that in one sense Blake did indeed achieve the mystic's oneness with Christ, but when he did it had little to do with seeing ghosts and spirits and talking man to man with God. 'Thy own Humanity learn to adore' and 'Everything that lives is holy', such statements sum up Blake's deepest insight when he did not doubt himself or his vision, and did not have to subject either to rational proof.

Shortly after this passage about Beulah there is a lovely burst of spring poetry. It is as if Beulah, no matter how inferior to Eternity, at least had the effect of taking Blake's mind off the

airless preoccupation with the Hayley-Satan conspiracy and sent
it out of doors into the bright sea air at Felpham:

> Thou hearest the Nightingale begin the Song of
>   Spring.
> The Lark sitting upon his earthy bed, just as the morn
> Appears, listens silent; then springing from the waving
>   Cornfield, loud
> He leads the Choir of Day: trill, trill, trill, trill,
> Mounting upon the wings of light into the Great Expanse,
> Reechoing against the lovely blue & shining heavenly Shell,
> His little throat labours with inspiration; every feather
> On throat & breast & wings vibrates with the effluence Divine.
> All Nature listens silent to him, & the awful Sun
> Stands still upon the Mountain looking on this little Bird
> With eyes of soft humility & wonder, love & awe,
> Then loud from their green covert all the Birds begin their
>   Song.

This Nature is no vague and terrifying Mundane Shell, but an
earth made out of lovely Minute Particulars such as this small
vibrating skylark, through any one of which eternity may be
glimpsed. And this is Beulah, nothing else. Another passage
almost as lovely follows, reminding us that Blake was capable
of seeing 'heaven in a wildflower'. Notice particularly the
curiously different effect given by the crimson rose on her bed
from that in 'The Sick Rose'.

> Thou perceivest the Flowers put forth their precious Odours,
> And none can tell how from so small a Center comes such
>   sweets,
> Forgetting that within that Center Eternity expands
> Its ever during doors . . .
>   First the Wild Thyme
> And Meadow-sweet, downy & soft waving among the reeds,
> Light springing on the air, lead the sweet Dance: they wake
> The Honeysuckle sleeping on the Oak; the flaunting beauty
> Revels along upon the wind; the White-thorn, lovely May,
> Opens her many lovely eyes listening; the Rose still sleeps,
> None dare to wake her; soon she bursts her crimson curtain'd
>   bed
> And comes forth in the majesty of beauty . . .

But while all nature bursts forth in joy,

> Milton oft sat upon the Couch of Death & oft
> conversed
> In vision & dream beatific with the Seven Angels of the
> Presence,
> 'I have turned my back upon these Heavens builded on cruelty;
> My Spectre still wandering thro' them follows my Emanation,
> He hunts her footsteps thro' the snow & wintry hail & rain.
> The Idiot Reasoner laughs at the Man of Imagination,
> And from laughter proceeds to murder by undervaluing
> calumny.

The last two lines show the kind of 'murder' Blake attributed to Hayley. Such, probably, was the attempt 'to bereave my life' he mentions in his epigram about Hayley. The lines about the Spectre of Blake–Milton are almost identical with lines in the lyric, 'My Spectre around me night & day'.

Milton, by entering into Blake, has tried to overcome the errors formerly perpetrated by his own puritanical Urizen-bound conscience. But he has not succeeded so far, and cannot redeem or be united with his wife as yet. Presumably Blake is bound to the same extent as Milton is bound and it is clear that Blake thinks of Ololon as his wife as well as Milton's, and Jerusalem, too, is in the state of Ololon. There is some reason for this all-round identification in that Milton and Blake are deluded by the same dictates of Urizen that delude Albion.

A short statement by the Angels of the Divine Presence sums up what has happened to Albion as man and country since Milton's God has had him in thrall. Blake's views about individuals versus states once more make their appearance:

> We are not Individuals but States . . .
> We were Angels of the Divine Presence, & were Druids in
> Annandale,
> Compell'd to combine into Form by Satan, the Spectre of Albion,
> Who made himself a God & destroyed the Human Form
> Divine . . .
> Distinguish therefore States from Individuals in those States.
> States Change, but Individual Identities never change nor
> cease.
> You cannot go to Eternal Death in what can never Die . . .
> The Imagination is not a State: it is the Human Existence
> itself.
> Affection or love becomes a State when divided from Imagination.

The discussion between Milton and the Angels takes place around what seems to be the death couch of Albion. Blake insists in a very moving passage that the death of Albion is somehow identical with the death of Christ, and that, like Christ, Albion will rise again. Christ is always with Albion even though Albion in his sickness has banished Christ from his soul:

Thus they converse with the Dead, watching round the Couch of
  Death;
For God himself enters Death's Door always with those that
  enter
And lays down in the Grave with them, in Visions of Eternity,
Till they awake & see Jesus & the Linen Clothes lying
That the Females had woven for them, & the Gates of their
  Father's House.

And this is the very moment, when Albion is at death's door, that the Christ within him spoke to Jerusalem, telling her not to be Vala, in the passage I quoted earlier: 'When I first married you', etc.

And as Albion lies dying, the Daughters of Beulah ask Jerusalem. 'Is terror chang'd to pity? O wonder of Eternity.' But it is still too early for Albion's resurrection and for Jerusalem to become herself all at once. Blake tells us that there is yet another dire state of the soul to be traversed first. Once again Blake's over-usage of nonsense names mars what he is saying:

And the Four States of Humanity in its Repose
Were shewed them. First of all Beulah, a most pleasant Sleep
On Couches soft with mild music, tended by flowers of Beulah,
Sweet Female forms, winged or floating in the air spontaneous,
The Second State is Alla, & the third State Al-Ulro:
But the Fourth State is dreadful, it is named Or-Ulro.
The First State is in the Head, the Second is in the Heart,
The Third in the Loins & Seminal Vessels, & the Fourth
In the Stomach & Intestines, terrible, deadly, unutterable.
And he whose Gates are open'd in those Regions of his Body
Can from those Gates view all these wondrous Imaginations.

This last terrible state of Or–Ulro is still to be traversed by Milton and Ololon, and presumably by Blake and his wife and by Albion and Jerusalem. For Ololon, although not yet become Jerusalem, is nevertheless wholly in sympathy with her husband, and she tries through understanding to help him through his living death. She chooses to go with him in his illness, giving up altogether Vala's position of hurt pride. She has looked his suffering full in the face and is familiar with all its fearful stages of unreality and will-to-hurt, yet never wavers from her own position. Thus in many ways she is indistinguishable from Jerusalem with whom at times she seems to merge, although she still belittles her own capacity for spiritual truth, and this is what offends Blake–Milton. For not to doubt her own value is a very important part of Jerusalem's wholeness. But at any rate Ololon dares to look suffering full in the face where Thel or Vala, each for a different reason, would have fled,

> Where lie in evil death the Four Immortals pale & cold
> And the Eternal Man, even Albion, upon the Rock of Ages.

Ololon is afraid, but none the less in an effort to understand and so help, she will look at the most terrifying aspects of the living death that Albion is enduring:

> And Ololon looked down into the Heavens of Ulro in fear.
> They said: 'How are the Wars of man, which in Great Eternity
> Appear around in the External Spheres of Visionary Life,
> Here render'd Deadly within the Life & Interior Vision?
> How are the Beasts & Birds & Fishes & Plants & Minerals
> Here fix'd into a frozen bulk subject to decay & death?

In other words, Ololon is still doubtful whether these are true visions granted by Christ, since they seem to kill rather than to inspire Albion to further effort. Nevertheless, she looks with pity and forgiveness at the terrible nightmare, which is her own, too, for as Vala she was forced to play her part. She is now in the state of Beulah where no strife can come. 'Into this pleasant Shadow, Beulah, all Ololon descended.'

> Those Visions of Human Life & Shadows of Wisdom &
>   Knowledge
> Are here frozen to unexpansive deadly destroying terrors
> And War & Hunting, the Two Fountains of the River of Life,

Are become Fountains of bitter Death & of corroding Hell, . . .
O dreadful Loom of Death! O piteous Female forms compell'd
To weave the Woof of Death! . . .
Where once the Cherubs of Jerusalem spread to Lambeth's
    Vale . . .
So spake Ololon in reminiscence astonish'd . . .
Even of Los & Enitharmon & all the Sons of Albion
And his Four Zoas terrified & on the verge of Death.'

And now Ololon, seen as the personification of all the Daughters
of Beulah within Jerusalem, confesses her crime of not having
stood firm and fourfold, of not having remained the wife that
Albion had married just when he needed her most,

                    falling down
Prostrate before the starry Eight asking with tears forgiveness,
Confessing their crime with humiliation & sorrow.

The starry eight are the Four Zoas and their emanations. In
a flash of insight Ololon within Jerusalem participates in Albion's
mental hell. She sees not only the part she has played in creating
it, but also the way out. It is in the realm of imagination, that
of Los and Enitharmon, that this healing vision comes to her,
and it is on this level that she can make successful contact with
Albion:

O how the Starry Eight rejoic'd to see Ololon descended,
And now that a wide road was open to Eternity
By Ololon's descent thro' Beulah to Los & Enitharmon! . . .
There is a Moment in each Day that Satan cannot find,
Nor can his Watch Fiends find it; but the Industrious find
This Moment & it multiply, & when it once is found
It renovates every Moment of the Day if rightly placed.
In this Moment Ololon descended to Los & Enitharmon.

Ololon then descends to Blake's garden at Felpham with
the Lark who is 'Los's Messenger'[1]:

When on the highest lift of his light pinions he arrives
At that bright Gate, another Lark meets him, & back to back
They touch their pinions, tip tip, & each descend
To their respective Earths & there all night consult with Angels

[1] On this plate is the famous drawing of Blake's cottage at Felpham
with Ololon descending.

177

Of Providence & with the eyes of God all night in slumbers
Inspired, & at the dawn of day send out another Lark . . .
Lark met the Female Ololon descending into my Garden . . .
For Ololon step'd into the Polypus within the Mundane Shell.
They could not step into the Vegetable Worlds without becoming
The enemies of Humanity, except in a Female Form,
As One Female Ololon & all its mighty Hosts
Appear'd, a virgin of twelve years: nor time nor space was
To the perception of the Virgin Ololon, but as the
Flash of lightning, but more quick the Virgin in my Garden
Before my Cottage stood . . .
Walking in my Cottage Garden, suddenly I beheld
The Virgin Ololon & address'd her as a Daughter of Beulah.

Ololon in the plural represents all the Daughters of Beulah together. As a single female form she represents Jerusalem in the state of Beulah. As the 'virgin of twelve years' she bears some resemblance to the Virgin Mary when she visited the temple. But so many of Blake's ideas are completely new interpretations of lines and images that begin in the Scriptures, that it is not advisable here to follow up such interesting and complicated sea-changes. The phrase, 'and all its mighty hosts' applied to Ololon as the Daughters of Beulah who are sometimes Guardian Angels, makes the reader wonder just how much Blake intended his doctrine of emanations or eons to coincide with the gnostic beliefs concerning eons and the hierarchy of angels flowing down to created matter. As usual, whatever Blake took from his reading, he made completely his own.

Ololon asks to see Milton. Milton appears in Blake s garden as all that is satanic and Urizen-bound in his own beliefs. All of Milton's errors, summed up in the Covering Cherub of the Church, confront Ololon:

So Ololon utter'd in words distinct the anxious thought:
Mild was the voice but more distinct than any earthly.
That Milton's Shadow heard, & condensing all his Fibres
Into a strength impregnable of majesty & beauty infinite,
I saw he was the Covering Cherub & within him Satan
And Rahab in an outside which is fallacious within,
Beyond the outline of Identity, in the Selfhood deadly;
And he appear'd the Wicker Man of Scandinavia, in whom
Jerusalem's children consume in flames among the Stars.
Descending down into my Garden, a Human Wonder of God

> Reaching from heaven to earth, a Cloud, & Human Form,
> I beheld Milton with astonishment & in him beheld
> The Monstrous Churches of Beulah, the Gods of Ulro dark,
> Twelve monstrous dishumaniz'd terrors, Synagogues of Satan . . .

The divisions of this Covering Cherub include:

> Osiris, Isis, Orus in Egypt, dark their Tabernacles on Nile
> Floating with solemn songs & on the Lakes of Egypt nightly
> With pomp even till morning break & Osiris appear in the sky . . .
> All these are seen in Milton's Shadow, Who is the Covering
>   Cherub,
> The Spectre of Albion in which the Spectre of Luvah inhabits.

'The Spectre of Albion in which the Spectre of Luvah inhabits': this is to say that Christ is hidden somewhere in all this spectrous covering just as he is hidden in Orc.[1]

Blake stands and views the ruined Albion, a spectacle as poignant as any waste land. Place names fuse with the characters in this passage, which is very fine. Albion, once a fourfold man and country united to his bride, the holy city of Jerusalem, is now a ruin, mated to Babylon.

> I stood . . . & beheld its desolations:
> A ruin'd Man, a ruin'd building of God, not made with hands:
> Its plains of burning sand, its mountains of marble terrible:
> Its pits & declivities flowing with molten ore & fountains
> Of pitch & nitre: its ruin'd palaces & cities & mighty works:
> Its furnaces of affliction, in which his Angels & Emanations
> Labour with blacken'd visages among its stupendous ruins,
> Arches & pyramids & porches, colonades & domes,
> In which dwells Mystery, Babylon; here is her secret place
> From hence she comes forth on the Churches in delight;
> Here is her Cup fill'd with its poisons in these horrid vales,
> And here her scarlet Veil woven in pestilence & war;
> Here is Jerusalem bound in chains in the Dens of Babylon.

Milton finally takes a stand against his own Spectre who wants to continue this ruination. He announces his intention of casting

[1] See frontispiece. Plate 38 of the British Museum copy has one of the loveliest drawings Blake ever made: Albion and Jerusalem lie asleep with peaceful grave expressions, and each lies with an arm thrown across the other. It is night and they are in the mossy curve of a rock, a calm blue sea lapping around them. A great sea-bird hovers motionless, its wings outstretched over them, gazing intently at the sleeping lovers.

off his Spectre altogether along with the false doctrines of the
Covering Cherub which he has hitherto believed.

> Satan! my Spectre! I know my power thee to annihilate . . .
> Thy purposes & the purposes of thy Priests & of thy Churches
> Is to impress on men the fear of Death, to teach
> Trembling & fear, terror, constriction, abject selfishness.
> Mine is to teach Men to despise death & to go on
> In fearless majesty, annihilating Self, laughing to scorn
> Thy Laws & terrors, shaking down thy Synagogues as webs.

But Satan means to oppose the idea of Christ as sole God,

> Till All Things become One Great Satan, in Holiness
> Oppos'd to Mercy, & the Divine Delusion, Jesus, be no more.

But at the very moment of this manifesto of Satan's there is an
indication of God's power:

> Suddenly around Milton on my Path the Starry Seven
> Burn'd terrible; my Path became a solid fire, as bright
> As the clear Sun, & Milton silent came down on my Path.
> And there went forth from the starry limbs of the Seven, Forms
> Human, with Trumpets, innumerable, sounding articulate
> As the Seven spake; & they stood in a mighty Column of Fire
> Surrounding Felpham's Vale, reaching to the Mundane Shell,
>   Saying:
> 'Awake, Albion awake! reclaim thy Reasoning Spectre, Subdue
> Him to the Divine Mercy. Cast him down into the Lake
> Of Los that ever burneth with fire ever & ever, Amen!
> Let the Four Zoas awake from Slumbers of Six Thousand Years.'

Satan hears the command to Albion to awake and put his
tyrannical reason in its proper place, forgiving and respecting
his own Humanity. Satan trembles as Albion tries to raise
himself from the death couch:

> Then Albion rose up in the Night of Beulah on his Couch
> Of dread repose; seen by the visionary eye, his face is toward
> The east, toward Jerusalem's Gates:

That is, although Albion still appears to be desperately ill and
rejecting Jerusalem, unseen to the eye he is looking towards
her hopefully. Although he falls back upon his couch in groans

of pain, the perceptive eye can see that a change for the good has taken place, and he is hoping to be reunited with his emanation. He wants to 'bathe in the Waters of Life; to wash off the Not Human', all those attempts to be something other than human which are the delusions caused by Urizen.

> groaning he sat above
> His rocks, London & Bath & Legions & Edinburgh
> Are the four pillars of his Throne: his left foot near London
> Covers the shades of Tyburn: his instep from Windsor
> To Primrose Hill stretching to Highgate & Holloway.
> London is between his knees, its basements fourfold;
> His right foot stretches to the sea on Dover's cliffs, his heel
> On Canterbury's ruins; his bosom girt with gold involves
> York, Edinburgh, Durham & Carlisle, & on the front
> Bath, Oxford, Cambridge, Norwich; his right elbow
> Leans on the Rocks of Erin's Land, Ireland, ancient nation;
> His head bends over London; he sees his embodied Spectre
> Trembling before him with exceeding great trembling & fear.
> He views Jerusalem & Babylon, his tears flow down.
> He mov'd his right foot to Cornwall, his left foot to the rocks of
>   Bognor.
> He strove to rise to walk into the Deep, but strength failing
> For bad, & down with dreadful groans he sunk upon his Couch.

For some time now Jerusalem has been herself, but Albion still fears that she is Vala, just as he still fears his own emotional nature as evil. As these changes take place within Albion, we find that Urizen has weakened in his struggle with Milton in Blake's garden. Ololon cheers Milton–Blake on, and fears for him. But she needn't have worried, Blake tells us. Milton is now seeing clearly:

> But turning toward Ololon in terrible majesty Milton
> Replied: 'Obey thou the Words of the Inspired Man.
> All that can be annihilated must be annihilated
> That the Children of Jerusalem may be saved from slavery . . .
> To bathe in the Waters of Life; to wash off the Not Human,
> I come in Self-annihilation & in the grandeur of Inspiration,
> To cast off Rational Demonstration by Faith in the Saviour. . . .
> To take off his filthy garments & clothe him with Imagination,
> To cast aside from Poetry all that is not Inspiration . . .
> To cast off the Idiot Questioner who is always questioning

181

But never capable of answering, who sits with a sly grin
Silent plotting when to question, like a thief in a cave,
Who publishes doubt & calls it knowledge, whose Science is
Despair . . .
These are the destroyers of Jerusalem, these are the murderers
Of Jesus, who deny the Faith & mock at Eternal Life.'

Then Ololon speaks, remembering the Vala-like role she was
forced to play under Milton's religion which was that of Urizen.
She wants to know what her role will be in this new dispensation,
fearing that it will be no better:

Then trembled the Virgin Ololon & reply'd in clouds of despair:
'Is this our Feminine Portion, the Six-fold Miltonic Female?
Terribly this Portion trembles before thee, O awful Man.
Altho' our Human Power can sustain the severe contentions
Of Friendship, our Sexual cannot, but flies into the Ulro.
Hence arose all our terrors in Eternity; & now remembrance
Returns upon us; are we Contraries, O Milton, Thou & I?
O Immortal, how were we led to War the Wars of Death?
Is this the Void outside of Existence which if enter'd into
Becomes a Womb? & is this the Death Couch of Albion?
Thou goest to Eternal Death & all must go with thee.'

There is poignance and beauty in Ololon's recognition that her
sexual nature needs more than the platonic love of friendship, and
no matter how much she tries to play the role of friend alone,
her sexual nature makes her behave like Vala when it is un-
fulfilled. With tenderness she wonders how their love for each
other could have ended in sexual warfare, and with a daring
that Thel would never achieve asks whether this death they are
in now is not the slow womb of rebirth. And yet, she wonders
whether she will not once more be forced to play Vala–Eve.

But Christ himself answers her, telling her that she is
redeemed. He shows her a vision of what is to come when Albion
is once more fourfold and reunited with Jerusalem. Blake in his
garden sees this vision, too. It is a curiously negative and wistful vision to end this prophetic book compared with the vision
that ended *The Four Zoas* and that to come in *Jerusalem*. It is a
vision very much in the future tense and one that is seen from
the couch of sickness, rather than an affirmation of fourfold

being already accomplished. But none the less it has a strange
loveliness:

> Then as a moony Ark Ololon descended to Felpham's Vale
> In Clouds of blood . . . with one accord the Starry Night became
> One Man, Jesus the Saviour, wonderful! round his limbs
> The Clouds of Ololon folded as a garment dipped in blood . . .

> And I beheld the Twenty-four Cities of Albion
> Arise upon their Thrones to Judge the Nations of the Earth;
> And the Immortal Four in whom the Twenty-four appear Four-
> fold
> Arose around Albion's body. Jesus wept & walked forth
> From Felpham's Vale clothed in Clouds of blood, to enter into
> Albion's bosom, the bosom of death, & the Four surrounded him
> In the Column of Fire in Felpham's Vale; then to their mouths
> the Four
> Applied their Four Trumpets & them sounded to the Four winds.

> Terror struck in the Vale I stood at that immortal sound.
> My bones trembled, I fell outstretch'd upon the path
> A moment, & my Soul return'd into its mortal state
> To Resurrection & Judgement in the Vegetable Body,
> And my sweet Shadow of Delight stood trembling by my side.

> Immediately the Lark mounted with a loud trill from Felpham's
> Vale,
> And the wild Thyme from Wimbledon's green & impurpled hills.

Part Four

JERUSALEM

'Rejoice, O Jerusalem, and come together all you that love her.' ISAIAH 66

JERUSALEM

'Jerusalem! dissembler Jerusalem!' BLAKE

'I saw the holy city, the new Jerusalem, coming down from
heaven from God, prepared as a bride adorned for her
husband.' APOCRYPHA 21

FREUD tells us that an artist possesses his fantasy while the
madman is possessed by his. In his final prophetic book,
Jerusalem, Blake emerges from a welter of conflicts as the artist
in full control of his material, which is the stuff of fantasy. The
reader leaves behind any doubts he may have had concerning
Blake's sanity, even though there are serious lapses into eccentricity in *Jerusalem*. He leaves behind, too, a feeling that Blake's
poetic power had diminished in direct ratio to the growth of his
claims as seer and mystic. For, despite the many passages in
Jerusalem that are not poetry, and whatever one may feel about
the unwieldy shape of a prophetic book in contrast to the delicacy
of Blake's early lyrics, the reader of *Jerusalem* cannot help
knowing that he is in the presence of a great poet who moves
with tranquillity and ease and power through a difficult element.

It is clear that by the time he wrote *Jerusalem* Blake had
overcome those turbulent doubts of himself and of his vision
caused by his lack of a sympathetic audience. *Jerusalem* is a
triumphant affirmation of his vision that no neglect can repress,
and Blake never found an audience during his lifetime. None
the less, there are in this great dramatic poem, marring it so
much that it is tempting to consider it as a very great failure,
traces of that careless eccentricity which might not have been
allowed to stand had Blake had even one sympathetic ear. It is a
great pity that Blake and Coleridge never met. Coleridge would

187

have understood both Blake's genius and his weakness, and would have been firm in his encouragement of the one and criticism of the other, forcing Blake to see that his interminable lists of private devils and counties and towns add nothing to those breathtaking psychological insights which emerge only when the poetry is dramatic rather than discursive.

I am not sure that it is altogether a fault that because we come to *Jerusalem* with an understanding of the map of the psyche drawn up so painfully in *The Four Zoas*—the schematic explanation of how the fourfold man came to be divided from his emanation—we are immediately able to comprehend a much richer poetic presentation of the same situation in *Jerusalem*. There is much less psychological geometry in *Jerusalem* and much less didactic explanation of the inner worlds of the protagonists. Blake no longer tells us what is happening on each level of Albion's being and the corresponding reaction within Jerusalem, moving the faculties around like distracted chessmen. Rather we are shown from the point of view of the whole person just what each lapse from fourfold humanity looks and feels like. Albion and Jerusalem are always before us as dramatic characters, as they rarely were in the earlier poems. In *The Four Zoas* we were told of the dire events that took place on each level of Albion's consciousness, but for all their insight, the accounts had a sameness that was both boring and confusing. Blake himself seemed bored with the repetition, and didn't bother to change his terms or descriptions for each set of faculties. The inevitable 'shrieks' and 'howls' with which he carelessly obscured an insight into breakdown that was deep but not deep enough, is offensive to the reader. His very attempt to distinguish between each level of being seemed to underscore the undifferentiated quality of his descriptions.

The Four Zoas, despite its very remarkable exploration of the world of breakdown, is not primarily a work of imagination. Its appeal is not the appeal of poetry. It is, rather, a feat of intellect, an ordering of dark irrational areas by sheer will of the mind. It puts Urizen in his place by using Urizen's own weapons with all their power and limitation. It has the fascination of a kind of mental game or geometry. *Jerusalem*, on the other hand, is the work of Los, imagination that is once more

188

the friend of Christ and of the two lovers who are struggling to be reunited. Although it is readily comprehensible to a sympathetic reader who has skipped over *The Four Zoas*, *Jerusalem* is the structure built on the four-square plan laid down in *The Four Zoas*, a myth that even in its bare mosaic outline was dangerously potent. *Jerusalem* adds an entire new dimension to Blake's myth, a dimension which has both a softening and a clarifying effect on his theme, and an infinitely enriching one.

Blake wrote *Jerusalem* after his return to London from Felpham, and after his misunderstanding with Hayley had blown over completely. His preface, 'To the Public', refers to his Felpham years: 'After my three years slumber on the banks of the Ocean, I again display my Giant forms to the Public.' He continues in what is surely a half ironic tone, speaking to his non-existent public: 'My former Giants & Fairies having receiv'd the highest reward possible, the *love* & *friendship* of those with whom to be connected is to be *blessed* . . . Therefore, *dear* Reader, *forgive* what you do not approve, & *love* me for this energetic exertion of my talent.'[1]

Blake promises his readers that 'Heaven, Earth & Hell, henceforth shall live in harmony'. 'The Marriage of Heaven & Hell' proved to be a troubled one, and *The Four Zoas*, which relates these tribulations, is indeed 'The Bible of Hell' that Blake promised his readers. But now there is to be peace and 'a Heaven in Hell's despite'.

In *Jerusalem* Blake has recovered some, though by no means all, of his control over words, a control that largely disappeared after *The Book of Thel*. Even though *Jerusalem* came to him as a vision dictated by the Eternals, Blake tells us that he gave considerable thought to the verse form:

'When this Verse was first dictated to me I consider'd a Monotonous Cadence, like that used by Milton & Shakespeare & all writers of English Blank Verse, derived from the modern bondage of Rhyming, to be a necessary & indispensable part of Verse. But I soon found that in the mouth of a true Orator such monotony was not only awkward, but as much a bondage as rhyme itself. I therefore have produced a variety in every line, both of cadence & number of syllables. Every

---

[1] The italicized words are, significantly, words which Blake tried to erase from the copper plate.

word & every letter is studied & put into its fit place; the terrific numbers are reserved for the terrific parts, the mild & gentle, for the mild & gentle parts, & the prosaic for inferior parts; all are necessary to each other. Poetry Fetter'd, Fetters the Human Race.'

If Blake was aware that not all of *Jerusalem* is poetry, his announcement that for the 'inferior parts' he has used prosaic cadences may be a form of disarmament. However, the theory of poetry he puts forth is a modern and a valid one.

The frontispiece to *Jerusalem* is a full-page drawing of 'Los As he enter'd the Door of Death for Albion's sake'. The illustrations to this prophecy are among the finest Blake ever did, and certainly the colours he used in the 'Stirling' copy are his most magnificent with their strong sombre greeny-blacks and blue-greys and browns, the gold-tipped roses and gold-flecked greens, and the delicate washes of lemon and blue and pink and violet. The title-page is adorned with one of those lovely fantastic illustrations of human figures sweeping on bat-wings, moth-wings, bird-wings, all the wings of nature rather than of angels. As they fly they seem to be watching uneasily and with fear or resignation the struggles of Vala to be freed from her trance-bound cocoon into the beauty of a starry-winged moth. The full title of the poem is: *Jerusalem the Emanation of the Giant Albion.*

Jerusalem begins on a note of strong and quiet joy which rises like a mounting wave in the poem, even in the most troubled passages, and ebbs to the serene and inevitable conclusion. The whole of this first section of the poem is the purest poetry. At the head of the page children float in a midnight-blue sky filled with stars, racing clouds and a crescent moon, as one of Blake's sibylline women crouches brooding and wrapped in a cocoon of smoky-blue veils. Her arms are outstretched prophetically while a naked male figure seated carelessly beside her stares at the sky.

> Of Sleep of Ulro! and of the passage through
> Eternal Death! and of the awaking to Eternal Life.

> This theme calls me in sleep night after night, & ev'ry morn
> Awakes me at sunrise, then I see the Saviour over me
> Spreading his beams of love, & dictating the words of this mild
> song.

Awake! awake O sleeper of the land of shadows, wake! expand!
I am in you and you in me, mutual in love divine:
Fibres of love from man to man thro' Albion's pleasant land.
In all the dark Atlantic vale down from the hills of Surrey
A black water accumulates; return Albion! return!
Thy brethren call thee, and thy fathers, and thy sons,
Thy nurses and thy mothers, thy sisters and thy daughters
Weep at thy soul's disease, and the Divine Vision is darken'd:
Thy Emanation that was wont to play before thy face,
Beaming forth with her daughters into the Divine bosom:
Where hast thou hidden thy Emanation, lovely Jerusalem
From the vision and fruition of the Holy-one?
I am not a God afar off, I am a brother and friend;
Within your bosoms I reside, and you reside in me:
Lo! we are One; forgiving all Evil; Not seeking recompense;
Ye are my members O ye sleepers of Beulah, land of shades!
But the perturbed Man away turns down the valleys dark:
'Phantom of the over heated brain! shadow of immortality!
Seeking to keep my soul a victim to thy Love! which binds
Man, the enemy of man, into deceitful friendships,
Jerusalem is not! her daughters are indefinite:
By demonstration man alone can live, and not by faith.
My mountains are my own, and I will keep them to myself:
The Malvern and the Cheviot, the Wolds, Plinlimmon &
        Snowdon
Are mine: here will I build my Laws of Moral Virtue:
Humanity shall be no more, but war & princedom & victory!'

So spake Albion in jealous fears, hiding his Emanation
Upon the Thames and Medway, rivers of Beulah, dissembling
His jealousy before the throne divine, darkening, cold!

The first thing to notice is that Blake, as the narrator, is semi-
detached from the still-troubled Albion he tells us about. Blake
is no longer so inextricably caught in Albion's illness that the
very telling of it is tortured and incoherent. Blake's tone is clear
and sure and full of the certainty that Albion's joyous release is
near at hand even though Albion himself is without hope. With
love and untroubled pity, in his own voice and in that of Christ,
he summons Albion to awake, seeing him still turning away
down dark and tortuous valleys of the mind, still a victim to the
father-god, calling Christ a phantom of the overheated brain.
Albion still denies love and faith and the peace of Beulah
because he cannot 'prove' them and guarantee their continued

existence before accepting them. Rather than risk happiness, he denies its possibility, negating Jerusalem, his wife, and keeping her as well as himself from fulfilment in love and children and that playing before the face of God which the good life must be. He is full of suspicion and jealousy, keeping his mountains and his rivers to himself, excluding Jerusalem, dissembling and hiding from himself his aching need for her, preventing out of jealous fear the mergence of England and Jerusalem. With absolute simplicity and rightness Blake in a few phrases unites the conception of Albion as a man with that of Albion as a land, avoiding the long lists in which he once equated parts of Albion's anatomy with places in England. In fact, it is remarkable how, in this lucid opening passage, Blake covers much of the difficult ground we have stumbled over in the previous prophetic books. Complex images and states of mind now fall simply and unerringly into place like the bits of glass in a kaleidoscope pattern. There is no need for didactic elaboration and over-insistence, for Blake's images once more convey all they are meant to convey with immediate significance and without in any way stopping the flow of narrative. And this is not merely because the reader has been conditioned by the earlier prophetic books, although this helps. It is more because Blake himself is now in full control of his material, and this gives it a new depth and vitality rather than the stale familiarity one might expect from terms and images to which one had simply grown accustomed.

Blake is one with Albion in a different way than in the earlier poems. As narrator we see him standing clear of Albion's illness, commenting on it. But without any warning his voice can blend with that of Albion, and the reader at once comprehends that Blake's relation to Albion is much closer than that of dispassionate observer. Blake is speaking of Albion s illness, his 'passage through Eternal Death', as the dark stage of a journey that he himself has taken and remembers well, although he is now beckoning to Albion from a point beyond 'the awaking to Eternal Life'. Realizing with thankfulness that Christ has been with him even when he thought himself deserted, Blake tells Albion to lay aside his rational doubts and to have faith even if he can see no reason to do so.

The tone of *Jerusalem* is the tone of Christian tragedy in contradistinction to Greek tragedy, and certainly in contradistinction to that self-pitying egoism which Orc–Albion confuses with tragedy and which is a romantic falsification of both the Christian view and the classical view of man's condition. The keynote of Christian tragedy is one of joy and radiant hope, even lightheartedness, in the face of all weakness and sorrow, rather than the calm recognition and relentless expiation of human error which marks Greek tragedy, or the deliberate wallowing in despair (dis-pair, dividedness), disease (dis-ease in the human condition) and Evil (Eve-ill) which characterizes tragedy of the 'romantic' school. And who is to say which is the more 'realistic' or 'romantic'—Albion's hopeless pessimism which is so aware of death and sin that life seems worthless, or Blake's regained optimism which is *willing* to live and love and even laugh despite a deep understanding of imperfection and suffering, and despite the lure of death?

In the passage I have quoted, as in much of *Jerusalem,* time and space shift and merge just as the voice of the poet blends with that of Christ and Albion, and sometimes with that of Los. This is

> the voice of the Bard!
> Who Present, Past, & Future sees;
> Whose ears have heard
> The Holy Word
> That walk'd among the ancient trees,
> Calling the lapsed Soul . . .

The mists of primeval Druid England swirl about the eighteenth-century husband and wife battling for stability, and the thin wintry sunshine of England often gives way to the rich gold light of Palestine. The black waters that accumulate beneath the moonlight of Albion's land belong to Hecate and all that in us has ever given heed to the magical wonder and mystery of nature. And yet these misted outlines are not confusions of time and space and mood caused by an irresponsible imagination. The cumulative effect of such strange openings in time and space is much more significant than were all the long-winded historical parallels drawn in the earlier prophetic books. Such half-stated effects as these are vitally relevant to the resolution of *Jerusalem*, which is the radiant coming together of the human lovers in God, but is also the transfiguration of all creation, the building of the holy city on England's druid shore, and the triumph of Christ's humanity over the moral laws and mystery of natural religion. Or rather than triumph, it is the absorption of all that is pagan into Christianity, where it is transformed.

Blake knew as much about occult lore and the secret rituals of early mystery religions as anyone of his day. He terms them all druidism and natural religion. Often he describes rites of sacrifice such as occurred in these mystery cults. But by far the most important rite that he describes—and indeed this ritual in its full psychological import is the theme of *Jerusalem*—is the rite that so shocked Herodotus when he found it being practised in one of its forms among the Babylonians. This is the ceremony that anthropological students of today know as the *hieros gamos*, or sacred marriage, and is the feminine equivalent of Orc's ritual consummation with Vala which was suggested in *The Four Zoas*.

Jung and his followers have discovered that in the fantasy world of many disturbed patients there is evidenced the need to re-enact in some imaginative form such archetypal situations as are externalized in many pagan rituals. I think that Blake would welcome this Jungian 'discovery' as confirmation of something he had intuitively known and tried to express.

For Blake is saying in *Jerusalem* that Albion's bride will never be a stable mature wife able to help her husband in his illness unless she first experiences some symbolic re-enactment and resolution of her parent-bound sexual conflicts and guilts. And Blake backs up this theory with detailed description of a rite that can be no other than the *hieros gamos* of the pagan world, although, of course, he does not use this name. Relentlessly he makes Jerusalem go through with it against her will. Sexual conflicts re-enacted within a religious context should be seen as the norm, universal, as something to be passed through ritualistically without guilt. Or at least in pagan religions this was so: a rite such as the sacred marriage was the feminine equivalent of an initiation into manhood. Blake would like to introduce the idea of initiation into Christianity, for it is just at this point that Christianity falls down, averting its eyes from such questions as if they did not exist. Like Orc, too often the pious Christian feels he is compelled to exclude from his religion all that is passionate and 'pagan'.

Over and over Blake tells us that natural religion is simply a religion of parent gods, and must be discouraged in the light of a greater revelation. But he knows, too, that within the individual as within the race, before the door of the heart is ready to open to and embrace the truths of Christ, the Human Son, there is a necessary phase of parental authority. Indeed, the passing need for natural religion and stern parental gods or guides is the condition on which Christianity must rest. 'Man must & will have Some Religion,' Blake knows. And since 'All deities reside in the human breast,' 'All Religions are One' only when 'the true Man is the source, he being the Poetic Genius.' Although Blake roundly scolded the Deists of his day, who, in the face of Christ's revelation, continue to preach natural religion much as it was preached by the Druids, he does not condemn the Druids in their historical time. For their religion was an expression of their poetic genius just as today Christianity is an expression of ours. It is only when Blake finds the moral righteousness and dualism that preaches vengeance for sin, whether he finds it in Druid or Greek or Christian, that he is loud in condemnation. But whatever Blake finds in pagan beliefs that he attributes to the poetic genius, he feels free to absorb into his version of Christianity if he finds need for it.

This is why Blake is able without a word of apology to incorporate into his history of the new Jersusalem, indeed, as its most crucial factor, a ritual of initiation that even Herodotus thought 'wholly shameful'. I will take opportunity here to outline this ritual and to give my own comments on its psychological significance, since I feel that Blake's poem, *Jerusalem*, cannot be understood in all its richness without an awareness of the part that this pagan ritual plays in it.

In certain mystery religions of the ancient world there was the rite known as the Sacred Marriage or *hieros gamos*. In it, a young girl who was betrothed, before she was considered mature enough to be a wife and mother, had to make a ritual dedication of her virginity. She was required to go to the temple, and there, herself representing the earth goddess, have ritual intercourse with a representative of the sky god, sometimes a priest, often a passing stranger.

This marked, of course, an initiation into womanhood, an acceptance of her own amoral passions which she joined to the controlling power of the god, thereby making herself ever after responsible for them, and giving them meaning. All that in her longs to abandon herself to the instinctual forces of nature joins forces rather than ranges itself against all that in her seems to forbid instinct and is afraid of it.

We today who have no such rite tend to divide in guilt and fear the father-god and barbaric mother within, that is, our own passionate earthy nature and the articulating guide of intellect or spirit. Or else we seek in our personal relationships a tortuous and abortive substitute for such a rite. Does not the struggle of romantic lovers to be united with an unattainable ideal rather than a person represent, in truth, this same striving to be united with the other half of oneself?

Only beyond such a ritual possession of the unattainable, a symbolic marriage in which the desire to partake for a moment of the mother-goddess or father-god is once and for all accepted, lies the balance and contentment necessary for human love and worship and creation. Only beyond such a union can we ourselves be born consciously for the first time, fully aware of the worst and the best in us without undue pride or fear.

And this is so because the lonely god within no longer has to condemn, but lives at home in the world, taking to himself and articulating in joy that poignant and beautiful life which can be known only through the earth-flowering earth-returning senses; seeking and finding the exact thought or Word to bound and make meaningful the exquisite impact of creation on his senses.

And as Frazer describes this sacred marriage or prostitution in *The Golden Bough*[1]:

'In Cyprus it appears that before marriage all women were formerly obliged by custom to prostitute themselves to strangers at the sanctuary of the goddess, whether she went by the name of Aphrodite, Astarte, or what not. Similar customs prevailed in many parts of Western Asia. Whatever its motive, the practice was clearly regarded, not as an orgy of lust, but as a solemn religious duty performed in the

[1] *The Golden Bough*, abridged edition, New York, 1942, p. 330.

service of that great Mother Goddess of Western Asia whose name varied, while her type remained constant, from place to place. Thus at Babylon every woman, whether rich or poor, had once in her life to submit to the embraces of a stranger at the temple of Mylitta, that is, of Ishtar or Astarte, and to dedicate to the goddess the wages earned by this sanctified harlotry. The sacred precinct was crowded with women waiting to observe the custom. Some of them had to wait there for years. At Heliopolis or Baalbec in Syria, famous for the imposing grandeur of its ruined temples, the custom of the country required that every maiden should prostitute herself to a stranger at the temple of Astarte, and matrons as well as maids testified their devotion to the goddess in the same manner. The emperor Constantine abolished the custom, destroyed the temple, and built a church in its stead. In Phoenician temples women prostituted themselves for hire in the service of religion, believing that by this conduct they propitiated the goddess and won her favour. "It was a law of the Amorites, that she who was about to marry should sit in fornication seven days by the gate." At Byblus the people shaved their heads in the annual mourning for Adonis. Women who refused to sacrifice their hair had to give themselves up to strangers on a certain day of the festival, and the money which they thus earned was devoted to the goddess. A Greek inscription found at Tralles in Lydia proves that the practice of religious prostitution survived in that country as late as the second century of our era. It records of a certain woman, Aurelia Aemilia by name, not only that she herself served the god in the capacity of a harlot at his express command, but that her mother and other female ancestors had done the same before her; and the publicity of the record, engraved on a marble column which supported a votive offering, shows that no stain attached to such a life and such a parentage. In Armenia the noblest families dedicated their daughters to the service of the goddess Anaitis in her temple of Acilisena, where the damsels acted as prositutes for a long time before they were given in marriage. Nobody scrupled to take one of these girls to wife when her period of service was over.'

It is interesting that Herodotus was altogether shocked by the custom of sacred prostitution, and even Frazer seems to see no reason for it. The emperor Constantine, too, even though, as Bede tells us, he tried whenever possible to absorb pagan customs into Christianity rather than destroy them, was also so dismayed by this ritual that he altogether forbade its practice. Only Blake, forerunner of so much that psychology is only now discovering, saw that such a rite played a vital psychological role in the maturing of a young girl into a responsible woman. Paradoxically, it is the equivalent of such

197

a 'shocking' rite that Albion's young wife, like the race itself, must somehow manage to perform in fantasy before she can go beyond and become Jerusalem, the mature woman who represents the citadel of the soul, rather than Babylon who stands for the earthly fleshly aspect of woman that looms all out of proportion until it is dedicated and so subdued. And to accomplish this, Jerusalem must lay aside all the 'nice' conventional ideas of what Christian piety is, and reach back beyond the vitiated symbols to the human conflict that underlies them, recognizing it as her own, and one that must be perpetually resolved anew.

This pagan act of Jerusalem's can be seen as the culmination and resolution in Blake's mind of the paradox represented on the one hand by Thel's flight from the passions and Ololon's child-wife innocence, and, on the other, by Oothoon's deliberate plucking of the flower of love and Vala's harlot-goddess promiscuity. This act represents, in short, not only the marriage of the two sides of ourselves, but the marriage of heaven and hell. It is an abandonment that may appear shocking, but it is also a necessary dedication.

Jerusalem as Thel, as Oothoon, and as Vala, has been seeking some such rite as this in which to confirm her own integrity, and by giving in to her own instinct, find the values to control it. Until she can achieve such a resolution of her own conflict, she flees in horror from her own passions and from her husband, like the virginal Thel. He, full of the same conflict, begins to feel that his love for her is brutal violence. Or, changing tack, Jerusalem in her state of insecurity can equally well veer from Thel to Vala, becoming irresponsible over-emphasized passion in an intense effort to accept and 'prove' her own femininity of which she is secretly afraid. Then she welcomes the stern condemnation of Albion's spectre which is like a projection of her own 'father-god' conscience. Like Oothoon in the early *Visions of the Daughters of Albion* she may dare, on theory, to pluck the flower of love, but she is made to feel hopelessly guilty about it, both by her husband and by the condemning father within herself.

The trouble with Albion and Jerusalem is that neither of them before marriage achieved that integration of instinct and reason which is maturity and without which a stable relationship between a man and woman is impossible. Each has to use the other as a parent figure in an effort to achieve the inner marriage, and each becomes to the other a stern god or looming goddess instead of a beloved human being. And, unfortunately, each struggles against such a fantasy union instead of once giving in to it. And so the abortive humourless attempts occur again and again. As Orc, Albion's consummation with Vala, the mother goddess in Jerusalem, was an attempt to achieve this *hieros gamos*. But in his case it is the 'masculine' god of reason that he must propitiate, atone to (or become at-one with), so that he can put his own reason in its proper place as a guide to passion rather than an implacable judge of all that is soft and yielding. Just as Jerusalem must for once allow herself to be swept away by the tide of her own instinct in order to find that she must control it by the values of *logos*, so Albion must be in a sense swept away by the rational laws of the father-god in order to find that they must be tempered by all that is warm and shadowy and transient. He yields to a necessary madness, a going out of his mind in order to discover the bounds and limits to the power of reason. She yields to a kind of madness of the body, a shameful abandonment to her femininity in order to discover the limits she must impose on her Vala-instincts. It is paradoxical that when Albion is trying to be all 'masculine' reason, he is neither god-like nor masculine, but a kind of weak hermaphrodite. Similarly, when Jerusalem is behaving like Vala, she is not a goddess nor attractive in a feminine way. It is only when each unites with the factors of the opposite sex that are latent within every man or woman, that Albion, accepting his 'feminine' emotions, becomes truly a man, and Jerusalem, accepting 'masculine' values, becomes for the first time a woman.

I have devoted a good deal of space to outlining the concept of the *hieros gamos*. Although Jerusalem's inner marriage occurs towards the end of Blake's long poem, it is as well to keep the theme clearly in mind, for Blake leads up to it in his own way, and often obscures his effects by passages of inferior verse that add little to his theme. This happens at the end of the fine passage I first quoted in which Albion, refusing the divine vision, turns 'away down the valleys dark'. Blake seems to be

giving the reader a beautiful invocation of Christ, but ends with
a dampening list of devils:

> Trembling I sit day and night, my friends are astonish'd at me,
> Yet they forgive my wanderings. I rest not from my great task!
> To open the Eternal Worlds, to open the immortal Eyes
> Of Man inwards into the Worlds of Thought; into Eternity
> Ever expanding in the Bosom of God, the Human Imagination.
> O Saviour pour upon me thy Spirit of meekness & love!
> Annihilate the Selfhood in me: be thou all my life!
> Guide thou my hand, which trembles exceedingly upon the rock
> of ages,
> While I write of the building of Golgonooza, & of the terrors of
> Entuthon:
> Of Hand & Hyle & Coban, of Kwantock, Peachey, Brereton,
> Slayd & Hutton:
> Of the terrible sons & daughters of Albion, and their Generations.

These devils are never anything more than names: they play no
part whatsoever in the action. Blake soon defaults again from
telling us about the 'Eternal Worlds' that can unfold within
Albion and his bride, to give us further exasperating lists. I
quote a short sample:

> Scofield, Kox, Kotope and Bowen, revolve mightily upon
> The Furnace of Los . . .
> Cambel & Gwendolyn & Conwenna & Cordella & Ignoge.
> And these united into Rahab in the Covering Cherub on
> Euphrates,
> Gwiniverra & Gwinefred & Gonorill & Sabrina beautiful,
> Estrild, Mehetabel & Ragan, lovely Daughters of Albion.

It is maddening to find many passages of this sort obscuring the
flow of fine narrative and poetry in *Jerusalem*. I do not want to
quote any more of such passages, but simply to extricate all
that is clear and moving in the poem from the overgrowth of
Blake's eccentricity.

When Albion turns once again from the divine vision, in her
pain and insecurity at his denial of all she means to him,
Jerusalem is powerless to remain herself. He has annihilated
her psychologically, and 'Jerusalem is scatter'd abroad like a
cloud of smoke thro' non-entity.' She feels that she is negated
and dissipated by his attitude unless she reacts as Vala and

asserts the rights of instinctual nature that he repudiates. And so each of the lovers wanders away from the divine vision in opposite lonely directions, she as Vala, he as his spectral self, 'Abstract Philosophy warring in enmity against Imagination.' Not even the Daughters of Beulah or Los, who is now Albion's staunch friend, can console Jerusalem. Whatever the terrors of Albion's illness, she, too, has her dark night of the soul.

The Starry Wheels revolv'd heavily over the Furnaces,
Drawing Jerusalem in anguish of maternal love,
Eastward, a pillar of a cloud with Vala upon the mountains
Howling in pain, redounding from the arms of Beulah's
    Daughters,
Out from the Furnaces of Los above the head of Los.
A pillar of smoke writhing afar into Non-Entity, redounding
Till the cloud reaches afar outstretch'd among the Starry Wheels
Which revolve heavily in the mighty Void above the Furnaces.

O what avail the loves & tears of Beulah's lovely Daughters!
They hold the Immortal Form in gentle bands & tender tears,
But all within is open'd into the deeps of Entuthon Benython,
A dark and unknown night, indefinite, unmeasurable, without end,
Abstract Philosophy warring in enmity against Imagination
(Which is the Divine Body of the Lord Jesus, blessed for ever),
And there Jerusalem wanders with Vala upon the mountains.
Attracted by the revolutions of those Wheels the Cloud of smoke
Immense, and Jerusalem & Vala weeping in the Cloud
Wander away into the Chaotic Void, lamenting with her
    Shadow
Among the Daughters of Albion, among the Starry Wheels,
Lamenting for her children, for the sons & daughters of Albion.

Imagination, Los in Albion and Enitharmon in Jerusalem, can heal to the same extent it can distort. Christ instead of Orc can be born on the level of imagination if the parent powers are mature instead of irresponsible quarrelling children like Los and Enitharmon. All of Orc's energy is bound in fearful impotent rage against these terrible parents instead of released, like the energy of Christ, in life and love and light. But when Albion and Jerusalem drift apart in this way, no matter how much Los wants to help, he is hindered to the extent that he, too, is divided from his emanation. In pity Los watches Jerusalem and

endures the beratings of the Spectre for the sake of his friend
Albion.[1]

> Los heard her lamentation in the deeps afar! his tears fall
> Incessant before the Furnaces, and his Emanation divided in
>   pain, . . .
> For as his Emanation divided, his Spectre also divided
> In terror of those starry wheels: and the Spectre stood over Los
> Howling in pain: a black'ning Shadow, black'ning dark & opake
> Cursing the terrible Los, bitterly cursing him for his friendship
> To Albion, suggesting murderous thoughts against Albion.

Los stamps his foot in rage at the Spectre's disloyal suggestions,
but he also weeps, terrified that the Spectre will persuade him
to turn against his friend, for 'still the Spectre divided, and still
his pain increas'd'. The Spectre bends all efforts

> To devour Los's Human Perfection; but when he saw that Los
> Was living, panting like a frighted wolf and howling
> He stood over the Immortal, in the solitude and darkness.

But in spite of the Spectre's bullying, Los remains alive and
'answer'd unterrified to the opake blackening Fiend'. The
Spectre is determined to destroy Los's friendship for Albion
which has so far prevented him from gaining complete power
over the Eternal Man. Imagination is the one level on which
Albion can still function, although the Spectre has crippled and
distorted all of his other faculties. Craftily the Spectre tells Los
that Albion is destroying him, and he slyly suggests that Albion
has won Los's emanation away from him and made Los a
laughing-stock. He peppers these lies with grains of truth,
accurately summing up Albion's inner chaos as we have seen
it in the earlier prophetic books.

> And thus the Spectre spoke: Wilt thou still go on to destruction?
> Till thy life is all taken away by this deceitful Friendship?
> He drinks thee up like water, like wine he pours thee
> Into his tuns; thy Daughters are trodden in his vintage.
> He makes thy Sons the trampling of his bulls, they are plow'd
> And harrow'd for his profit! lo! thy stolen Emanation
> Is his garden of pleasure! all the Spectres of his Sons mock
>   thee . . .

[1] An illustration shows Los pausing by his Furnace, listening to the
Spectre.

I saw it indignant, & thou art not moved!
This has divided thee in sunder, and wilt thou still forgive?
Oh! thou seest not what I see, what is done in the Furnaces.
Listen, I will tell thee what is done in moments to thee unknown:
Luvah was cast into the Furnaces of affliction and sealed,
And Vala fed in cruel delight the Furnaces with fire:
Stern Urizen beheld; urg'd by necessity to keep
The evil day afar, and if perchance with iron power
He might avert his own despair: in woe & fear he saw
Vala incircle round the Furnaces where Luvah was clos'd.
With joy she heard his howlings, & forgot he was her Luvah
With whom she liv'd in bliss in times of innocence & youth.

Los replies calmly to this speech, saying that he knows that
Albion has done worse things than these, but that they haven't
yet caused him to withdraw his love and friendship. He advises
the Spectre to befriend Albion, too, despite all of the just causes
for irritation that Albion has given both of them. Only love
and pity and forgiveness can heal Albion's perversity, although
firmness in the right place is also necessary.

Los answer'd: 'Altho' I know not this, I know far worse than this:
I know that Albion hath divided me, and that thou, O my Spectre,
Hast just cause to be irritated: but look stedfastly upon me:
Comfort thyself in my strength; the time will arrive,
When all Albion's injuries shall cease, and when we shall
Embrace him tenfold bright, rising from his tomb in immortality.
They have divided themselves by Wrath, they must be united by
Pity: let us therefore take example & warning, O my Spectre.
O that I could abstain from wrath! O that the Lamb
Of God would look upon me and pity me in my fury . . .
Pity must join together those whom wrath has torn in sunder,
And the Religion of Generation which was meant for the
    destruction
Of Jerusalem, become her covering, till the time of the End.
O holy Generation, Image of regeneration!
O point of mutual forgiveness between Enemies!
Birthplace of the Lamb of God incomprehensible!

Los threatens his Spectre just as in *The Four Zoas* Albion
threatened Urizen, knowing that often the simple pointing out
of the right choice is not enough to defeat the perverse forces
that fight against it. He reinforces his idealistic views of turning
the other cheek and forgiveness with a realistic warning that he

is quite aware of the Spectre's perversity and desire for revenge, and if necessary, will take strong measures to keep him in his place, forgiving *hard*!

> I know thy deceit & thy revenges, and unless thou desist
> I will certainly create an eternal Hell for thee. Listen!
> Be attentive! be obedient! Lo the Furnaces are ready to receive thee!
> I will break thee into shivers, & melt thee in the furnaces of death.
> I will cast thee into forms of abhorrence & torment if thou
> Desist not from thy own will & obey not my stern command:
> I am clos'd up from my children: my Emanation is dividing,
> And thou my Spectre art divided against me. But mark,
> I will compell thee to assist me in my terrible labours: To beat
> These hypocritic Selfhoods on the Anvils of bitter Death.

The Spectre feigns submission to Los's commands, but is waiting his chance to rebel, as Los well knows:

> While Los spoke, the terrible Spectre fell shudd'ring before him
> Watching his time with glowing eyes to leap upon his prey . . .
> He saw that Los was the sole, uncontroll'd Lord of the Furnaces.
> Groaning he kneel'd before Los's iron-shod feet on London Stone,
> Hung'ring & thirsting for Los's life, yet pretending obedience,
> While Los pursu'd his speech in threat'nings loud & fierce.
> Thou art my Pride & Self-righteousness: I have found thee out,
> Thou art reveal'd before me in all thy magnitude & power.
> Thy Uncircumcised pretences to Chastity must be cut in sunder:
> Thy holy wrath & deep deceit cannot avail against me.

The deceits and perversity of the Spectre are Albion's as well since he has turned away from the divine vision and given credence to Urizen's spectral laws. Los laments to see the Eternal Man in this state:

> I saw the limbs form'd for exercise, contemn'd, & the beauty of
> Eternity, look'd upon as deformity, & loveliness as a dry tree.
> I saw disease forming a Body of Death around the Lamb
> Of God, to destroy Jerusalem, & to devour the body of Albion
> By war . . .
> Awkwardness arm'd in steel, folly in a helmet of gold;
> Weakness with horns & talons: ignorance with a rav'ning beak:

Every Emanative joy forbidden as a Crime
And the Emanations buried alive in the earth with pomp of
        religion:
Inspiration deny'd: Genius forbidden by laws of punishment:
I saw terrified . . .

And Los realizes that the abstract 'Reasoning Power' of the
Spectre is 'A murderer of its own Body: but also a murderer of
every Divine Member.'

                    it is the Reasoning Power,
An Abstract objecting power, that Negatives every thing.
This is the Spectre of Man: the Holy Reasoning Power,
And in its Holiness is closed the Abomination of Desolation.

It is in this context that Los speaks the lines that are so often
quoted in Blake's own voice, and can be misleading:

The Spectre weeps, but Los unmov'd by tears or threats remains.
'I must Create a System, or be enslav'd by another Man's.
I will not Reason & Compare: my business is to Create'. . .

And Los cries to the Spectre:

            Obey my voice & never deviate from my will
And I will be merciful to thee: be thou invisible to all
To whom I make thee invisible, but chief to my own Children,
O Spectre of Urthona: Reason not against their dear approach
Nor them obstruct with any temptations of doubt & despair;
O Shame, O strong & mighty Shame I break thy brazen fetters.

Blake speaks so often about the spectral doubt and shame and
despair that destroys the unborn children of Albion and Jerusalem, that it is tempting to wonder whether this is what kept
William and Catherine Blake from having children. Blake of all
poets should have had children to sing his songs to.
    It is the Spectre who speaks of children as the sinful fruit of
passion:

The Spectre answer'd. Art thou not asham'd of those thy Sins
That thou callest thy Children? lo the Law of God commands
That they be offered upon his Altar: O cruelty & torment
For thine are also mine! I have kept silent hitherto,

Concerning my chief delight, but thou hast broken silence.
Now I will speak my mind! Where is my lovely Enitharmon,
O thou my enemy, where is my Great Sin? She is also thine.

'Despair! I am Despair,' cries the Spectre, 'O that I could cease
to be.' He tells Los that he was 'Created to be the great example
of horror & agony', and that 'Prayer is vain. I call'd for compassion: compassion mock'd.' He is the cosmic sufferer, full of
self-hatred and self-pity, enjoying the picture he paints of his
own Lucifer-like wickedness, the 'dark tears' of self-pity
running 'down his shadowy face' as he wails:

> Life lives on my
> Consuming: & the Almighty hath made me his Contrary,
> To be all Evil, all reversed & for ever dead: knowing
> And seeing life, yet living not: how can I then behold
> And not tremble? how can I be beheld & not abhorr'd?

So great is the egotistical pride of the Spectre that in confessing
to his own perversity he does not confess to ordinary dull sinful-
ness, but must be the *most* contemptible, Evil itself, God's
contrary, anti-Christ. He must be all important in his fallen
magnificence. He is incapable of seeing his own behaviour in
perspective. He must be all good or all evil, and always the
centre of the universe.

Only Los within Albion labours selflessly to keep Albion
from being dominated by the Spectre, 'striving with Systems
to deliver Individuals from those Systems'. Within Jerusalem
the Daughters of Beulah watch and respond to Los's labours:

> But when the joy of meeting was exhausted in loving embrace,
> Again they lament. O what shall we do for lovely Jerusalem?
> To protect the Emanations of Albion's mighty ones from
>   cruelty? . . .
>   Scofield is bound in iron armour:
> He is like a mandrake in the earth . . .
> He shoots beneath Jerusalem's walls to undermine her
>   foundations:
> Vala is but thy Shadow, O thou loveliest among Women:
> A shadow animated by thy tears, O mournful Jerusalem!
> Why wilt thou give to her a Body whose life is but a Shade?
> Her joy and love a shade; a shade of sweet repose:
> But animated and vegetated, she is a devouring worm:
> What shall we do for thee, O lovely mild Jerusalem?

Vala, as well as Orc, can be the invisible worm that destroys the sick rose, the feminine shadow that is as ghostly but as inhibiting as the masculine spectre. The reference to the soldier Scofield as a demon who undermines Jerusalem's walls is one more indication that Jerusalem and Catherine Blake are closely identified, for it was Catherine's security in her cottage at Felpham that was undermined when the soldier accused Blake of treason. And the following passage about Lambeth, beloved by Jerusalem, preparing itself for the return of the bride, is another indication that Blake closely linked the adventures of Albion and Jerusalem with events in his own domestic life. For the Blakes, after the disturbing time at Felpham with Hayley and with Scofield, were glad to plan their return to London, although they had arrived at Felpham with high hopes.

> What are these golden builders doing? . . . is that
> Mild Zion's hills, most ancient promontory, near mournful
> Ever weeping Paddington? is that Calvary and Golgotha
> Becoming a building of pity and compassion? Lo!
> The stones are pity, and the bricks, well wrought affections
> Enamel'd with love & kindness, & the tiles engraven gold,
> Labour of merciful hands: the beams & rafters are forgiveness:
> The mortar & cement of the work, tears of honesty: the nails
> And the screws & iron braces, are well wrought blandishments,
> And well contrived words, firm fixing, never forgotten,
> Always comforting the remembrance: the floors, humility:
> The ceilings, devotion: the hearths, thanksgiving.
> Prepare the furniture, O Lambeth, in thy pitying looms;
> The curtains, woven tears & sighs, wrought into lovely forms
> For comfort: there the secret furniture of Jerusalem's chamber
> Is wrought: Lambeth! the Bride, the Lamb's Wife, loveth thee.
> Thou art one with her & knowest not of self in thy supreme joy.
> Go on, builders in hope, tho' Jerusalem wanders far away
> Without the gate of Los: among the dark Satanic wheels.

With this building going on Los does not despair altogether although he is often tempted to do so when he sees Albion, apparently dead, separated from the divine vision and from his emanation. 'God is within, & without: he is even in the depths of Hell!' Los keeps reassuring himself. And as he reaffirms his faith that Albion will live again, the golden builders,

      appear'd within & without incircling on both sides
The Starry Wheels of Albion's Sons with Spaces for Jerusalem,
And for Vala the shadow of Jerusalem, the ever mourning Shade:
On both sides, within & without beaming gloriously.

They build the spiritual fourfold London, every gate and wall of
it foursquare like Jerusalem, even though Jerusalem still
wanders away as Vala, and Albion seems dead. There is an
illustration here of an ugly bejewelled Vala, swooping through
the air, while another drawing shows the recumbent Albion,
dreaming of Jerusalem who appears in a vision of glory beneath
a rainbow that arches over Albion.

Only the side of the city that turns 'toward Eden is walled up,
till time of renovation'. 'The third Gate in every one is clos'd
as with a threefold curtain of ivory & fine linen & ermine', until
Albion's awakening, and his reunion with Jerusalem.

    And every part of the city is fourfold: & every inhabitant,
        fourfold.
    And every pot & vessel & garment & utensil of the houses,
    And every house, fourfold.

But even though this building is going on in Albion's
spiritual capitol, Golgonooza, still all 'around Golgonooza lies
the land of death eternal: a land of pain and misery and despair
and ever brooding melancholy'.

    The Vegetative Universe opens like a flower from Earth's center,
    In which is Eternity. It expands in Stars to the Mundane Shell
    And there it meets Eternity again, both within and without,
    And the abstract Voids between the Stars are the Satanic Wheels.
    There is the Cave; the Rock; the Tree; the Lake of Udan-Adan:
    The Forest, and the Marsh, and the Pits of bitumen deadly:
    The Rocks of solid fire: The Ice valleys: the Plains
    Of burning sand; the rivers, cataract & Lakes of Fire:
    The Islands of the fiery Lakes: the Trees of Malice, Revenge,
    And black Anxiety . . .
    The land of darkness flamed, but no light, & no repose:
    The land of snows, of trembling, & of iron hail incessant:
    The land of earthquakes: and the land of woven labyrinths:
    The land of snares & traps & wheels & pit-falls & dire mills . . .
        above: beneath: on all sides surrounding
    Golgonooza: Los walks round the walls night and day.

He views the City of Golgonooza, & its smaller Cities . . .
Permanent, & not lost nor vanish'd, & every little act,
Word, work & wish, that has existed, all remaining still . . .
Shadowy to those who dwell not in them, meer possibilities:
But to those who enter into them they seem the only substances,
For every thing exists & not one sigh nor smile nor tear,
One hair nor particle of dust, not one can pass away.

Los stands on the wall of the city and sees in panoramic survey all that has happened to Albion, the Eternal Man, since his Fall:

He views the Cherub at the Tree of Life, also the Serpent,
Orc the first born, coil'd in the south: the Dragon Urizen:
Tharmas, the Vegetated Tongue, even the Devouring Tongue:
A threefold region, a false brain: a false heart:
And false bowels . . . Los also views the Four Females:
Ahania, and Enion, and Vala and Enitharmon lovely,
And from them all the lovely beaming Daughters of Albion.
Ahania & Enion & Vala, are three evanescent shades:
Enitharmon is a vegetated mortal Wife of Los:
His Emanation, yet his Wife till the sleep of death is past . . .
And Los beheld the mild Emanation Jerusalem eastward bending
Her revolutions toward the Starry Wheels in maternal anguish,
Like a pale cloud arising from the arms of Beulah's Daughters.

But suddenly Blake breaks in in his own voice:

　　　　　such is my awful Vision.
I see the Four-fold Man, The Humanity in deadly sleep,
And its fallen Emanation. The Spectre & its cruel Shadow.
I see the Past, Present & Future, existing all at once
Before me; O Divine Spirit sustain me on thy wings!
That I may awake Albion from his long & cold repose.
For Bacon & Newton sheath'd in dismal steel their terrors hang
Like iron scourges over Albion. Reasonings like vast Serpents
Infold around my limbs, bruising my minute articulations.

Blake turns his eyes with foreboding on the state of European civilization:

I turn my eyes to the Schools & Universities of Europe,
And there behold the Loom of Locke, whose Woof rages dire
Wash'd by the Water-wheels of Newton: black the cloth
In heavy wreathes folds over every Nation . . .

I see Albion sitting upon his Rock in the first Winter, . . .
The Soldier's Fife, the Harlot's shriek, the Virgin's dismal groan,
The Parent's fear, the Brother's jealousy, the Sister's curse.

One of Blake's long irritating lists follows:

And the Forty Counties of England are thus divided in the Gates:
Of Reuben, Norfolk, Suffolk, Essex. Simeon, Lincoln, York,
Lancashire.
Levi, Middlesex, Kent, Surrey. Judah, Somerset, Glouster,
Wiltshire.

And so on. The long list ends with a remarkable passage that
would seem to indicate that Blake had a theory about eternal
situations that take place in imagination or fantasy, very close
to the modern theory of archetypes:

All things acted on Earth are seen in the bright Sculptures of
Los's Halls, & every Age renews its powers from these Works,
With every pathetic story possible to happen from Hate or
Wayward Love, & every sorrow & distress is carved here,
Every Affinity of Parents, Marriages & Friendships are here
In all their various combinations wrought with wondrous Art,
All that can happen to Man in his pilgrimage of seventy years.

The following passage makes it difficult to tell whether it
was Albion's Spectre or the shocked Emanation who first saw
love as guilty. But none the less, the feeling of guilt born of
Urizen's taboos is soon felt by the Emanation who withdraws
into a religion of chastity and cruel hypocritical love:

The Spectre of the Living pursuing the Emanations of the Dead.
Shudd'ring they flee: they hide in the Druid Temples in cold
chastity:
Subdued by the Spectre of the Living & terrified by the undisguis'd
desire.
For Los said: Tho' my Spectre is divided: as I am a Living Man
I must compell him to obey me wholly: that Enitharmon may not
Be lost: & lest he should devour Enitharmon: Ah me!
Piteous image of my soft desires & loves: O Enitharmon!
I will compell my Spectre to obey: I will restore to thee thy
Children.
No one bruises or starves himself to make himself fit for labour.

Tormented with sweet desire for these beauties of Albion,
They would never love my power if they did not seek to destroy
Enitharmon: Vala would never have sought & loved Albion
If she had not sought to destroy Jerusalem: such is that false
And Generating Love: a pretence of love to destroy love:
Cruel hipocrisy unlike the lovely delusions of Beulah:
And cruel forms, unlike the merciful forms of Beulah's Night.
They know not why they love nor wherefore they sicken & die,
Calling that Holy Love, which is Envy, Revenge & Cruelty,
Which separated the stars from the mountains: the mountains
    from Man,
And left Man, a little grovelling Root, outside of Himself. . . .
So Los in secret with himself communed & Enitharmon heard
In her darkness & was comforted: yet still she divided away
In gnawing pain from Los's bosom in the deadly Night. . . .
Suspended over her he hung: he infolded her in his garments
Of wool: he hid her from the Spectre, in shame & confusion of
Face.

At the foot of Plate 8 there is a drawing of Vala, naked, and harnessed to an enormous green-gold moon which rides a midnight sky, all but a crescent of it in darkness. This drawing, of course, symbolizes Vala's helpless subjugation to the forces of nature. Jerusalem as Vala is like the moon goddess herself, a cold impersonal vehicle through which the passions of nature flow indiscriminately.

There is much in Albion that is violent and primeval, and Vala is that part of Jerusalem which has the capacity for delighted response to his strong passion, which is, of course, a very important part of married love. But if this nature force is not controlled by the individual—the Virgin Mary is often pictured as standing on the crescent moon signifying her control over nature rather than rejection of it—it looms too large and is feared, becoming destructive in its alternate eruption and suppression. Quite possibly Blake was familiar with the Hindu doctrine of the veil of Maya, and his conception of Vala may have been consciously or unconsciously based on this oriental belief. The veil of Maya is the beautiful changing veil of Nature and appearance which in its magical and often delusive moods, can hide or obscure the bare reality of the spirit. If Jerusalem sees herself wholly as Vala as Albion does at times, which is quite natural, then indeed all is lost. For Vala, that

beautiful femaleness that attracts Albion in his moments of
desire is only one side of Jerusalem, and if the moments of
passion result in children, it must be that 'Vala produc'd the
Bodies, Jerusalem gave the Souls'. An illustration portrays a
tormented Albion and Jerusalem lying apart, but from each
rushes a child, and the children embrace between the lovers. If
moments of desire are regarded simply as physical passion, the
meaning of love is lost. As Vala, Jerusalem seems to be the
direct contrary of Albion, and represents all that tries to lure
him away from the preoccupations of the soul, rather than a
whole person who is a companion of the spirit as well as of the
body. Instead of Albion's counterpart she seems 'Babylon . . .
the Goddess Virgin-Mother' and he withdraws from her and
becomes the condemning priest of Urizen, 'Jealous of Jerusalem's children, asham'd of her little-ones', and of joyous
family life. In terrified revulsion he sees her as his 'Great Sin'
and cries:

> Cast! Cast ye Jerusalem forth! The Shadow of delusions!
> The Harlot daughter! Mother of pity and dishonourable
>   forgiveness!
> Our Father Albion's sin and shame! . . . No more the sinful
>   delights
> Of age and youth, and boy and girl, and animal and herb,
> And river and mountain, and city and village, and house & family,
> Beneath the Oak & Palm, beneath the Vine and Fig-tree,
> In self-denial! . . . sinful Jerusalem. To build
> Babylon the City of Vala, the Goddess Virgin-Mother.
> She is our Mother! Nature! Jerusalem is our Harlot-Sister
> Return'd with Children of pollution to defile our House
> With Sin and Shame. Cast! Cast her into the Potter's field.
> Her little ones, she must slay upon our Altars: and her aged
> Parents must be carried into captivity, to redeem her Soul,
> To be for a Shame & a Curse, and to be our Slaves for ever.

Such are the sick imaginings and conflicts raging in Albion's
mind as he lies motionless in apparent sleep. Blake moves into
magnificent poetry as he gives us a glimpse of the fallen
Albion, man and country, in which the many levels of meaning
compress effortlessly into a rich whole rather than spread themselves out in thin prosy analysis.

In a dark & unknown Night,
Outstretch'd his Giant beauty on the ground in pain & tears.
His Children exil'd from his breast, pass to and fro before him,
His birds are silent on his hills, flocks die beneath his branches,
His tents are fall'n: his trumpets, and the sweet sound of his harp,
Are silent on his clouded hills, that belch forth storms & fire.
His milk of Cows & honey of Bees, & fruit of golden harvest,
Is gather'd in the scorching heat, & in the driving rain:
Where once he sat he weary walks in misery and pain,
His Giant beauty and perfection fallen into dust:
Till from within his wither'd breast grown narrow with his woes,
The corn is turn'd to thistles & the apples into poison:
The birds of song to murderous crows, his joys to bitter groans:
The voices of children in his tents to cries of helpless infants:
And self-exiled from the face of light & shine of morning.
In the dark world, a narrow house! he wanders up and down,
Seeking for rest and finding none! and hidden far within,
His Eon weeping in the cold and desolated Earth.

A drawing shows Albion stretched out in sickness in a sunset landscape, mourning children leaving him. It is perhaps unnecessary to point out how this passage with its unmistakably Blakean images and biblical cadence succeeds in conveying within a small and luminous space almost all of those insights about life-hatred and its poisoning effect that Blake has given us elsewhere in long-winded and clumsy explanation. There is no clumsiness in this passage. Here, as in the *Songs*, Blake is complete master of his material. His touch on it is quiet and radiant. He gives us tragedy, not with a heavy hand, but in all its delicate searing light and shade, from some point beyond tragedy where he understands it clearly and calmly. Although he insists less, he understands immeasurably more than he did in the earlier poems where he was trying desperately to extricate himself from anguish by cut-and-dried precepts. He has even learned a kind of hands-off policy in treating Albion's illness, instead of rushing in as once he might have, shouting 'You've got to be fourfold. I'll tell you how'. Now he simply presents the illness, recognizing that it must run its course and the very worst happen before healing begins. But the feeling of hope is much stronger. Although he does not say it, even at this blackest point he is sure and we are sure that healing will come and Albion and Jerusalem will be reunited.

The piling up of images in this passage to suggest Albion's overflowing natural abundance and its simultaneous poisoning by Albion's darkening soul, is masterful. We move, the horizon narrowing inexorably, from the golden harvest gathered in 'scorching heat' and 'driving rain', to knowledge that it is not nature that is being unfriendly, but Albion's very soul that has withered in spectral self-hatred. He has shut himself away from the shining morning into a narrow windowless house. The final image, conveyed largely by suggestion, is narrower yet. It is an image of two tombs, that of Albion in his self-inflicted living death, and that of Jerusalem in the desolate earth to which he has doomed her. Psychologically speaking, he has succeeded in killing both himself and his emanation, which is what he wants, or rather, what his Spectre wants. Like Hamlet, like Ahab in *Moby Dick*, and like the hero of Henry James' story, *The Beast in the Jungle*, Albion is so much the artist of round-about self-suicide, that he wills to destroy not only himself but all that could conceivably give him pleasure. He hates 'the low, enjoying power', in himself and in others.

And here, with Albion and Jerusalem at their lowest ebb, begins the story proper of *Jerusalem*. This is the point where Jerusalem, out of her tomb in the 'cold and desolated earth', begins to flower into herself. It is with her as it is with the seed that must fall into the earth and die before it can live.

But until then both she, as Vala, and he, as the Spectre, are 'Raging against their Human natures'. Any attempt, as in the following passage, to come together in love is too intense and open to the reaction of shame, because, although the desire provoked by Vala is very strong, it is no stronger than the corresponding taboos of the Spectre. It is significant that the rising tide of Albion's desire for his wife is presided over by a stormy moon. Radiant soft moonlight is the light of Beulah, but the intense troubling magical moon belongs more to Vala and the goddess of Nature. Plate 24 shows a crescent moon riding a wave like a boat or cradle, a strange feline figure outstretched in its curve. The following passage, in its poignant picture of desire, clouded and confused as it is by over-intensity and false shame, is one of the most tender and most fully realized in the poem: it marks a noble attempt to recover Beulah:

Albion's Circumference was clos'd: his center began dark'ning
Into the Night of Beulah, and the Moon of Beulah rose
Clouded with storms: Los, his strong Guard, walk'd beneath the
    Moon
And Albion fled inward among the currents of his rivers.

He found Jerusalem upon the River of his City soft repos'd
In the arms of Vala, assimilating in one with Vala,
The Lilly of Havilah: and they sang soft thro' Lambeth's vales,
In a sweet moony night & silence that they had created,
With a blue sky spread over with wings and a mild moon,
Dividing & uniting into many female forms: Jerusalem
Trembling; then in one comingling in eternal tears,
Sighing to melt his Giant beauty on the moony river.
But when they saw Albion fall'n, upon mild Lambeth's vale:
Astonish'd, Terrified, they hover'd over his Giant limbs.
Then thus Jerusalem spoke, while Vala wove the veil of tears:

Weeping in pleadings of Love, in the web of despair.
Wherefore hast thou shut me into the winter of human life,
And clos'd up the sweet regions of youth and virgin innocence,
Where we live, forgetting error, not pondering on evil,
Among my lambs & brooks of water, among my warbling birds:
Where we delight in innocence before the face of the Lamb,
Going in and out before him in his love and sweet affection.

Vala replied weeping & trembling, hiding in her veil.

When winter rends the hungry family and the snow falls
Upon the ways of men hiding the paths of man and beast,
Then mourns the wanderer: then he repents his wanderings & eyes
The distant forest: then the slave groans in the dungeon of stone,
The captive in the mill of the stranger, sold for scanty hire.
They view their former life: they number moments over and over:
Stringing them on their remembrance as on a thread of sorrow.
Thou art my sister and my daughter: thy shame is mine also:
Ask me not of my griefs! thou knowest all my griefs.

Jerusalem answer'd with soft tears over the valleys.

O Vala what is Sin? that thou shudderest and weepest
At sight of thy once lov'd Jerusalem! What is Sin but a little
Error & fault that is soon forgiven; but mercy is not a Sin
Nor pity nor love nor kind forgiveness: O! if I have sinned
Forgive & pity me! O! unfold thy Veil in mercy and love!

Slay not my little ones, beloved Virgin Daughter of Babylon,
Slay not my infant loves & graces, beautiful daughter of Moab.
I cannot put off the human form, I strive but strive in vain.
When Albion rent thy beautiful net of gold and silver twine,
Thou hadst woven it with art, thou hadst caught me in the bands

Of love: thou refusedst to let me go: Albion beheld thy beauty,
Beautiful thro' our Love's comeliness, beautiful thro' pity.
The Veil shone with thy brightness in the eyes of Albion,
Because it inclos'd pity & love; because we lov'd one another.
Albion lov'd thee: he rent thy Veil: he embraced thee: he lov'd
    thee!
Astonish'd at his beauty & perfection, thou forgavest his furious
    love:
I redounded from Albion's bosom in my virgin loveliness:
The Lamb of God receiv'd me in his arms, he smil'd upon us:
He made me his Bride & Wife: he gave thee to Albion.
Then was a time of love: O why is it passed away!

Jerusalem is looking back to the beginning of their love before
guilt spoiled everything. This is the way it must be again, but
only after each has resolved their inner conflicts can it come to
pass that neither will feel ashamed of love, and she will, though
a wife, redound 'from Albion's bosom in my virgin loveliness'
after each embrace. Only after her inner marriage of the parents
within, who war just as passion and reason war, will she again
be Albion's bride and also the Bride of Christ, the Son, who is in
Albion, and who once watched their love with approval rather
than the condemnation of Urizen. Jerusalem, in an effort to
redeem Vala, tells Vala that Christ 'gave thee to Albion' for
his enjoyment: Christ does not frown on human passion as so
many think.

With magnificent insight Blake sees that Albion plays father
to Jerusalem's immaturity just as she plays mother to his bound
child, Orc. But although she, as Vala, in an effort to achieve
her inner marriage, is here uniting with the father-god in
Albion, Albion is still sunk in his spectral shame. This will
continue until Jerusalem leaves the realms of fantasy and sees
her marriage in its true light. Now, in a titanic struggle to
accomplish her fantasy marriage, Jerusalem even addresses her
husband as 'Albion! my Father Albion!' Filled with doubt and
shame, he cries to her:

O Vala! O Jerusalem! do you delight in my groans!
You O lovely forms, you have prepared my death-cup:
The disease of Shame covers me from head to feet: I have no
 hope.
Every boil upon my body is a separate & deadly Sin.
Doubt first assail'd me, then Shame took possession of me:
Shame divides Families, Shame hath divided Albion in sunder:

First fled my Sons, & then my Daughters, then my wild
 Animations,
My Cattle next, last ev'n the Dog of my Gate; the Forests fled,
The Corn-fields, & the breathing Gardens outside separated,
The Sea: the Stars: the Sun: the Moon: driv'n forth by my
 disease.
All is Eternal Death unless you can weave a chaste
Body over an unchaste Mind! Vala! O that thou wert pure!
That the deep wound of Sin might be clos'd up with the Needle,
And with the Loom . . .
Jerusalem! dissembler Jerusalem! I look into thy bosom:
I discover thy secret places. Cordella! I behold
Thee whom I thought pure as the heavens in innocence & fear:
Thy Tabernacle taken down, thy secret Cherubim disclosed.
Art thou broken? Ah me, Sabrina, running by my side:
In childhood what wert thou? unutterable anguish! Conwenna!
Thy cradled infancy is most piteous. O hide, O hide!
Their secret gardens were made paths to the traveller:
I knew not of their secret loves with those I hated most,
Nor that their every thought was Sin & secret appetite.

This passage is powerful and moving up to here. Even the
strange names—Cordella! Conwenna!—add something to
Albion's tortured and pathetic mistrust of his wife's virtue, and
his wrung cry, full of an unwilling tenderness: 'Jerusalem! dissembler Jerusalem!' Albion half knows that his suspicions and
jealousies are unfounded, and again his tenderness emerges in
his wonderings about what she was like as a child, leaping and
running in play, or as a helpless baby. But again comes the
suspicion that 'the traveller' has had free access to those secret
gardens and places that only a husband should know, and that
the traveller was one of 'those I hated most'. The passage continues with an annoying list of devils, headed, perhaps significantly in this context of the 'traveller', by 'Hyle', a faintly
disguised anagram for 'Hayley'.

Albion, thinking for once of the unborn children that he has murdered by his attitude, cries:

> I hear my Children's voices,
> I see their piteous faces gleam out upon the cruel winds . . .
> I see them distant from my bosom scourg'd along the roads,
> Then lost in clouds; I hear their tender voices! clouds divide:
> I see them die beneath the whips of the Captains . . .
> Are the Dead cruel? are those who are infolded in moral Law
> Revengeful? O that Death & Annihilation were the same!

The following passage is fine dramatic poetry which speaks for itself. Vala and Jerusalem are now on the same side, and at one with the moon goddess, who, controlled by love and pity, presides over Beulah just as uncontrolled she rules Vala's pagan magical world. The moon of Beulah is now rising despite Albion's doubts and fears. Both Vala and Jerusalem understand that they must stand together, even though Jerusalem is still half in the fantasy world and has not yet married Vala, the mother within herself, to the father-god of her conscience.

> Then Vala answer'd spreading her scarlet Veil over Albion.
> Albion thy fear has made me tremble; thy terrors have surrounded
> me . . .
> All Love is lost! terror succeeds & Hatred instead of Love,
> And stern demands of Right & Duty instead of Liberty.
> Once thou wast to me the loveliest Son of heaven: but now
> Where shall I hide from thy dread countenance & searching eyes?
> I have looked into the secret Soul of him I loved
> And in the dark recesses found Sin & can never return.[1]

> Albion again utter'd his voice beneath the silent Moon.

> I brought Love into light of day to pride in chaste beauty,
> I brought Love into light & fancied Innocence is no more.

> Then spoke Jerusalem. O Albion! my Father Albion!
> Why wilt thou number every little fibre of my Soul,
> Spreading them out before the Sun like stalks of flax to dry?
> The Infant Joy is beautiful, but its anatomy
> Horrible, ghast & deadly: nought shalt thou find in it
> But dark despair & everlasting brooding melancholy.[1]

[1] These lines are the same as those spoken by Enion and Tharmas in *The Four Zoas.*

Then Albion turn'd his face toward Jerusalem & spoke.

Hide thou, Jerusalem, in impalpable voidness, not to be
Touch'd by the hand nor seen with the eye: O Jerusalem,
Would thou wert not & that thy place might never be found.
But come, O Vala, with knife & cup: drain my blood
To the last drop: then hide me in thy Scarlet Tabernacle.
For I see Luvah whom I slew, I behold him in my Spectre,
As I behold Jerusalem in thee, O Vala dark and cold.

Jerusalem then stretch'd her hand toward the Moon & spoke.

Why should Punishment Weave the Veil with Iron Wheels of War,
When Forgiveness might it Weave with Wings of Cherubim?

Jerusalem asks Albion why they must punish and annihilate
each other, when it could all be so lovely as it has been and as
it should be, if only forgiveness could reign instead of fear and
vengeance. Some indication is given of the extent of Albion's
psychological destructiveness in his words: 'O Jerusalem,
Would thou wert not & that thy place might never be found.'
So terrible are his spectral taboos that he feels that in loving her
he is being destroyed, and would rather destroy her instead, or
at least pretend she does not exist. And yet in his reply to
Jerusalem's question as to why they cannot forgive instead of
punish, there is a point. He says that forgiveness is impossible
because they are not in a true relation of husband and wife, but
an incestuous one of parent and child. It is this false relationship
that each tries to punish the other for. Blake's remarkable
understanding of the realm of archetypes is apparent in these
lines:

Loud groan'd Albion from mountain to mountain & replied.

Jerusalem! Jerusalem! deluding shadow of Albion!
Daughter of my phantasy! unlawful pleasure! Albion's curse!
I came here with intention to annihilate thee; But
My soul is melted away, inwoven within the Veil.
Hast thou again knitted the Veil of Vala, which I for thee
Pitying rent in ancient times. I see it whole and more
Perfect and shining with beauty! But thou! O wretched Father!

Jerusalem reply'd, like a voice heard from a sepulcher:
Father! once piteous! Is Pity a Sin? Embalm'd in Vala's bosom
In an Eternal Death for Albion's sake, our best beloved.

219

Thou art my Father & my Brother: Why hast thou hidden me,
Remote from the divine Vision, my Lord & Saviour?
Trembling stood Albion at her words in jealous dark despair,

He felt that Love and Pity are the same; a soft repose:
Inward complacency of Soul: a Self-annihilation.

I have err'd! I am ashamed! and will never return more:
I have taught my children sacrifices of cruelty: what shall I
    answer?
I will hide it from Eternals! I will give myself for my Children!
Which way soever I turn, I behold Humanity and Pity!

He recoil'd: he rushed outwards: he bore the Veil whole away.
His fires redound from his Dragon Altars in Errors returning,
He drew the Veil of Moral Virtue, woven for Cruel Laws,
And cast it into the Atlantic Deep . . . Albion sunk
Down in pallid languor: These were his last Words . . .
But thou, deluding Image, by whom imbu'd the Veil I rent,
Lo here is Vala's Veil whole, for a Law, a Terror & a Curse!
And therefore God takes vengeance on me: from my clay-cold
    bosom
My children wander, trembling victims of his Moral Justice.
His snows fall on me and cover me, while in the Veil I fold
My dying limbs. Therefore O Manhood, if thou art aught
But a meer Phantasy, hear dying Albion's Curse!

Albion, as he almost visibly disintegrates before our eyes,
curses Christ and all life because he himself has lost the will to
live, the will to manhood. Almost immediately he regrets his
curse, but plaintively asks what the meaning of life can possibly
be when it is so filled with betrayal and destruction. The
following passage brings to mind the curious legend which persists, although it may well be apocryphal, of the visitor who
found William and Catherine Blake wandering naked in their
garden which was supposed to be the Garden of Eden. The
following lines are, at any rate, a poignant description of a
frank joy in human love and beauty that is slowly turned to
shame and dividedness:

What have I said? What have I done? O all-powerful Human
    Words!
You recoil back upon me in the blood of the Lamb slain in his
    Children:

Two bleeding Contraries, equally true, are his Witnesses
    against me.
We reared mighty Stones: we danced naked around them:
Thinking to bring Love into light of day, to Jerusalem's shame:
Displaying our Giant limbs to all the winds of heaven: sudden
Shame seiz'd us, we could not look on one another for abhorrence:
    the Blue
Of our Immortal Veins & all their Hosts fled from our Limbs
And wander'd distant in a dismal Night clouded & dark:
The Sun fled from the Briton's forehead: the Moon from his
    mighty loins.

In anguish Albion asks what it all means:

O what is Life & what is Man? O what is Death? Wherefore
Are you my Children, natives in the Grave to where I go?
Or are you born to feed the hungry ravenings of Destruction,
To be the sport of Accident! to waste in Wrath & Love, a weary
Life, in brooding cares & anxious labours, that prove but chaff?
O Jerusalem, Jerusalem, I have forsaken thy Courts,
Thy Pillars of ivory & gold; thy Curtains of silk & fine
Linen: the Pavements of precious stones: thy Walls of pearl
And gold, the Gates of Thanksgiving, thy Windows of Praise: . . .
Stretching their Wings sublime over the Little-ones of Albion!
O Human Imagination, O Divine Body I have crucified,
I have turned my back upon thee into the Wastes of Moral Law:
There Babylon is builded in the Waste, founded in Human
    desolation.
O Babylon, thy Watchman stands over thee in the night,
Thy severe Judge all the day long prove thee, O Babylon,
With provings of destruction, with giving thee thy heart's desire.
But Albion is cast forth to the Potter, his children to the Builders,
To build Babylon because they have forsaken Jerusalem.

The destructive testings and severe judgements of Albion's
spectre as he hovers over Jerusalem, eager to prove her Babylon,
are all indicated in this passage. The note of insanity is struck,
although if Albion only knew it he is insane only in the sense
that he is crazy about his wife, and is afraid to admit it. We are
shown, none the less, along with Albion's neurotic perversity, the
very real regret of the true Albion for what he is doing to
Jerusalem, turning her into what he condemns because he is
afraid of loving her too much as she is. The two things exist
side by side: fear of abundant love and poisoned waste.

The Walls of Babylon are Souls of Men: her Gates the Groans
Of Nations: her Towers are the Miseries of once happy Families.
Her Streets are paved with Destruction, her Houses built with
    Death.
Her Palaces with Hell & the Grave; her Synagogues with
    Torments
Of ever-hardening Despair, squar'd & polish'd with cruel skill.
Yet thou wast lovely as the summer cloud upon my hills
When Jerusalem was thy heart's desire in time of youth & love . . .
Albion cover'd the whole Earth . . .
The footsteps of the Lamb of God were there: but now no more,
No more shall I behold him, he is clos'd in Luvah's Sepulcher.
Yet why these smitings of Luvah, the gentlest mildest Zoa?
If God was Merciful this could not be: O Lamb of God,
Thou art a delusion and Jerusalem is my Sin!

And just as Albion cries that Christ is a delusion, he sees Christ:

Dost thou appear before me who liest dead in Luvah's Sepulcher?
Dost thou forgive me? thou who wast Dead & art Alive?
Look not so merciful upon me, O thou Slain Lamb of God!
I die! I die in thy arms tho' Hope is banish'd from me.

With Albion's magnificent Faustian cry as he dies a spiritual
death, sustained by the arms of Christ whom he has just rejected,
the action of the first chapter of *Jerusalem* comes to a close.

And there was heard a great lamenting in Beulah: all the Regions
Of Beulah were moved as the tender bowels are moved: & they
    said: . . .
Descend, O Lamb of God, & take away the imputation of Sin.

A beautiful illustration, the bodies grouped roughly in the form
of a Celtic Cross, shows two Daughters of Beulah ministering
to the tortured Albion, who kneels, head and body thrown back,
and stars and moon and sun tattooed on his body. Above, her
arms outstretched protectively is a third Daughter of Beulah
with serene grave countenance.

Chapter 2 begins with the prose exhortation that Blake
calls: 'To the Jews'. Its argument is calculated to disarm readers
who might question Blake's statement that England and Jerusalem were once united, and can be again. An illustration shows
a fiery figure appearing to a timid observer, and the legend:
'Jerusalem is named Liberty'.

'Jerusalem the Emanation of the Giant Albion! Can it be? Is it a Truth that the Learned have explored? Was Britain the Primitive Seat of the Patriarchal Religion? If it is true, my title-page is also True, that Jerusalem was & is the Emanation of the Giant Albion. It is True, and cannot be controverted. Ye are united, O ye Inhabitants of Earth, in One Religion: the Religion of Jesus: the most Ancient, the Eternal & the Everlasting Gospel. The Wicked will turn it to Wickedness, the Righteous to Righteousness. Amen! Huzza! Selah!

'All things Begin & End in Albion's Ancient Druid Rocky Shore. . . . You have a tradition, that Man anciently contain'd in his mighty limbs all things in Heaven & Earth: this you received from the Druids. But now the Starry Heavens are fled from the mighty limbs of Albion.'

The first five stanzas, which I quote, of the lyric which follows this prose manifesto, are a fulfilment of the prophecy in the famous lyric from *Milton* known as 'Jerusalem'. Albion and Jerusalem are one:

> The fields from Islington to Marybone,
> To Primrose Hill and Saint John's Wood,
> Were builded over with pillars of gold,
> And there Jerusalem's pillars stood.
>
> Her little-ones ran on the fields,
> The Lamb of God among them seen,
> And fair Jerusalem his Bride,
> Among the little meadows green.
>
> Pancrass & Kentish-town repose
> Among her golden pillars high:
> Among her golden arches which
> Shine upon the starry sky.
>
> The Jew's-harp-house & the Green Man,
> The Ponds where Boys to bathe delight,
> The fields of Cows by Willan's farm,
> Shine in Jerusalem's pleasant sight.
>
> She walks upon our meadows green:
> The Lamb of God walks by her side:
> And every English Child is seen,
> Children of Jesus & his Bride.

Blake should have ended the lyric here, for this far it is lovely and a unity. But he tries to give in addition a complicated and technical resumé of the lapses, psychological, spiritual, and historical, which have separated Albion and Jerusalem. He uses mythological names and ideas which seem top-heavy and out of place in the fragile form of a lyric. After this summary there are seven stanzas about the Spectre which are also complete and can stand alone:

> He wither'd up sweet Zion's Hill,
> From every Nation of the Earth;
> He wither'd up Jerusalem's Gates,
> And in a dark Land gave her birth.
>
> He wither'd up the Human Form,
> By laws of sacrifice for sin,
> Till it became a Mortal Worm;
> But O! translucent all within.
>
> The Divine Vision still was seen,
> Still was the Human Form Divine,
> Weeping in weak & mortal clay,
> O Jesus, still the Form was thine.
>
> And thine the Human Face, & thine
> The Human Hands & Feet & Breath,
> Entering thro' the Gates of Birth,
> And passing thro' the Gates of Death.
>
> And O thou Lamb of God whom I
> Slew in my dark self-righteous pride,
> Art thou return'd to Albion's Land?
> And is Jerusalem thy Bride?
>
> Come to my arms & never more
> Depart; but dwell for ever here:
> Create my Spirit to thy Love:
> Subdue my Spectre to thy Fear.
>
> Spectre of Albion! warlike Fiend!
> In clouds of blood & ruin roll'd:
> I here reclaim thee as my own,
> My Self-hood! Satan! arm'd in gold.

Chapter 2 opens with Albion again completely at the mercy of his Spectre. He has become altogether the condemning father of Jerusalem, her 'every Act a Crime, and Albion the punisher & judge'.

And Albion spoke from his secret seat and said:
All these ornaments are crimes, they are made by the labours
Of loves, of unnatural consanguinities and friendships,
Horrid to think of when enquired deeply into; and all
These hills & valleys are accursed witnesses of Sin.

Albion is now determined 'In Shame & Jealousy to annihilate Jerusalem' rather than admit his passionate love for her which his Spectre condemns as soft and idolatrous and sinful, an obsession of two imperfect human beings for one another that offends the perfectionist god of Reason. Jerusalem represents as Vala all that Albion fears in himself—violent and destructive emotions that prevent the clear omnipotence of reason. Hence, he wants to cut himself off from her, annihilate her and that which she represents in himself. But with this alienation he also destroys all that Jerusalem in her positive aspect stands for, in himself as well as in her own right—the ability to feel and believe and be loyal, to apply imagination and love and faith to a particular limited human situation and work for it because it seems good, although by no means perfect or absolute. It never occurs to Albion that the law of 'Be ye perfect' is fulfilled when two weak beings struggle to fulfil an ideal of love that entails forgiveness of imperfection and sin over and over again. Albion as the Spectre rejects in himself all 'feminine' softness and emotion, and he must condemn it in Jerusalem, too. Jerusalem as Vala will have nothing to do with 'masculine' law and control. Neither realizes that they are making any relationship impossible, yet each clamours for a guaranteed perfect partner. Just as the emotional side of a man is his link to woman, her spiritual side is her connective in dealing with man. So, too, man's emanation is his connective in dealing with mankind in general, for it is able to bridge gaps that law and sweet reasonableness alone cannot:

Man is adjoin'd to Man by his Emanative portion,
Who is Jerusalem in every individual Man: and her
Shadow is Vala, builded by the Reasoning power in Man.
O search & see; turn your eyes inward; open, O thou World
Of Love & Harmony in Man: expand thy ever lovely Gates.

There can be no love and harmony while Albion is trying to annihilate Jerusalem just as he is trying to cut off his own emotional nature. This is psychological castration. Nor can there be any peace while Jerusalem, as Vala, even though she means no harm, is unable to explain her position to Albion, having annihilated the bridge of reasonableness. For she has cut herself off from her own spiritual conscience and suffers Albion's persecution more or less inarticulately, feeling guilty.

One often wishes that Jerusalem, instead of automatically behaving like Vala simply because it is expected and easiest, would for once stand up to Albion when he thinks up new reasons to condemn her. And *then*, if he persists in his ridiculous accusations, go away rather than be destroyed by him. He might even find out that he doesn't like it much without her. As things are, Albion simply keeps her around to torture: he would rather die than admit that she is necessary for his well-being, and that it is natural and good for men and women to live together. He criticizes Jerusalem and will not claim her as his wife, but neither will he let her go: that would be like giving up a part of himself. He does his best to drive her away and get rid of her and his own feeling for her, but he never really frees her. And so he tortures her and himself, plotting 'In Shame & Jealousy to destroy Jerusalem'. And she, afraid of losing him, puts up with this treatment until she reaches exploding point and then Vala erupts in irrational ways. It would be far better if, in comparative calm and at some judicious moment, she deliberately hurled a flower pot or plate against the wall, knowing that her anger is justified, and that she can control it. As it is, she suppresses her anger, afraid that one outburst will prove Albion right in saying that she always behaves like Vala.

The more deadly and intense and gloomy this Thurberesque warfare between men and women becomes, the more ludicrous and unnecessary it appears to the outsider except as a manifestation of Albion's sick and perverse mind. In itself the problem is nothing that should loom so large except to the immature mind. Blake, in exploring the forest of married love, makes his lovers stick on a problem that is usually simply material for a few cat-and-dog squabbles and yields most gracefully to a humorous touch, being no more than the inescapable differences, in emphasis rather than in kind, in the psychology of men and women. These are differences that neither can help, and without which life would be less interesting, but which each can intensify to war level by refusing to put out the connective bridges that each possesses. Albion refuses to be 'loving' so Jerusalem refuses to be 'logical'. It is as simple as that, and as difficult. And its difficult and serious side brings us back once more to the concept of the *hieros gamos* that must take place in the psychology of each, before either is able and willing to put out a connective bridge. Each must meet the other half-way, so that he, in offering emotional understanding, is a brother and friend as well as a lover, and she, in being reasonable, proves a sister and companion as well as mistress and wife. However, Albion in his present state is capable of using even her most reasonable behaviour against her, saying that she is like a sister or mother or daughter and therefore he mustn't love her as a wife, just as at other moments he desires her so much that he says she is too much like a harlot in tempting him.

Only when the necessary bridges have been lowered and crossed can this warfare between the sexes be rendered harmless and channelled into the mock warfare and mischievous make-believe which alone can make marriage safe yet keep it from being dull. The emotional conflicts that fill Albion and Jerusalem with dire foreboding and gloom should, in a sound marriage, be discharged in that half serious, half playful, and altogether charming expression of fantasy needs that always exist no matter how mature the man or woman: that of a man for a mother, a mistress, an ideal, an intelligent companion, and sometimes a daughter; and that of a woman for a father, an ardent lover, someone to tell things to, a god, and a son. And last but not least, is the desire of a man for a wife and a woman for a husband, and of both for children.

But again and again the Spectre prevents Albion from admiring such an interesting human lot, telling him that it is lowly and shameful:

I am your Rational Power, O Albion, & that Human Form
You call Divine, is but a Worm Seventy inches long
That creeps forth in a night & is dried in the morning sun.

Hearing this, 'Albion's Emanation which he had hidden in Jealousy' appears, 'deflecting back to Albion in Sexual Reasoning, Hermaphroditic'. As Vala she speaks to Albion:

> I was a City & a Temple built by Albion's Children!
> I was a Garden planted with beauty, I allured on hill & valley
> The River of Life to flow against my walls & among my trees.
> Vala was Albion's Bride & Wife in great Eternity:
> The loveliest of the daughters of Eternity, when in day-break
> I emanated from Luvah over the Towers of Jerusalem,
> And in her Courts among her little Children, offering up
> The Sacrifice of fanatic love! why loved I Jerusalem?
> Why was I one with her embracing in the Vision of Jesus?
> Wherefore did I loving create love, which never yet
> Immingled God & Man, when thou & I hid the Divine Vision
> In cloud of secret gloom which behold involves me round about?
> Know me now Albion: look upon me, I alone am Beauty:
> The Imaginative Human Form is but a breathing of Vala:
> I breathe him forth into the Heaven from my secret Cave,
> Born of the Woman to obey the Woman, O Albion the mighty.

But to Albion, even though Vala insists that she was once one with lovely Jerusalem, she appears as the looming and terrifying goddess Nature, mate of the god of light, queen of dim moonlit grottoes. As such her lure seems to him a kind of death, emasculating rather than delighting him.

> Art thou Vala? replied Albion, image of my repose!
> O how I tremble! how my members pour down milky fear!
> A dewy garment covers me all over, all manhood is gone!
> At thy word & at thy look death enrobes me about
> From head to feet, a garment of death & eternal fear.
> Is not that Sun thy husband & that Moon thy glimmering Veil?
> Are not the Stars of heaven thy Children? art thou not Babylon?
> Art thou Nature Mother of all? is Jerusalem thy Daughter?
> Why have thou elevate inward, O dweller of outward chambers,
> From grot & cave beneath the Moon, dim region of death . . .
>   O Vala!
> In Eternity they neither marry nor are given in marriage.
> Albion the high Cliff of the Atlantic is become a barren Land.

And Los, seeing the weakening effect that Albion's cowardly subservience to the goddess has on him, cries:

What may Man be? who can tell! but what may Woman be,
To have power over Man from Cradle to corruptible Grave?
There is a Throne in every Man, it is the Throne of God,
This Woman has claim'd as her own & Man is no more!

Albion has nothing positive left in him: he is completely
passive: 'Doubt is my food day & night'. Los, seeing that
'Albion goes to Eternal Death' because his vision of life has so
narrowed down, cries in scorn and sarcasm:

If Perceptive Organs vary, Objects of Perception seem to vary:
If the Perceptive Organs close, their Objects seem to close also.
Consider this, O mortal Man: O worm of sixty winters, said Los,
Consider Sexual Organization & hide thee in the dust.

Even the Eternals laugh heartily at Albion's foolish fears and
self-created troubles. They are all scornful of Albion's weakness.

And many of the Eternal Ones laughed after their manner:
Have you known the Judgment that is arisen among the
Zoas of Albion; where a Man dare hardly to embrace
His own Wife, for the terrors of Chastity that they call
By the name of Morality.

But others of the Eternals do not laugh, realizing that to Albion
his torment is all too real, no matter how ridiculous it seems to
the outside eye. It is a question of dire importance to him to
know whether he is full of moral virtue or of sick inhibition in
obeying Urizen's laws: he cannot distinguish one from the
other. These Eternals chide those who laugh at Albion's
foolish fears:

Then those in Great Eternity who contemplate on Death
Said thus: 'What seems to Be, Is, To those to whom
It seems to Be, & is productive of the most dreadful
Consequences to those to whom it seems to Be, even of
Torments, Despair, Eternal Death; but the Divine Mercy
Steps beyond and Redeems Man in the Body of Jesus. Amen.'

For Jerusalem to give too much sympathetic understanding to
Albion is as bad for him as is the crude attempt to laugh him
out of his fears. It is worse in fact, for sympathy makes him

perversely harden himself to shut out the very love that he craves. Los,

> when he saw blue death in Albion's feet
> Again he join'd the Divine Body, following, merciful,
> While Albion fled more indignant: revengeful covering
> His face and bosom with petrific hardness, and his hands
> And feet, lest any should enter his bosom and embrace
> His hidden heart: his Emanation wept & trembled within him:
> Uttering not his jealousy, but hiding it as with
> Iron and steel, dark and opake, with clouds & tempests brooding:
> His strong limbs shudder'd upon his mountains high and dark.
>
> Turning from Universal Love petrific as he went,
> His cold against the warmth of Eden rag'd with loud
> Thunders of deadly war (the fever of the human soul)
> Fires and clouds of rolling smoke! but, mild, the Saviour
>   follow'd him,
> Displaying the Eternal Vision, the Divine Similitude,
> In loves and tears of brothers, sisters, sons, fathers, and friends.

Albion is being as contrary and self-destructive as he knows how. He shuts out the radiance that was once within him, and even when Christ follows him he flees, hard and indignant and jealous. He is feverish and trembling, not because there is anything physically wrong with his 'strong limbs', but because he has deliberately worked himself into a state, like a child having a tantrum in order to gain attention which he immediately rejects querulously. An ordinary mortal might feel, at a time like this, compelled to put a small bomb under Albion in lieu of the spanking he deserves. But Christ only follows him, asking Albion's forgiveness if anything has been done to offend him. Christ speaks persuasively, as all men,

> Saying, Albion! Our wars are wars of life, & wounds of love,
> With intellectual spears & long winged arrows of thought:
> Mutual in one another's love and wrath all renewing
> We live as One Man: for contracting our infinite senses
> We behold multitude: or expanding, we behold as one.
> As One Man all the Universal Family: and that One Man
> We call Jesus the Christ: and he in us, and we in him,
> Live in perfect harmony in Eden the land of life,
> Giving, receiving, and forgiving each other's trespasses.
> He is the Good Shepherd, he is the Lord and master:

He is the Shepherd of Albion, he is all in all,
In Eden: in the garden of God: and in heavenly Jerusalem.
If we have offended, forgive us, take not vengeance against us.
Thus speaking, the Divine Family follow Albion:
I see them in the Vision of God upon my pleasant valleys.

But Albion is lost in self-pity: he flees from his Saviour as from his wife and friends and from his own dignity, bent on self-destruction. Los, who is his staunchest friend and who has remained with him through thick and thin, tries to speak to him.

Los was the friend of Albion who most lov'd him. In Cambridge-
    shire
His eternal station, he is the twenty-eighth, & is four-fold.
Seeing Albion had turn'd his back against the Divine Vision,
Los said to Albion. Whither fleest thou? Albion reply'd.
I die! I go to Eternal Death! the shades of death
Hover within me & beneath, and spreading themselves outside
Like rocky clouds, build me a gloomy monument of woe:
Will none accompany me in my death? or be a Ransom for me
In that dark Valley? I have girded round my cloke, and on my
    feet
Bound these black shoes of death, & on my hands, death's iron
    gloves.
God hath forsaken me, & my friends are become a burden,
A weariness to me, & the human footstep is a terror to me.

Los answered, troubled, and his soul was rent in twain:
Must the Wise die for an Atonement? does Mercy endure
    Atonement?
No! It is Moral Severity, & destroys Mercy in its Victim.
So speaking not yet infected with the Error & Illusion
Los shudder'd at beholding Albion, for his disease
Arose upon him pale and ghastly: and he call'd around
The friends of Albion: trembling at the sight of Eternal Death.
The four appear'd with their Emanations in fiery
Chariots . . .
Albion is sick! said every Valley, every mournful Hill
And every River: our brother Albion is sick to death.
He hath leagued himself with robbers: he hath studied the arts
Of unbelief: Envy hovers over him: his Friends are his
    abhorrence:
Those who give their lives for him are despised:
Those who devour his soul, are taken into his bosom:

To destroy his Emanation is their intention.
Arise! awake, O Friends of the Giant Albion!
They have perswaded him of horrible falshoods:
They have sown errors all over his fruitful fields!

Although Albion's illness is due to his own perversity in
rejecting the Divine Vision of love that follows him, even
Christ's solicitude does not prevent Albion from being very
close to spiritual death. What is to be done? One of the most
beautiful illustrations that Blake ever made shows, in superb
colours, Jerusalem, surrounded by a radiant light, sustaining the
body of Albion as he falls back under the shadowy tree of life.
Below, the body is laid out on the death couch, and covered with
a rich clinging material that seems to merge with silver roots
and rocks. A great spectral bird broods over him, rose-coloured
wings outstretched above the bier.

Nothing but mercy can save him! nothing but mercy, interposing
Lest he should slay Jerusalem in his fearful jealousy.
O God, descend! gather our brethren, deliver Jerusalem!
But that we may omit no office of the friendly spirit,
Oxford, take thou these leaves of the Tree of Life: with eloquence,
That thy immortal tongue inspires present them to Albion:
Perhaps he may receive them, offer'd from thy loved hands.

So spoke, unheard by Albion, the merciful Son of Heaven
To those whose Western Gates were open, as they stood weeping
Around Albion: but Albion heard him not: obdurate, hard,
He frown'd on all his Friends, counting them enemies in his
    sorrow.

This, then, is all that can be done: to continue loving and
forgiving Albion, but without letting Albion know, for he only
tries to destroy love when he knows it is present. So Christ
absents himself, and seems to have deserted Albion as Albion
claims he has been deserted. Jerusalem, guided by Los and
Christ, says to Albion, 'Albion, I cannot be thy Wife', seeming
to reject him as he has been driving her away. And then she
flees in order to save herself, whisked away by the Daughters of
Beulah to stay invisible as Christ will stay invisible until Albion
himself knows that he needs them and calls them back. Else he
will destroy her, or force her to destroy herself.

> mild Jerusalem sought to repose in death & be no more.
> She fled to Lambeth's mild Vale and hid herself beneath
> The Surrey Hills . . . Jerusalem cannot be found; Hid
> By the Daughters of Beulah, gently snatch'd away, and hid in
> Beulah.

But the Four Zoas, the faculties within Albion who cannot absent themselves, turn upon him, partly in guilt at the part they have played in his illness:

> They kneel'd around the Couch of Death in deep humiliation
> And tortures of self-condemnation while their Spectre rag'd
> within.
> The Four Zoas in terrible combustion rage,
> Drinking the shuddering fears & loves of Albion's Families,
> Destroying by selfish affections the things that they most admire,
> Drinking & eating, & pitying & weeping, as at a tragic scene,
> The soul drinks murder & revenge, & applauds its own holiness.
> They saw Albion endeavouring to destroy their Emanations . . .
> In the terrible Family Contentions of those who love each other.

Los is the only one of the faculties who stands absolutely firm as Albion's friend, and he is tremendously angered by the weak default of the other Zoas who moan for Christ's return but squabble foolishly among themselves, making matters worse. He scolds them:

> Then Los grew furious raging: Why stand we here trembling
> around
> Calling on God for help; and not ourselves in whom God dwells
> Stretching a hand to save the falling Man; are we not Four
> Beholding Albion upon the Precipice ready to fall into
> Non-Entity . . .
> I see America clos'd apart, & Jerusalem driven in terror
> Away from Albion's mountains, far away from London's spires:
> I will not endure this thing: I alone withstand to death,
> This outrage! Ah me! how sick & pale you all stand round me!
> Ah me! pitiable ones! do you also go to death's vale?
> All you my Friends & Brothers, all you my beloved companions:
> Have you also caught the infection of Sin & stern Repentance?
> I see Disease arise upon you.

They stand uneasy and silent, but then rise as one to Los's challenge. They try to bear Albion back against his will 'with kindest violence' to the Divine Vision he has strayed from. But it is no good: Albion cannot be saved against his will. He resists them, and as soon as they let go of 'their awful charge' back he rolls on greased wheels to his deliberate self-destruction.

> So Los spoke. Pale they stood around the House of Death:
> In the midst of temptations & despair: . . . at length they rose
> With one accord in love sublime, & as on Cherubs' wings
> They Albion surround with kindness violence to bear him back
> Against his will thro' Los's Gate to Eden: Four-fold, loud,
> Their wings waving over the bottomless Immense: to bear
> Their awful charge back to his native home: but Albion, dark,
> Repugnant, roll'd his Wheels backward into Non-Entity.

Albion does not want to be helped. If his friends manage to pull him together, as soon as they let go Albion loses shape again, oozing into his old amorphous self-pity like an amoeba. An illustration shows Albion borne in a little ark with wings by a group of angelic figures. One thing at least has been achieved in that the Zoas are now united and stand by with love and compassion even if they cannot actively help Albion against his will. This is what Christ is doing and what Jerusalem has learned that she must do, that is to do nothing, loving in silence and letting Albion think as he is determined to think that nobody loves him. It is a risk for the Zoas and for Jerusalem, for Albion may well destroy himself, and with him they too will be destroyed, for their well-being depends almost wholly on his. But even so, they have learned to love, expecting nothing and doing nothing, allowing Albion to discover for himself the worst as well as the best within him, the things he is afraid to discover. The risk must be taken that if Albion *does* choose death, it is their funeral too. It must be his choice:

> But as the Will must not be bended but in the day of Divine
> Power: silent calm & motionless, in the mid-air sublime,
> The Family Divine hover around the darken'd Albion.

It is no use at all to force Albion to make the right choice until he himself wills it, of his own volition calling back the Divine Vision of love just as he himself banished it. Until then his own faculties, even his imaginative genius, like his emanation

and like Christ, must simply stand by and wait, 'silent calm &
motionless', making no fuss in risking their own death as well
as witnessing Albion's. The Zoas, understanding this,

> And feeling the damps of death they with one accord delegated
>   Los,
> Conjuring him by the Highest that he should watch over them
> Till Jesus shall appear: & they gave their power to Los.

They realize that Albion, in all his perfection of form and talents,
is of himself nothing without the animating Divine Vision. It was
this vision which gave life to his perfection, and his attempt to do
without it that has put him into his pitiable state:

>   this Man whose great example
> We all admir'd & lov'd, whose all benevolent countenance, seen
> In Eden, in lovely Jerusalem, drew even from envy
> The tear: and the confession of honesty, open & undisguis'd,
> From mistrust and suspition. The Man is himself become
> A piteous example of oblivion. To teach the Sons
> Of Eden, that however great and glorious, however loving
> And merciful the Individuality; however high
> Our palaces and cities, and however fruitful our fields
> In Selfhood, we are nothing: but fade away in morning's breath.
> Our mildness is nothing: the greatest mildness we can use
> Is incapable and nothing: none but the Lamb of God can heal
> This dread disease: none but Jesus: O Lord, descend and save.

An illustration shows God and Jerusalem being drawn along by
strange clumsy beasts in a chariot made of snakes. God, his
face grave and compassionate, holds Jerusalem, who is in
widow's veils, close to him, and rests his face against her head.

All of England's cities pray for Albion together with the
Zoas. Cities such as learned Oxford beg Albion to 'reason not on
both sides' as he has been doing, on the one hand aspiring to a
god-like perfection through Reason, and on the other condemning and destroying himself and all who care for him by this
same rational power which pronounces him imperfect and
contemptible. Instead of doubting and analysing all life away he
should be content to 'Repose in Beulah's night, till the Error is
remov'd' by Christ himself. By rationalizing his sense of guilt
into 'a Religion of Generation to destroy by Sin and atonement

happy Jerusalem', Albion is making a hell in heaven's despite. He is taking to himself the power of being his own witness, judge, and jury, and himself his own hell. This is the one power that must be left to Christ, and Christ is much more ready to forgive Albion for being human than Albion is himself.

Albion prefers to sit, brooding palely on Evil, passive himself, but studying closely the behaviour of others so that he can condemn them. He lists their crimes in his diseased mind only to find that they are projections of the crimes for which he condemns himself:

> Thus Albion sat, studious of others in his pale disease;
> Brooding on evil; but when Los open'd the Furnaces before him,
> He saw that the accused things were his own affections,
> And his own beloveds: then he turn'd sick: his soul died within
>   him.

As early as *The Songs of Experience* Blake implied that evil of every kind—sickness, crime, war, cruelty, even destructiveness in animals—is caused by the dis-ease of the human mind, its inability to accept its environment and see it as good, and its proud tendency to think itself too good for its surroundings. This is what Los now tells Albion: he begs him to stop trying to be god-like 'in self-glorying and pride', and instead accept 'a limit of Opakeness, and a limit of Contraction'. Only then will Albion become truly god-like for the first time, discovering that,

> there is no limit of Expansion; there is no Limit of
>   Translucence,
> In the bosom of Man for ever from eternity to eternity.

The expansion and radiant quality is all within when man accepts his human lot of being 'the Image of God surrounded by Four Zoas', that is, a human being functioning harmoniously on all levels—imagination, intellect, emotion and instinct—because he is Christ-centred. There is no need to prove one's own intellect a god when this harmony exists.

But Albion turns on Los, using him as a scapegoat on which to blame all of his troubles, even though Los is his best friend:

Albion spoke in his dismal dreams: O thou deceitful friend,
Worshipping mercy & beholding thy friend in such affliction:
Los! thou now discoverest thy turpitude to the heavens.
I demand righteousness & justice. O thou ingratitude!

Los, sustained by Christ, is able to answer Albion with strength
and justice, even telling Albion to vent all of his fury on him if it
will keep him from destroying others:

Los answer'd. Righteousness & justice I give thee in return
For thy righteousness; but I add mercy also, and bind
Thee from destroying these little ones; am I to be only
Merciful to thee and cruel to all that thou hatest?
Thou wast the Image of God surrounded by the Four Zoas.
Three thou hast slain: I am the Fourth, thou canst not destroy me.
Thou art in Error; trouble me not with thy righteousness.
I have innocence to defend, and ignorance to instruct:
I have no time for seeming, and little arts of compliment,
In morality and virtue: in self-glorying and pride . . .
Therefore I break thy bonds of righteousness; I crush thy
      messengers;
That they may not crush me and mine; do thou be righteous,
And I will return it; otherwise I defy thy worst revenge;
Consider me as thine enemy: on me turn all thy fury:
But destroy not these little ones, nor mock the Lord's
      annointed:
Destroy not, by Moral Virtue, the little ones whom he hath
      chosen;
The little ones whom he hath chosen in preference to thee.

Los, who is imagination, and whose vision is that of Christ and
the value of human life and love, warns Albion against the
tempting life-hatred, with its spurious air of moral virtue, which
Albion has fallen into. Albion's righteousness is of the holier-
than-thou variety. By sheer will power he suppresses that
virility and *joie de vivre* which marked his greatness. With
puritan prudery he maintains that it must be wrong to do anything one wants to do. All that is pleasurable is *ipso facto* sinful.
He rejects the flowering earth and all natural pleasures just
because they are lovely. Gradually he elevates his life-hatred
into a code, and develops an arrogant pride in his appearance of
virtue, and in his 'difference' in looking for something 'higher'
than the ordinary pleasures of life which are there for anyone to

taste. He sits brooding about how virtuous and intelligent and righteous he is, yet he *does* nothing at all, because anything he does will be contaminated by 'ordinary' life. Even he realizes that all of his gifts, which, in Beulah, he was content to focus on whatever he was doing at a given moment, are now entirely wasted. 'O! I have utterly been wasted', he cries.

In freeing himself from the laws of life that govern 'ordinary' mortals, and setting himself and those around him much more rigorous rules of behaviour, Albion in fact plays havoc with all those unspoken courtesies and loyalties of human intercourse which make life bearable. He feels no compunction in destroying life if it is necessary to his secret codes. Los, imagination, is afraid that Albion will set up a similar theory of art: that is, he might claim that the only art worth having is an art that is out of touch with life which is its enemy, an art that is aloof and cerebral and unpolluted by actual life. Blake himself came dangerously near such a theory of art when he was caught in Albion's state of mind and could say: 'That which can be made Explicit to the Ideot is not worth my care.' But this was after Blake's profound and lucid *Songs* failed to reach every heart as they should have done. Los is determined that while he governs the realm of imagination, Albion will not push his life-hatred this far. Albion has already nearly destroyed all that is alive and natural and warm in Jerusalem as in himself. He loved her, but she was life and therefore as dangerous to his gloom as the flowering earth in spring, of which she constantly reminds him in her bright loveliness. Life is the enemy. Life is the malignant force, binding the intellect to the meaningless wheel of procreation, enslaving the genius of the individual. This is Albion's fallacious way of thinking, forgetting that a mind or art which cuts itself off from life is not only barren but mad, feeding endlessly on stale fantasy and empty ideas.

But Albion in his mood of life-hatred believes that 'Man lives by deaths of Men'. All of his cities 'repent of their human kindness', and Jerusalem wanders 'in the regions of the dead'. Even Los's realm of imagination is being forced by Albion's attitude to build the Mundane Shell and 'the Net & Veil of Vala'. Los is almost overcome in his lonely stand against Albion's self-destruction, until Christ 'like a silent Sun' appears to say: 'Fear not, O little Flock, I come: Albion shall rise again.'

Blake tells again how when Albion's Spectre first 'rose a Shadow from his wearied intellect', Albion walked with Vala instead of Jerusalem, and Albion and Luvah, Vala's rightful husband, fought over the Emanation—

> And the vast form of Nature like a serpent roll'd between,
> Whether of Jerusalem's of Vala's ruins congenerated we know not.

And Blake tells how only two escaped from the general destruction caused by the Spectre in Albion and Jerusalem. And these two were Los and his wife, Enitharmon: in life-giving imagination 'They had been on a visit to Albion's children.'

> Being not irritated by insult, bearing insulting benevolences,
> They perceived that corporeal friends are spiritual enemies:
> And the Divine hand was upon them bearing them thro' darkness,
> Back safe to their Humanity as doves to their windows:
> Therefore the Sons of Eden praise Urthona's Spectre in Songs
> Because he kept the Divine Vision in time of trouble.

These two keep on an even keel, keeping sight of the important things, and bearing Albion's insulting behaviour with tolerant good humour. And Los, the good friend, enters Albion's interior landscape to search out Albion's tempters and robbers:

> Fearing that Albion should turn his back against the Divine
>   Vision
> Los took his globe of fire to search the interiors of Albion's
> Bosom, in all the terrors of friendship, entering the caves
> Of despair & death, to search the tempters out, walking among
> Albion's rocks & precipices: caves of solitude & dark despair.
> And saw every Minute Particular of Albion degraded & murder'd,
> But saw not by whom . . . But Los
> Search'd in vain; clos'd from the minutia he walk'd, difficult
> He came down from Highgate thro' Hackney & Holloway
>   towards London . . .
>   thence thro' the narrows of the River's side
> And saw every minute particular, the jewels of Albion, running
>   down
> The kennels of the streets & lanes as if they were abhorr'd.

Every Universal Form was become barren mountains of Moral
Virtue: and every Minute Particular harden'd into grains of
    sand:
And all the tendernesses of the soul cast forth as filth & mire.
Among the winding places of deep contemplation intricate.

Seeing that Albion has thrown out all love and softness as
polluting, Los does not know of whom to enquire his way in
this barren inner landscape. 'Enquiring in vain of stones and
rocks he took his way, for human form was none.' Los does not
know what to do to evict the criminals in Albion's soul, for to
Christ the judge and punisher is the only criminal, and Albion
now does nothing but judge and punish himself and those he
once loved: Los does not want to add to this vengeance.

What shall I do? What could I do, if I could find these Criminals?
I could not dare to take vengeance: for all things are so
    constructed
And Builded by the Divine hand that the sinner shall always
    escape,
And he who takes vengeance alone is the criminal of Providence:
If I should dare to lay my finger on a grain of sand
In way of vengeance, I punish the already punish'd; O whom
Should I pity if I pity not the sinner who is gone astray?
O Albion, if thou takest vengeance, if thou revengest thy wrongs,
Thou art for ever lost!

Meanwhile Jerusalem is feeling guilty as if she had actually
committed the crimes Albion accuses her of, and as if love really
were sinful. But it is not Albion who is now berating her, but
Vala, the mother goddess within herself with whom she has
not yet come to terms in the *hieros gamos* of the soul. Instead,
she allows Vala to storm at her with wild accusations:

And thou, O harlot daughter, daughter of despair, art all
This cause of these shakings . . . hence we turn thee forth,
For all to avoid thee; to be astonish'd at thee for thy sins:
Because thou art the impurity & the harlot; & thy children,
Children of whoredoms.

One does not admire Jerusalem's meek submissiveness to all of
Albion's ill-treatment. It is born, not so much of her own mild-

ness and gentleness, but of her insecurity and not knowing and trusting what she is. She feels guilty about her own femininity, and so she allows Vala to say outrageous things, making her the scapegoat for all of Vala's own misbehaviour. An illustration shows Jerusalem as she should be: Jerusalem stands, without obscuring veils, her children playing happily around her. Jerusalem is frowning and speaking firmly to Vala who is being mysterious and prophetic and tricksy beneath her veils. The illustration on the opposite plate shows Albion and Jerusalem as they really are, Albion tearing his hair and Vala recoiling at his accusations and trampling on Jerusalem.

Albion, 'the Punisher', dies one more spiritual death, crying, 'Hope is banish'd from me'.

> These were his last words, and the merciful Saviour in his arms
> Receiv'd him, in the arms of tender mercy, and repos'd
> The pale limbs of his Eternal Individuality
> Upon the Rock of Ages.

And even though Albion's 'Death is for a period' only, Jerusalem is drawn away by the Daughters of Beulah, and there is deep mourning:

> From this sweet Place Maternal Love awoke Jerusalem:
> With pangs she forsook Beulah's pleasant lovely shadowy
>   Universe
> Where no dispute can come: created for those who Sleep.
> Weeping was in all Beulah, and all the Daughters of Beulah
> Wept for their Sister, the Daughter of Albion, Jerusalem:
> When out of Beulah the Emanation of the Sleeper descended,
> With solemn mourning out of Beulah's moony shades and hills,
> Within the Human Heart, whose Gates closed with solemn sound.
> And this is the manner of the terrible Separation.

And yet Erin, one of the Daughters of Beulah, warns against blaming Albion and Jerusalem:

> they are blameless & Iniquity must be imputed only
> To the State they are enter'd into that they may be deliver'd . . .
> Learn therefore, O Sisters, to distinguish the Eternal Human
> That walks among the stones of fire, in bliss & woe
> Alternate, from those States or Worlds in which the Spirit travels.

And Erin prays:

> Come Lord Jesus, Lamb of God descend! for if, O Lord!
> If thou hadst been here, our brother Albion had not died.
> Arise sisters! Go ye & meet the Lord, while I remain.
> Behold the foggy mornings of the Dead on Albion's cliffs:
> Ye know that if the Emanation remains in them
> She will become an Eternal Death, an Avenger of Sin,
> A self-righteousness: the proud Virgin-Harlot! Mother of War!

Chapter 2 ends with the reply of the Daughters of Beulah:

> Come, O thou Lamb of God, and take away the remembrance of
> Sin.
> To Sin & to hide the Sin in sweet deceit, is lovely!
> To sin in the open face of day is cruel & pitiless! But
> To record the Sin for a reproach, to let the Sun go down
> In a remembrance of the Sin, is a Woe & a Horror,
> A brooder of an Evil Day, and a Sun rising in blood!
> Come then, O Lamb of God, and take away the remembrance of
> Sin.

Chapter 3 is prefaced by the prose passage which Blake calls
'To the Deists', and by the lyric 'I saw a Monk of Charlemaine'. The illustration at the head of the chapter shows Vala
seated on a sun-flower throne in all her magnificence, with her
head resting dolefully on her hands.

In this chapter everything moves swiftly towards the accomplishment of Jerusalem's ritual prostitution, which, once
achieved, will wed the two sides of her soul which are in conflict,
and make her a stable wife able to help Albion. Los prepares
the way for this, both 'Babylon come up to Jerusalem', and,

> The Mystic Union of the Emanation in the Lord; Because
> Man divided from his Emanation is a dark Spectre,
> His Emanation is an ever-weeping melancholy Shadow:
> But she is made receptive of Generation thro' mercy.

Once Jerusalem accepts both the 'mother' and the 'father' in
herself, both the emotions and the logos, the feminine principle
and the masculine principle, then she will be able to give herself
freely to her husband, unaffected by his guilt feelings, and her-

self full of a serenity that will help Albion to achieve his own integration:

> In Great Eternity, every particular Form gives forth or Emanates
> Its own peculiar Light, & the Form is the Divine Vision,
> And the Light is his Garment. This is Jerusalem in every Man,
> A Tent & Tabernacle of Mutual Forgiveness, Male & Female
>   Clothings.
> And Jerusalem is called Liberty among the Children of Albion.

But until Jerusalem can first free herself from being tyrannized over by her own archetypal parents, she makes Albion's sickness worse instead of better. Their fantasies fit into each other as into grooves, exacerbating each other. For Albion, a victim of his own archetypal parents, projects on to Jerusalem the mother-goddess, Vala, and if she is not herself seeing very clearly, she allows him to do this and becomes caught in his fantasy network of guilt and revenge:

> The silent broodings of deadly revenge, springing from the
> All powerful parental affection, fills Albion from head to foot.

The turning point comes when the Eternals, seeing this, and seeing that

> . . . the Spectre like a hoar frost & a Mildew rose over Albion,
> Saying, I am God, O Sons of Men! I am your Rational Power!

decide that things have gone altogether too far. There is a conclave, and 'an eternal deed was done', when they decree that man's emotional and sexual nature must be freed from the spectral guilt surrounding it:

> Let the Human Organs be kept in their perfect Integrity,
> At will Contracting into Worms, or Expanding into Gods,
> And then, behold! what are these Ulro Visions of Chastity?

We come nearer and nearer to the initiation in which Jerusalem, if she is to be the chaste wife of Albion, must first play out, as if in a theatre or religious ritual, that she is a harlot, all that she is afraid that she may become. Through being one with the goddess she submits her amoral flesh to the will of the God. The cities of England cry like a Greek chorus, while an illustration shows Albion dreaming of two women—

> What is a Wife & what is a Harlot? What is a Church? & what
> Is a Theatre? are they Two & not One? Can they Exist Separate?

It is as Vala, the harlot, that Jerusalem must go to this ritual, in all her pagan magical beauty. She must consent to guilt, for simply pretending that Albion is her moralistic father has made matters worse rather than better. For once in her life abandoning herself to the instincts of wilfully seductive femininity, which are the instincts of Nature herself, she will discover powers of control that she has long been afraid she did not have. Because she has been afraid that the Vala in her would break out in destructive ways, she has in fact been Vala's victim, preaching chastity in moral pride, yet feeling as guilty as if she were sacrificing victims in secret groves.

The ceremony of confirmation in the Christian Church, coming as it does at puberty and symbolizing the marriage of the soul to Christ's values, *ought* to serve the purpose of such an initiation rite as the *hieros gamos*. In fact it does not, largely because the Church has carefully removed any suggestion that one must know what passion is before it can be controlled or denied, and that the confirmation is that of a young adult who knows his own amoral nature and wants to control it. The emphasis is put, rather, on the spotless bride of Christ aspect of the ceremony. Blake, to make the distinction quite clear, makes Jerusalem go first through a ritual that is wholly pagan and lustful. Blake makes it as lurid as he knows how, and what's more, repeats it several times. Only then, when this knowledge of the flesh has been learned, is Jerusalem ready to unite with Christ in her husband, and, through Christ, with God the Father. The final illustration of *Jerusalem* shows Jerusalem in complete joy flying to the embrace of God amidst the flames of the transfiguration. A mystic like Santa Teresa of Avila, or her friend, John of the Cross, can accomplish both sides of this union at one and the same time in a consummation with Christ that is both highly spiritual and highly erotic. But such mystics are few, and are frowned upon by the Church until the time that they cannot be ignored because of the miraculous conviction such a union with all that is good or God in themselves brings, and the capacities it unfolds in them to do wonderful things with this inner god as guide.

Jerusalem, however, is afraid to go through with the pagan ceremony: she thinks it is wrong and against Christ's teachings. But Christ himself appears to tell her that she, like so many others, is wrong only in trying to leave out of Christianity all that is passionate and pagan, and in trying to be impossibly 'good' without first putting into its proper place the desire to be 'bad'. He tells Jerusalem as she sits weeping, Vala's slave and victim rather than her master, that she is wrong not to go through with the ritual prostitution which is meant to free her to higher human concerns. It is included in the plan of salvation, this submission to sin in order to know forgiveness and control. Not only is she now bound to the wheels of Nature, Christ tells her, but the Divine Vision is equally bound. She is much nearer now to the spirit of paganism in all of her suppressed longings than she would be if she got rid of them and passed on to more mature concerns. In the words of the Scriptures, Christ is saying in effect: 'There are two testaments; the one from mount Sina, engendering unto bondage, which is Agar: for Sina is a mountain in Arabia, which hath affinity to that Jerusalem which is now, and is in bondage with her children: but that Jerusalem which is above is free, which is our mother' (Gal. 4). The only way for Jerusalem to become free is to pass through the binding laws of Sina, breaking them in order to know forgiveness of Sin and purity for the first time, and to learn that the only innocence of value is 'organiz'd innocence'. In a passage of lovely and tender persuasion Christ tells Jerusalem that Mary's submission of her flesh to God's will stood for exactly the same thing that this rite stood for in pre-Christian days and, like Mary, after it is accomplished, she will be freed to her husband and her children. . . . 'Thy sons are lovelier than Egypt or Assyria . . . O lovely Jerusalem!' At the end of this speech Jerusalem is convinced that she must submerge herself in the destructive element, and for once give in to all that in herself she is afraid of as much as Albion is. She and Mary become one:

The Divine Vision appear'd
On Albion's hills; often walking from the Furnaces, in clouds
And flames among the Druid Temples & the Starry Wheels,
Gather'd Jerusalem's Children in his arms & bore them like
A Shepherd, in the night of Albion which overspread all the Earth.
I gave thee liberty and life, O lovely Jerusalem,
And thou hast bound me down upon the Stems of Vegetation.
I gave thee Sheep-walks upon the Spanish Mountains, Jerusalem,
I have thee Priam's City and the Isles of Grecia lovely:
I gave thee . . . the Counties of Albion:
They spread out like a lovely root into the Garden of God.
They were as Adam before me: united into One Man,
They stood in innocence & their skiey tent reach'd over Asia . . .
Following thee as a Shepherd by the Four Rivers of Eden.
Why wilt thou rend thyself apart, Jerusalem?
And build this Babylon & sacrifice in Secret Groves,
Among the Gods of Asia: among the fountains of pitch & nitre.
Therefore thy Mountains are become barren, Jerusalem:
Thy Valleys, Plains of burning sand, thy Rivers, waters of death.
Thy Villages die of the Famine, and thy Cities
Beg bread from house to house, lovely Jerusalem.
Why wilt thou deface thy beauty & the beauty of thy little-ones
To please thy Idols, in the pretended chastities of Uncircum-
cision?
Thy Sons are lovelier than Egypt or Assyria . . . O lovely
Jerusalem!
They have perswaded thee to this, therefore their end shall come,
And I will lead thee thro' the Wilderness in shadow of my cloud,
And in my love I will lead thee, lovely Shadow of Sleeping
Albion.
This is the Song of the Lamb, sung by Slaves in evening time.

But Jerusalem faintly saw him, clos'd in the Dungeons of
Babylon.
Her Form was held by Beulah's Daughters, but all within unseen
She sat at the Mills, her hair unbound, her feet naked,
Cut with the flints; her tears run down, her reason grows like
The Wheel of Hand, incessant turning day & night without rest.
Insane she raves upon the winds, hoarse, inarticulate:
All night Vala hears, she triumphs in pride of holiness
To see Jerusalem deface her lineaments with bitter blows
Of despair, while the Satanic Holiness triumph'd in Vala,
In a Religion of Chastity & Uncircumcised Selfishness
Both of the Head & Heart & Loins, clos'd up in Moral Pride.

But the Divine Lamb stood beside Jerusalem, oft she saw
The lineaments Divine & oft the Voice heard, & oft she said.

246

O Lord & Saviour, have the Gods of the Heathen pierced thee:
Or hast thou been pierced in the House of thy Friends?
Art thou alive: & livest thou for evermore? or art thou
Not: but a delusive Shadow, a thought that liveth not.
Babel mocks, saying, there is no God nor Son of God:
That thou, O Human Imagination, O Divine Body, art all
A delusion: but I know thee, O Lord, when thou arisest upon
My weary eyes, even in this dungeon & this iron mill.
The Stars of Albion cruel rise: thou bindest to sweet influences:
For thou also sufferest with me altho' I beheld thee not:
And altho' I sin & blaspheme thy holy name, thou pitiest me:
Because thou knowest I am deluded by the turning mills,
And by these visions of pity & love because of Albion's death.

Thus spake Jerusalem, & thus the Divine Voice replied.

Mild Shade of Man, pitiest thou these Visions of terror & woe?
Give forth thy pity & love, fear not! lo I am with thee always.
Only believe in me that I have power to raise from death
Thy Brother Who Sleepeth in Albion: fear not, trembling Shade.
Behold: in the Visions of Elohim Jehovah, behold Joseph & Mary,
And be comforted, O Jerusalem, in the visions of Jehovah Elohim.

She looked & saw Joseph the Carpenter in Nazareth, & Mary,
His espoused Wife. And Mary said, If thou put me away from
    thee
Dost thou not murder me? Joseph spoke in anger & fury. Should I
Marry a Harlot & an Adulteress? Mary answer'd, Art thou
    more pure
Than thy Maker, who forgiveth Sins & calls again Her that is
    Lost?
Tho' She hates, he calls her again in love. I love my dear Joseph,
But he driveth me away from his presence, yet I hear the voice
    of God
In the voice of my Husband: tho' he is angry for a moment, he
    will not
Utterly cast me away: if I were pure, never could I taste the
    sweets
Of the Forgiveness of Sins; if I were holy, I never could behold
    the tears
Of love! of him who loves me in the midst of his anger in
    furnaces of fire.

Ah my Mary! said Joseph, weeping ever & embracing her closely
    in
His arms: Doth he forgive Jerusalem & not expect Purity from
    her who is

247

Polluted. I heard his voice in my sleep & his Angel in my
    dream: . . .
(saying)
There is none that liveth & Sinneth not. And this is the Covenant
Of Jehovah: If you Forgive one-another, so shall Jehovah
    Forgive You:
That He Himself may Dwell among You. Fear not then to take
To thee Mary thy Wife, for she is with Child by the Holy Ghost.

Then Mary burst forth into a Song: she flowed like a River of
Many Streams in the arms of Joseph, & gave forth her tears of joy
Like many waters . . . And I heard a voice among
The Reapers, Saying, Am I Jerusalem the lost Adulteress? or am I
Babylon come up to Jerusalem? And another voice answer'd
    Saying:
Does the voice of my Lord call me again? am I pure thro' his
    Mercy
And Pity? Am I become lovely as a Virgin in his sight, Who am
Indeed a Harlot drunken with the Sacrifice of Idols, does he
Call her pure as he did in the days of her Infancy, when she
Was cast out to the loathing of her person? . . . O Mercy,
    O Divine Humanity!
O Forgiveness & Pity & Compassion! If I were Pure I should
    never
Have known Thee: If I were Unpolluted I should never have
Glorified thy Holiness, or rejoiced in thy great Salvation.

Mary leaned her side against Jerusalem, Jerusalem received
The Infant into her hands in the Visions of Jehovah. Times
    passed on:
Jerusalem fainted over the Cross & Sepulcher. She heard the
    voice: . . .
Every Harlot was once a Virgin: every Criminal an Infant Love!

Repose on me till the morning of the Grave. I am thy life.
Jerusalem replied. I am an outcast: Albion is dead:
I am left to the trampling foot & the spurning heel:
A Harlot I am call'd, I am sold from street to street: . . .
And wilt thou become my Husband, O my Lord & Saviour?
Shall Vala bring thee forth? Shall the Chaste be ashamed also? . . .
Shall Albion arise? I know he shall arise at the Last Day!
I know that in my flesh I shall see God: but Emanations
Are weak, they know not whence they are, nor whither tend.

Christ tells Jerusalem to trust him even 'tho' thou seest me not
for a season, Even a long season, & a hard journey & a howling

wilderness.' With this comfort and vision Jerusalem must be
content, and, still against her judgement, go through with the
pagan *hieros gamos*, knowing that more than ever Albion will
probably condemn her as a 'Harlot, drunken with the Sacrifice
of Idols . . . Jerusalem the lost Adulteress.'

And so Jerusalem as 'Vala the Wife of Albion' is prepared
for this ritual in the midst of pagan magical splendour while
'The fires blaz'd on the Druid Altars'. She is one with the
moon goddess and with all the goddesses of pre-Christian
religions. A lovely illustration shows an enormous Druid arch
through which tiny figures move against a hilly landscape and
cloud-filled sky.

> Where the Human Victims howl to the Moon, & Thor & Friga
> Dance the dance of death . . .
> The Giants & the Witches & the Ghosts of Albion dance with
> Thor & Friga, & the Fairies lead the Moon along the Valley . . .
> Bleeding in torrents from Mountain to Mountain, a lovely
> Victim. . . .
> When the Druids demanded Chastity from Woman & all was lost.
>
> How can the Female be Chaste, O thou stupid Druid, cried Los,
> Without the Forgiveness of Sins?

And the God that Vala unites with in this *hieros gamos* is the
God that Albion has made of his Spectre. She, 'among the
Chaotic Rocks of the Druids', plays goddess-harlot to his condemning God, but for once they unite in pagan splendour
despite his frowns.

> Then the Spectre drew Vala into his bosom, magnificent,
> terrific,
> Glittering with precious stones & gold, with Garments of Blood
> & fire . . .
> Crimson with Wrath & green with Jealousy, dazzling with Love
> And Jealousy immingled, & the purple of the violet darken'd
> deep . . .
> A dark Hermaphrodite they stood frowning upon London's
> River . . .
> Drinking his Emanation in intoxicating bliss, rejoicing in Giant
> dance . . .
> Then he becomes her Priest & she his Tabernacle,
> And his Oak Grove, till the Victim rend the woven Veil.

And with almost frightening insight Blake points out that in this fantasy ritual marriage of harlot and God, victim and priest, each lover finds that he has killed the parent of his own sex in order to unite with the parent of the other:

> Astonish'd, terrified & in pain & torment, sudden they behold
> Their own Parent, the emanation of their murder'd Enemy,
> Become their Emanation and their Temple and Tabernacle:
> They knew not, this Vala was their beloved Mother, Vala
>   Albion's Wife.

These are things that the daylight consciousness of the ordinary housewife doing her chores and the reliable husband at his work cannot allow. And yet they are there, these amoral incestuous desires and murderous instincts as old and as inevitable as humanity itself. Long before such shocking admissions were generally tolerated, Blake fearlessly analysed such needs in all their complexity. If, he suggests, dark desires and baleful wishes are not allowed a harmless outlet and resolution in unashamed ritual, fantasy and play—play which can be creative in the manner of the arts, and ritual which can be permanent in religion—then they can cause inexplicable trouble, mixing themselves into actual relationships and activities, making the line between fantasy and actuality difficult to distinguish as it has become in the marriage of Albion and Jerusalem.

Blake knew well that it is in our 'modern civilizations' that the worst crimes of war, murder and sexual violence occur, erupting against all of our peace-loving efforts, partly because our puritan side will not admit until it is too late that we have such incredible desires, and partly because many of the rituals, games, and other practices which once served as safe outlets for such energies, are now surrounded with an aura of guilt because they are 'pagan', 'brutal', 'shameful', or even 'superstitious'. All initiation rites must now be disguised as something else, very probably as 'Art', and even here the moralists complain.

In unveiling these fantasy worlds in all their complexities, and in a wider context than do today's psychiatrists, Blake runs the risk of seeming overly intense, humourless and all that seems 'unhealthy' or even 'mad' to minds for whom the cut-

and-dried surface values have always been adequate. But once the surface values totter, rightly or wrongly there is no end to the complications that can invade what is basically a simple relation, making its story seem rather like a cosmic soap-opera.

To make his point quite clear, Blake does not stop with the simple accomplishment of Jerusalem's ritual union with the god. He elaborates upon the theme of primitive ritual and sacrifice, piling detail upon orgiastic detail, until it is apparent that we cannot ignore such rites, for they are one of the ways of satisfying all that in human nature thirsts for violence, magic, sacrifice, and sexual abandon.

> All the Daughters of Albion became One . . . even Vala . . .
> The Daughters of Albion clothed in garments of needle work
> Strip them off from their shoulders and bosoms, they lay aside
> Their garments, they sit naked upon the Stone of trial.
> The knife of flint passes over the howling Victim: his blood
> Gushes & stains the fair side of the fair Daughters of Albion. . . .
> They take off his vesture whole with their knives of flint:
> But they cut asunder his inner garments: searching with
> Their cruel fingers for his heart, & then they enter in pomp,
> In many tears: & there they erect a temple & an altar:
> They pour cold water on his brain in front to cause
> Lids to grow over his eyes in veils of tears: and caverns
> To freeze over his nostrils, while they feed his tongue from cups
> And dishes of painted clay. Glowing with beauty & cruelty,
> They obscure the sun & moon: no eye can look upon them . . .
> The Sun forgets his course . . . the Moon is leprous as snow . . .
> The Stars flee remote: the heaven is iron, the earth is sulphur,
> And all the mountains & hills shrink up like a withering gourd:
> As the Senses of Men shrink together over the knife of flint,
> In the hands of Albion's Daughters, among the Druid Temples.

Blake is not, of course, suggesting that such rituals would be a good thing to revive. He is simply saying that there is something in human nature which, before maturity and stability is attained, craves violence and degradation, and that we must recognize it and somehow within our Christian beliefs provide safe outlet for it. All of this fantasy is going on in Jerusalem's consciousness as she is united with Albion's Spectre who plays both god and victim to her 'goddess Nature, Mystery, Babylon . . . & hidden Harlot'. And such violence-craving immaturity exists only when

'The Feminine separates from the Masculine & both from Man, Ceasing to be His Emanations, Life to themselves assuming', in gloomy projections. It exists only when Albion rejects love or when Jerusalem is 'Ashamed to give Love openly to the piteous & merciful Man', but must, in order to satisfy her own insecure pride, become a goddess 'consuming lives of Gods & Man . . . Till God himself become a Male subservient to the Female'. And Blake cries,

> No Individual ought to appropriate to Himself
> Or to his Emanation, any of the Universal Characteristics . . .
> Of Eve, of the Woman, or of the Lord . . .
> When the Individual appropriates Universality
> He divides in Male & Female: & when the Male & Female
> Appropriate Individuality they become an Eternal Death . . .
> Unless we find a way to bind these awful Forms to our
> Embrace we shall perish annihilate, discover'd our Delusions.

Immaturity consists of the division out of pride and shame into male and female, the woman trying to be all femininity, the goddess herself, and the man trying to be a god, all masculine intellect, and each failing miserably. But each imposes their delusion on the other and fosters it, until the only way out is to embrace the unattainable god or goddess in the other amidst guilt and violence. If one does not consume in the embrace as Orc did, one may learn painfully that it is not necessary for a human being to be a deity, and that it is, in fact, much finer to give love openly to a limited and individual human being than to be in love with an idealized and cruel god or goddess. Jerusalem who as Vala forces Albion to play the part of unattainable god so that in uniting with him she may accomplish her *hieros gamos*, seems to him like an infinitely cruel goddess, and he her victim.

> Look! the beautiful Daughter of Albion sits naked upon the Stone,
> Her panting Victim beside her: her heart is drunk with blood,
> Tho' her brain is not drunk with wine: she goes forth from Albion
> In pride of beauty, in cruelty of holiness, in the brightness
> Of her tabernacle, & her ark & secret place: the beautiful Daughter
> Of Albion delights the eye of kings: their hearts & the
> Hearts of their Warriors glow hot . . .
> He sees the Twelve Daughters naked upon the Twelve Stones . . .
> Lo, they rest upon the Tribes, where their panting Victims lie.

Molech rushes into the kings in love to the beautiful Daughters,
But they frown & delight in cruelty . . . they sport before the kings,
Clothed in the skin of the Victim . . . he rejoices
In moral law & its severe penalties . . .
O beautiful Daughter of Albion! cruelty is thy delight,
O Virgin of terrible eyes who dwellest by Valleys of springs. . . .
In cruelties of holiness, to refuse the joys of love . . .
      I am drunk with unsatiated love:
I must rush again to War; For the Virgin has frown'd & refus'd.
Sometimes I curse & sometimes bless thy fascinating beauty.
Once Man was occupied in intellectual pleasures & energies,
But now my Soul is harrow'd with grief & fear & love & desire,
And now I hate & now I love & Intellect is no more:
There is no time for anything but the torments of love & desire . . .
Bearing the Images of various Species of Contention
And Jealousy & Abhorrence & Revenge & deadly Murder,
Till they refuse liberty to the Male: & not like Beulah
Where every Female delights to give her maiden to her husband.
The Female searches sea & land for gratifications to the
Male Genius: who in return clothes her in gems & gold
And feeds her with the food of Eden, hence all her beauty beams.

Blake goes on to compare the delights of Beulah with the
horrors of this divided existence which revels in false holiness
and secret amorousness. Blake cries indignantly that, in Beulah,

Embraces are Cominglings, from the Head even to the Feet,
And not a pompous High Priest entering by a Secret Place.

In Beulah the female

        Creates at her will a little moony night & silence
With Spaces of sweet gardens & a tent of elegant beauty:
Closed in by a sandy desart & a night of stars shining,
And a little tender moon & hovering angels on the wing.
And the Male gives a Time & Revolution to her Space
Till the time of love is passed in ever varying delights.
For All Things Exist in the Human Imagination,
And thence in Beulah they are stolen by secret amorous theft,
Till they have had Punishment enough to make them commit
    Crimes.
Hence rose the Tabernacle in the Wilderness & all its Offerings,
From Male & Female Loves in Beulah & their Jealousies.
The Jealousies became Murderous . . .
Therefore the Male severe & cruel fill'd with stern Revenge:
Mutual Hate returns & mutual Deceit & mutual Fear.

There follows in slightly different terms one more statement
of the union between Vala and the Spectre. In this version Vala
seduces the stern rational Spectre as he sits, a woman-hater,

> his Feminine Power unreveal'd
> Brooding Abstract Philosophy, to destroy Imagination, the
> Divine
> Humanity: A Three-fold Wonder, feminine, most beautiful,
> Threefold
> Each within other. On her white & even Neck, her Heart
> Inorb'd and bonified: with locks of shadowing modesty, shining
> Over her beautiful Female features, soft flourishing in beauty,
> Beams mild, all love and all perfection, that when the lips
> Receive a kiss from Gods or Men, a threefold kiss returns
> From the press'd loveliness; so her whole immortal form, three-
> fold,
> Three-fold embrace returns: consuming lives of Gods & Men . . .
> O who can withstand her power?
> Her name is Vala in Eternity.

The rest of chapter 3 is given over to an interminable list of
biblical names and place names, almost destroying Blake's
carefully achieved effect. The final plate shows Jerusalem
wound round in the embrace of a beautifully coloured snake
with man's head and torso: this is a symbolic representation
of her union with the Orc-like priest or god.

Chapter 4 starts out with the prose passage containing the
famous sentence: 'I know of no other Christianity and of no
other Gospel than the liberty both of body and mind to exercise
the Divine Arts of Imagination.' A beautiful illustration shows
a male figure, rather like Blake himself, his arms outstretched
in wonder and love before Christ who is crucified on a dimly
outlined tree.

A lovely lyric follows. Jerusalem, at last sure of herself and
of her own integrity, joyfully realizes that Albion shall live
again: she calls to him:

> England! awake! awake! awake!
> Jerusalem thy Sister calls!
> Why wilt thou sleep the sleep of death
> And close her from thy ancient walls?

Thy hills & valleys felt her feet,
Gently upon their bosoms move:
Thy gates beheld sweet Zion's ways:
Then was a time of joy and love.

And now the time returns again:
Our souls exult, & London's towers
Receive the Lamb of God to dwell
In England's green & pleasant bowers.

At the beginning of this chapter comes, too, the well-known quatrain:

I give you the end of a golden string,
Only wind it into a ball:
It will lead you in at Heaven's gate,
Built in Jerusalem's wall.

It seems to me that Blake makes one of his most damaging artistic errors at the beginning of this final chapter of *Jerusalem*. In the previous chapter and in the opening lyrics of Chapter 4 Blake has carefully paved the way for Albion's reawakening; 'Hell is open'd to Heaven' at last, it seems. Jerusalem has been brought through her baptism of fire and stands ready to unite with Albion and Christ. But instead of leading swiftly into the dénouement, which the harassed reader by now feels he deserves, Blake takes a fresh breath and launches forth on many pages of recapitulation which add no new insights to the story. Indeed, they complicate the plot by trying to redraft the theme in rather far-fetched historical terms, with only an occasional line of beauty, such as:

Humanity is become
A weeping Infant in ruin'd Jerusalem's folding Cloud.

Jerusalem in all her desolation is the theme of the illustration on plate 92.

Only after many careless and unnecessary pages is the connection made between Jerusalem's lovely song urging Albion to awake and the lifeless figure of Albion himself as he lies stretched out in the sleep of death:

Albion cold lays on his Rock: storms & snows beat round him,
Beneath the Furnaces & the starry Wheels & the Immortal Tomb.
Howling winds cover him: roaring seas dash furious against him:
In the deep darkness broad lightnings glare, long thunders roll.
The weeds of Death inwrap his hands & feet, blown incessant
And wash'd incessant by the for-ever restless sea-waves, foaming
    abroad
Upon the white Rock.

But Albion is no longer as lifeless as he looks. Already his
voice has been heard, speaking as Los:

> Jerusalem & Vala cease to mourn:
> His voice is heard from Albion . . .
> O lovely mild Jerusalem! . . .
> I see thy Gates of precious stones; thy Walls of gold & silver.
> Thou art the soft reflected Image of the Sleeping Man.

Albion recognizes and accepts Jerusalem as his Emanation,
seeing that she is Jerusalem and that Vala is only a part of her.
Without any doubt he claims her as 'Jerusalem: lovely Shadow
of Sleeping Albion', knowing that her habitat is 'where Beulah
lovely terminates in the hills & valleys of Albion'. Once more
he sees her as pure and lovely as she was when he first married
her, 'become lovely as a Virgin in his sight'. 'Come forth, O
lovely-one!' he calls, saying:

> I see thy Form, O lovely mild Jerusalem . . .
> Thy forehead bright; Holiness to the Lord: with Gates of pearl
> Reflects Eternity beneath thy azure wings of feathery down . . .
> From thy white shoulders shadowing, purity in holiness . . .
>   I see the River of Life, Tree of Life,
> I see the New Jerusalem descending out of Heaven
> Between thy Wings of gold & silver feather'd, immortal.

Albion is getting over his guilt about the 'crime' of being human
and generated, and the fact that the 'places of joy & love' are
'excrementitious'.[1] He realizes that there cannot be any
'consummate bliss without being Generated on Earth'. Albion
is now seeing so clearly that he even modifies his views, stated

[1] Yeats based one of his most successful poems, 'Crazy Jane Talks
with the Bishop', on this comment of Blake's.

in *Milton*, concerning the superiority of Eden, or Eternity where man talks 'man to man' about intellectual matters, to Beulah, which is the realm of the fearful emanation. He now stipulates that only with the approval of their Emanations and well-being of their families can man go off to talk man to man in Eternity, instead of, as before, going off in scorn of the weak emanation:

> When in Eternity Man converses with Man they enter
> Into each others Bosom (which are Universes of delight)
> In mutual interchange, and first their Emanations meet
> Surrounded by their Children: if they embrace & comingle
> The Human Four-fold Forms mingle also in the thunders of
> Intellect.
> But if the Emanations mingle not: with storms & agitations
> Of earthquakes & consuming fires they roll apart in fear.
> For Man cannot unite with Man but by their Emanations,
> Which stand both Male & Female at the Gates of each Humanity.
> How then can I ever again be united as Man with Man
> While thou, my Emanation, refusest my Fibres of dominion?
> When Souls mingle & join thro' all the Fibres of Brotherhood
> Can there by any secret joy on Earth greater than this?

Jerusalem is for the first time Albion's wife, and for the first time completely distinct from Albion's emotional nature or *anima* which has also hitherto been called his emanation. Now Albion's feminine side, his *anima*, is more rightly called Brittania, and when Jerusalem sings her song to awake Albion, Brittania awakens in Albion's bosom and pities him. It is she who has been the real Vala, the 'Jealous Wife'. No longer does he confuse the projection of his own *anima* with his wife as he once did when he saw 'England, who is Brittania, divided into Jerusalem & Vala'. His own lost *anima*, like Eurydice, is redeemed from the underworld of death.

> Time was Finished! The Breath Divine Breathed over Albion . . .
> And England who is Brittania awoke from Death on Albion's
> bosom:
> She awoke pale & cold . . .
> O piteous Sleep, O piteous Dream! O God, O God, awake! I have
> slain,
> In Dreams of Chastity & Moral Law I have Murdered Albion.

Such is Albion's awakening. He rises in wonderful righteous anger at the living death to which he has been subjected by his own Spectre and *anima*. And Brittania, adoring his stern rebukes, unites with him. This is Albion's comparatively simple *hieros gamos*, the inner marriage of the two sides of himself that frees him to the Divine Vision once more and makes him trust instead of fear the behaviour of his own emotions and of his wife.[1] Christ appears in the likeness of Los, knowing that Albion wants him again, and Albion asks pardon for his rebellion.

Her voice pierc'd Albion's clay cold ear, he mov'd upon the Rock:
The Breath Divine went forth upon the morning hills, Albion
    mov'd
Upon the Rock, he open'd his eyelids in pain: in pain he mov'd
His stony members, he saw England. Ah! shall the Dead live
    again?
The Breath Divine went forth over the morning hills, Albion rose
In anger: the wrath of God breaking bright, flaming on all sides
    around
His awful limbs: into the Heavens he walk'd, clothed in flames
Compelling Urizen to his Furrow, & Tharmas to his Sheepfold,
And Luvah to his loom . . . Los unwearied laboured . . .
Because he kept the Divine Vision in time of trouble.

As the Sun & Moon lead forward the Visions of Heaven & Earth
England, who is Brittania, enter'd Albion's bosom rejoicing,
Rejoicing in his indignation, adoring his wrathful rebuke.
She who adores not your frowns will only loathe your smiles.

As the Sun & Moon lead forward the Visions of Heaven & Earth
England, who is Brittania, enter'd Albion's bosom rejoicing.

Then Jesus appeared standing by Albion, as the Good Shepherd
By the lost Sheep that he hath found, & Albion knew that it
Was the Lord, the Universal Humanity, & Albion saw his Form
A Man, & they conversed as Man with Man, in Ages of Eternity.
And the Divine Appearance has the likeness and similitude of Los.

An illustration shows the Lord holding close to him the Emanation who looks up at him trustingly. Albion, understanding at last the terrible wonder of Christ's having died for him, rouses

[1] Orc's vision with Vala in *The Four Zoas* did not join the two sides of Albion, for Orc was consumed.

his cities and counties, and at last stands fourfold before God, all his evils having become

> Fountains of Living Waters, flowing from the Humanity Divine.
> And all the Cities of Albion rose from their Slumbers, and All
> The Sons & Daughters of Albion on soft clouds, Waking from
>   Sleep.
> Soon all around remote the Heavens burnt with flaming fires,
> And Urizen & Luvah & Tharmas & Urthona arose into
> Albion's Bosom: then Albion stood before Jesus in the Clouds
> Of Heaven, Fourfold among the Visions of God in Eternity.

And Albion calls joyously to Jerusalem his wife, and in his voice speaks not only Christ, but God the Father with whom Jerusalem unites in her consummation with her husband.

> Awake, Awake, Jerusalem! O lovely Emanation of Albion,
> Awake, and overspread all Nations as in Ancient Time.
> For lo! The Night of Death is past and the Eternal Day
> Appears upon our Hills: Awake, Jerusalem, and come away!
>
> So spake the Vision of Albion, & in him so spake in my hearing
> The Universal Father. Then Albion stretch'd his hand into
>   Infinitude,
> And took his Bow. Fourfold the Vision, for bright beaming
>   Urizen
> Lay'd his hand on the South & took a breathing Bow of curved
>   Gold,
> Luvah his hand stretch'd to the East & bore a Silver Bow bright
>   shining,
> Tharmas Westward a Bow of Brass pure flaming richly wrought,
> Urthona Northward in thick storms a Bow of Iron terrible
>   thundering.
>
> And the Bow is a Male & Female, & the Quiver of the Arrows of
>   Love
> Are the Children of his Bow . . .

And Blake sings the song of the fourfold man who trusts himself and trusts his wife: he is at one with Christ and with all of Creation. The tense is the past tense and the tone is one of lovely calm. All has been accomplished, and all is well for ever and ever between Albion and his bride, as the quiet ending testifies: 'And I heard the Name of their Emanations: they are named Jerusalem.' And in the illustration Jerusalem rushes rapturously to the arms of God, and around them are the flames of the consummation.

And every Man stood Fourfold, each Four Faces had, One to the
West,
One toward the East, One to the South, One to the North, the
Horses Fourfold.
And the dim Chaos brighten'd beneath, above, around! Eye as
the Peacock
According to the Human Nerves of Sensation, the Four Rivers of
the Waters of Life. . . .

The Four Living Creatures, Chariots of Humanity, Divine,
Incomprehensible,
In beautiful Paradises expand. These are the Four Rivers of
Paradise,
And the Four Faces of Humanity, fronting the Four Cardinal
Points
Of Heaven, going forward, forward irresistible from Eternity to
Eternity. . . .

And they conversed together in visionary forms dramatic, which
bright
Redounded from their Tongues in thunderous majesty . . . &
they walked
To & fro in Eternity as One Man, reflecting each in each &
clearly seen
And seeing: according to fitness & order . . .

All Human Forms identified, even Tree, Metal, Earth & Stone, all
Human Forms identified, living, going forth, & returning wearied
Into the Planetary lives of Years, Months, Days & Hours,
reposing
And then Awaking into his Bosom in the Life of Immortality.
And I heard the Name of their Emanations: they are named
Jerusalem.

FINIS

BIBLIOGRAPHY

The Complete Poetry of William Blake, The Modern Library, New York, 1946.

Jerusalem, William Blake, the 'Stirling' and the 'Rinder' copies as reproduced by the Blake Trust at the Trianon Press and distributed by Faber & Faber.

All of the original Blakes owned by the British Museum and the Fitzwilliam Museum.

Whatever I have used from other books of Blake criticism is noted in the text.

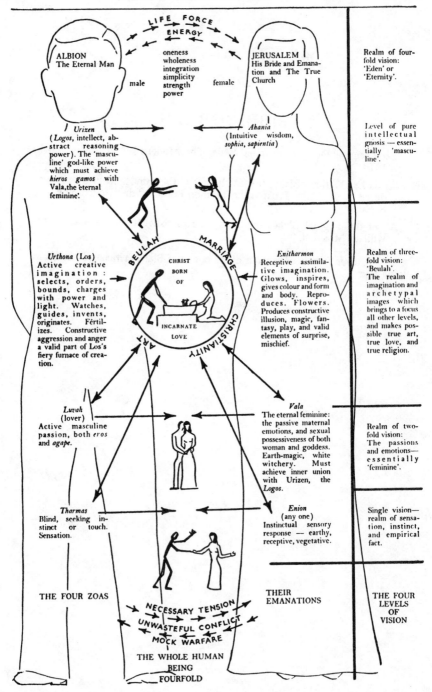

LIFE FORCE
ENERGY

ALBION
The Eternal Man

oneness
wholeness
integration
simplicity
strength
power

male   female

JERUSALEM
His Bride and Emana-
tion and The True
Church

Realm of four-
fold vision:
'Eden' or
'Eternity'.

Urizen
(*Logos*, intellect, ab-
stract   reasoning
power). The 'mascu-
line' god-like power
which must achieve
hieros gamos with
Vala, the eternal
feminine'.

Ahania
(Intuitive wisdom,
sophia, sapientia)

Level of pure
intellectual
gnosis — essen-
tially 'mascu-
line'.

Urthona (Los)
Active   creative
imagination :
**selects, orders,
bounds, charges
with power and
light.** Watches,
guides, invents,
originates. Fertil-
izes. Constructive
aggression and anger
a valid part of Los's
fiery furnace of crea-
tion.

BEULAH   MARRIAGE

CHRIST
BORN
OF

INCARNATE
LOVE

ART   CHRISTIANITY

Enitharmon
Receptive assimila-
tive imagination.
Glows, inspires,
gives colour and form
and body. Repro-
duces. Flowers.
Produces constructive
illusion, magic, fan-
tasy, play, and valid
elements of surprise,
mischief.

Realm of three-
fold vision:
'Beulah'.
The realm of
imagination and
archetypal
images which
brings to a focus
all other levels,
and makes pos-
sible true art,
true love, and
true religion.

Luvah
(lover)
Active masculine
passion, both *eros*
and *agape*.

Vala
The eternal feminine:
the passive maternal
emotions, and sexual
possessiveness of both
woman and goddess.
Earth-magic, white
witchery.   Must
achieve inner union
with Urizen, the
Logos.

Realm of two-
fold vision:
The passions
and emotions—
essentially
'feminine'.

Tharmas
Blind, seeking in-
stinct or touch.
Sensation.

Enion
(any one)
Instinctual sensory
response — earthy,
receptive, vegetative.

Single vision—
realm of sensa-
tion, instinct,
and empirical
fact.

THE FOUR ZOAS

THEIR
EMANATIONS

THE FOUR
LEVELS
OF
VISION

NECESSARY TENSION
UNWASTEFUL CONFLICT
MOCK WARFARE

THE WHOLE HUMAN
BEING
FOURFOLD

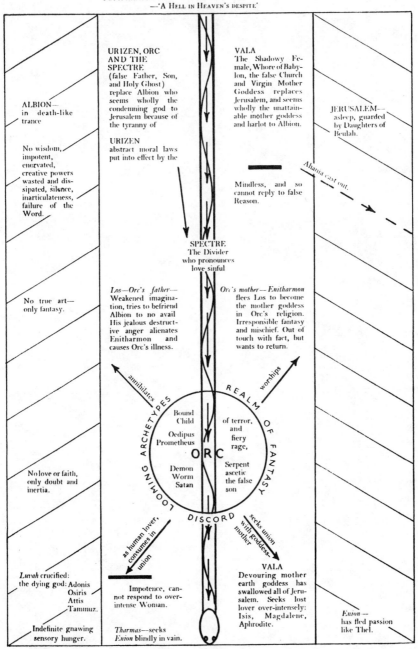

II. STATE OF SEPARATION AND BREAKDOWN,
COMPLEXITY AND WASTE: UNREAL RELATIONSHIP
—'A HELL IN HEAVEN'S DESPITE'

URIZEN, ORC
AND THE
SPECTRE
(false Father, Son,
and Holy Ghost)
replace Albion who
seems wholly the
condemning god to
Jerusalem because of
the tyranny of

URIZEN
abstract moral laws
put into effect by the

VALA
The Shadowy Fe-
male, Whore of Baby-
lon, the false Church
and Virgin Mother
Goddess replaces
Jerusalem, and seems
wholly the unattain-
able mother goddess
and harlot to Albion.

ALBION—
in death-like
trance

No wisdom,
impotent,
enervated,
creative powers
wasted and dis-
sipated, silence,
inarticulateness,
failure of the
Word.

JERUSALEM—
asleep, guarded
by Daughters of
Beulah.

Ahania cast out.

Mindless, and so
cannot reply to false
Reason.

SPECTRE
The Divider
who pronounces
love sinful

No true art—
only fantasy.

Los—Orc's father—
Weakened imagina-
tion, tries to befriend
Albion to no avail
His jealous destruct-
ive anger alienates
Enitharmon and
causes Orc's illness.

Orc's mother—Enitharmon
flees Los to become
the mother goddess
in Orc's religion.
Irresponsible fantasy
and mischief. Out of
touch with fact, but
wants to return.

annihilates
REALM
worships
OF
LOOMING ARCHETYPES
FANTASY

Bound
Child

of terror,
and
fiery
rage,

Oedipus
Prometheus

ORC

Serpent
ascetic
the false
son

No love or faith,
only doubt and
inertia.

Demon
Worm
Satan

DISCORD

as human lover,
consumes in
union

seeks union
with goddess
mother

Luvah crucified:
the dying god: Adonis
Osiris
Attis
Tammuz.

Impotence, can-
not respond to over-
intense Woman.

VALA
Devouring mother
earth goddess has
swallowed all of Jeru-
salem. Seeks lost
lover over-intensely:
Isis, Magdalene,
Aphrodite.

Indefinite gnawing
sensory hunger.

Tharmas—seeks
Enion blindly in vain.

Enion—
has fled passion
like Thel.

INDEX